D1031795

A PAIR OF ACES AND A TREY

A PAIR OF ACES
AND A TREY

1st Lieutenants William P. Erwin, Arthur E. Easterbrook,
and Byrne V. Baucom

America's Top Scoring World War I Observation Pilot
and Observers

ALAN L. ROESLER

CASEMATE

Philadelphia & Oxford

Published in the United States of America and Great Britain in 2023 by
CASEMATE PUBLISHERS
1950 Lawrence Road, Havertown, PA 19083, USA
and
The Old Music Hall, 106–108 Cowley Road, Oxford OX4 1JE, UK

Hardcover Edition: ISBN 978-1-63624-187-6
Digital Edition: ISBN 978-1-63624-188-3

A CIP record for this book is available from the British Library

Printed and bound in the United Kingdom by CPI Group (UK) Ltd, Croydon, CR0 4YY

For a complete list of Casemate titles, please contact:

CASEMATE PUBLISHERS (US)
Telephone (610) 853-9131
Fax (610) 853-9146
Email: casemate@casematepublishers.com
www.casematepublishers.com

CASEMATE PUBLISHERS (UK)
Telephone (0)1226734350
Email: casemate-uk@casematepublishers.co.uk
www.casematepublishers.co.uk

Front cover: top, George H. Williams Collection via Greg VanWyngarden; bottom, Courtesy Easterbrook Collection, US Air Force Museum, via Alan D. Toelle
Back cover: George H. Williams Collection via Greg VanWyngarden

Contents

Dedication

"Greatest U.S. Aviation Hero—Captain Erwin, Says Former Army Air Chief"

Several men, all brave and worthy, have been suggested as America's greatest aviation war hero. But without detracting from glory, I want to suggest a man who had four observers shot in his plane; a man who in a heavy two-seated observation plane outflew most pilots in light pursuit planes; a man who chased German aviators into their airdromes; and who, when shot down once by the Germans, simply jumped to the ground, wiped out a whole nest of machine gunners and made his way back to the American lines![1]

—COLONEL WILLIAM B. MITCHELL, US AIR SERVICE

This book is dedicated to the memory of William P. Erwin, who flew off into the setting sun on the western horizon for the last time on August 19, 1927. And to the memory of his courageous observer and later pilot Byrne V. Baucom, who also flew off into the westward horizon less than 10 months later, never to return. And to Arthur E. Easterbrook, who kept Erwin alive on so many occasions during the last two months of World War I.

And to:

My wife, Tara, my son Dr. Alexander Roesler, and my daughter Dr. Kimberly Roesler. May they continue their lives in service to others.

Preface

In 2012 I began receiving digital images of Victory Loan Flying Circus (VLFC), Mid-West Flight air show scenes from the grandson of one of the Spad VII pilots, 1st Lt. Franklin O. Carroll. Both Carroll and Capt. William P. Erwin flew in air shows in 23 different Midwestern cities between April 11 and May 10, 1919. Three of the dozen photographs in which Erwin appear are individual shots. Carroll had arranged his photograph album chronologically by city, supplying the necessary information about where they were taken. Newspapers confirm the dates and supply detailed descriptions of those air shows, verifying where and when the photographs were taken. Erwin was one of four designated "aces" (used hereafter to describe a pilot or observer with five confirmed victories) assigned to travel with this tour to help sell Victory Loan bonds in the aftermath of World War I, as well as fly during some of the air shows.

I studied the photographs and documented each day's events from newspaper accounts in several cities as the VLFC Mid-West Flight tour worked its way northward. Captain Erwin's contribution was noteworthy, if not always positive. The press media was typically eager to interview the pilots before air shows, and Captain Erwin was initially just as enthusiastic to relate his memory of his most recent past, as he was enthusiastic about being on this tour. After all, he had escaped the boredom of duty at Post Field, Oklahoma, had temporarily been promoted from 1st lieutenant to captain upon joining this tour, and had 30 days in which to perform aerobatics in front of awe-struck crowds with three other aces, all pursuit pilots, one of whom then qualified as the premier aerobatic pilot in the world. He also had plenty of time to visit his home, or prior home, in Chicago, not once, but three times during this tour.

I noted that Erwin was admonished by his executive officer while on this VLFC tour, after damaging his airplanes three times in landing accidents. The press media always misreported the number of his confirmed victories, but not those of the other three aces, and I did not understand why. Sometimes he spun stories to the media about his exploits in France and the details were not always the same, while the other three aces remained tight lipped. I wondered how he became a captain when all my reference sources listed him as a 1st lieutenant. Finally, after studying these VLFC air show events for seven years, during which I had documented his participation through either photographs or newspaper articles in several of these Midwestern cities, I knew it was time to sort out fact from fiction.

My story was not going to revolve around a simple recitation of combat reports, aerial victories, and awards for valor. I wanted to show how the work of aviation was integrated into the total war effort. I wanted to highlight the purpose and effect of the various aviation participants and focus on two key components: duty and bravery, particularly of Erwin, Byrne V. Baucom, and Arthur E. Easterbrook. Erwin had been in the 1st Aero Squadron less than a week before flying his first mission with Baucom, a fellow Texan, and a dependable, detail-oriented infantry officer beforehand. Easterbrook, another detail-oriented former infantry officer, did not arrive at the squadron until a month later. Their mission was to carry out daily orders of the divisions the First Army assigned them to. Their stories constantly reveal those key elements of heroism and duty first. Their aerial victory confirmations and later awards for valor were the acknowledgment for having gone above and beyond those orders and expectations. This required original documentation from a myriad of sources covering all units involved. When I used secondary sources, I cross-checked them with original source material, where possible.

Many of Lieutenant Erwin's exploits while teaming with Baucom and Easterbrook were previously published in the *Dallas Morning News* from September 30 to October 24, 1928, in a series of 25 articles on Erwin's life, titled "Erwin: From the War Letters and Diaries of an American Ace," by journalist John Peyton Dewey. Published only 10 years after World War I, without reference notes, they left the reader with having to accept everything at face value. While holding much factual information, some articles in the series have misleading or false, unsupported claims, inaccurate dates and times, or simply twist the facts to the extent that Erwin's version is different from several other eyewitness accounts of the same event. Occasionally, I had to rely upon the Erwin flight logs that predated my foremost reference source, *Gorrell's History of the American Expeditionary Forces Air Service, 1917–1919*, compiled by Colonel Edgar S. Gorrell, Assistant Chief of Staff of the Air Service, and his in-depth analysis of the performance and operations of American military aviation in World War I. The volume summarizing the 1st Aero Squadron is interrelated with multiple other volumes when trying to reconstruct the missions flown by Erwin, Baucom, and Easterbrook, as well as their military careers. Sometimes another squadron or balloon company was involved, and I needed to check their records for verification. I also needed to check American First Army records for victory claims in general orders, and daily reports, their final summarized reports sometimes overriding details given in the initial squadron's versions. While such first-hand source materials form the backbone of this book, Air Service/Air Corps newsletters and newspaper accounts were also primary information sources. I also relied upon the 1938 *American Armies and Battlefields in Europe* book and its supporting maps as a primary source, using other books and articles as secondary sources of information.

I needed to verify the information used in the 1928 *Dallas Morning News* series with other reference sources, or else consider it plausible and not be otherwise refuted. The most valuable aspect of the series was its ability to supply clues where to look for the other resource information I needed for verification. Trying to understand, research, sort out, and accurately portray all the discrepancies in William P. Erwin's life was not a simple task; for example, explaining why Erwin was not awarded the *Croix de Guerre* medal yet was still entitled to wear one. The contention that Erwin was previously nominated for the Congressional Medal of Honor by the 1st Aero Squadron was not discussed because I have never found supporting documentation from any other source.

Chapter Seven describes William P. Erwin's (Dallas's favorite son in 1927) participation in the Dole Air Race and his later loss on August 19, 1927, while searching for other participants lost during that race. The events that led to that fateful conclusion—from the time that he picked up his famous *Dallas Spirit* from the Swallow Airplane Company in Wichita, Kansas, to his final radio communication over the Pacific Ocean—are derived from the *Dallas Morning News* articles. The Frontiers of Flight Museum in Dallas displays Erwin's *Dallas Spirit* Swallow Monoplane NX941 replica, and a photograph of 1st Aero Squadron's Salmson 2A2 5464 "8," a postwar airplane received on March 31, 1919, on a display board beneath it. As such, his previous legacy, prior to the details presented in this biography, would ordinarily lead one to remember him as "Lone Star Bill" of the Dole Air Race. Now it becomes more obvious that his most important legacy instead lies in his service during World War I.

I would like to thank the World War I aviation experts who helped me in compiling this book, especially Alan D. Toelle, a former Marine captain and award-winning author and editor. Alan spent several decades developing a database of all the Salmson 2A2s flown by the 1st Aero Squadron, by serial number, from the first 17 they received on July 1, 1918, to the last two the squadron received on March 31, 1919. Alan also supplied daily tips, advice, databases, pilot logs, maps, high-resolution photo images, and edited my drafts over the course of several months. World War I aviation expert Steven A. Ruffin, a retired U.S. Air Force colonel, pilot, and award-winning author and editor, supplied my 50th Aero Squadron images, reviewed and edited my drafts over several months, and recommended manuscript formatting and editing changes. Special thanks also go to World War I aviation expert and noted author Greg VanWyngarden, for his advice and photographic images of Easterbrook, and to Franklin Otis Carroll for his images of Capt. William P. Erwin during the April–May 1919 VLFC tour. Lastly, thanks also to Patrizia Nava, Curator of Aviation Archives at University of Texas at Dallas (UTD), for her research assistance on the Byrne V. Baucom and George H. Williams Collections and Joseph A. Weisberg Papers.

Maps

Introduction

Texans William P. Erwin (pilot) and his observer Byrne V. Baucom flew and fought in support of the 1st and 42nd Divisions in the American Château-Thierry operations from July 21 to August 12, 1918. Together with Arthur E. Easterbrook, all three supported 2nd Division operations during the St. Mihiel operations between August 26 and September 18, 1918. All three of them supported the 1st, 35th, and 80th Divisions during the Meuse–Argonne offensive, from September 26–November 5, 1918. Their missions called for them to fly at altitudes between 20 meters and 3,000 meters, carrying out artillery surveillance/fire adjustment, infantry contact patrols, photography, and reconnaissance.

Working in an observation squadron in an open cockpit, being subject to attack by antiaircraft fire and German airplanes on every mission, was quite hazardous, with only learned skills, a sharpened awareness, and a bit of luck keeping their crews alive. Erwin, trained as a *chasse* (hunting) pilot at the 3rd Aviation Instruction Center (AIC), was not a typical observation pilot. After reaching the 1st Aero Squadron on July 19, 1918, he brought more pep and enthusiasm than any of the other men, while letting it be known that he was also looking for aerial victories. His two primary observers, Baucom and Easterbrook, were both infantry officers first, with prior experience serving with French and British squadrons. They combined deadly marksmanship with exceptional observation skills.

Flying as Erwin's observer, or even on the same missions with him, was indeed hazardous duty. By the time that Baucom arrived at the 1st Aero Squadron on July 25, Erwin had already flown his first mission and brought back a dead observer. The squadron suffered heavy casualties during operations in the Château-Thierry sector. Baucom nevertheless volunteered to fly missions with Erwin from the first day he arrived at the squadron, although they did not team up together on a regular basis until the start of the St. Mihiel offensive on September 12.

After Erwin's first 13 full days since arriving, five 1st Aero Squadron pilots (one of them Ernest Wold, Erwin's best friend since joining the squadron) and observers had already been killed and one was wounded after flying on missions with him. Three escorting 27th Aero Squadron pursuit pilots were also killed in action and three more made prisoners of war (one being wounded). Erwin nevertheless claimed an unconfirmed aerial victory, the black cross he later had painted on the fuselage side of his Salmson serving as his validation.

These casualties were five of the 16 total 1st Aero Squadron crew members killed during World War I, three in airplane accidents and 13 KIA. Three of those 13 died while flying on missions with Erwin, as well as two of the seven crewmen wounded in action while either flying with or serving as protection escorts for Erwin on missions. This wound total does not even include Easterbrook's double-victory flight, when a bullet went through his thumb, or his last mission, where a bullet grazed his face. Erwin, nicknamed the "unkillable" by the squadron, and Baucom meanwhile remained relatively unscathed. This was an incredible feat considering that between August 26 and November 6, 1918, Erwin flew for 89 hours and 20 minutes over the front lines, Baucom 57 hours and 15 minutes, and Easterbrook 49 hours and 45 minutes. It was especially so considering that they fired thousands of rounds of ammunition between them at air and ground targets, with Erwin compiling eight confirmed victories, three of these while flying with Baucom, and four confirmed victories shared with Easterbrook.[1]

Erwin's flight hours were at least double or triple those of 17 of the other 18 squadron pilots. He was also apparently flight commander of the second flight. Although "flight commander" does not appear in 1st Aero Squadron records, his hangar sergeant in charge of the second flight, Sgt. W. N. Buchard, wrote the damage assessment report of his Salmson after he returned from his first mission on August 1. In his September 4, 1918, letter home, he told his mother that his foremost, perhaps unrealistic, expectation was to be promoted to captain—and by his birthday on October 18. Much of this was based on his personal assessment that he had already flown about 60 hours over the front lines, while most pilots averaged only 15–20 hours of flight time before being shot down. Two 1st Aero Squadron officers promoted to captain prior to the Armistice, John G. Colgan (joined June 6, 1917) and squadron commander Arthur J. Coyle (joined August 9, 1917), had simply been in the squadron for a year longer than Erwin.[2]

Erwin's eight victories made him the highest-scoring American two-seater pilot. An observer ace from World War I is also a rarity in aviation history, and Easterbrook's five victory credits in lone combats scored entirely by him

"The Three Amigos"—The top three airmen of the 1st Aero Squadron, credited with nine of the squadron's 12 confirmed victories, are all 1st Lieutenants (left to right): Byrne V. Baucom (DSC), William P. Erwin (DSC), and Arthur E. Easterbrook (DSC). Baucom and Easterbrook had the most flight hours of any other observers over the front lines during the St. Mihiel and Meuse–Argonne offensives. Erwin had the most flight hours of any squadron pilot over the front lines during those campaigns and was the most aggressive and highest-scoring two-seater pilot in the U.S. Air Service. Only two other 1st Aero Squadron airmen won the DSC during the war. (George H. Williams via Greg VanWyngarden)

xviii • A PAIR OF ACES AND A TREY

and his pilot make him the highest-scoring American observer ace (according to U.S. Air Force Historical Study No. 133, June 1969). Although Baucom had been included on an initial list of 63 American officer aces credited with five victories, the American Expeditionary Forces, First Army Air Service's final compilation of confirmed victories, as of May 26, 1919, credited Baucom with three victories, hence "Trey" rather than "Ace."

These three airmen alone were awarded Distinguished Service Crosses and Oak Leaf Clusters and Bar a total of 10 times. They also accounted for nine of the 1st Aero Squadron's 13 confirmed victories.[3]

Erwin and Easterbrook were one of only two 1st Aero Squadron teams to score a double victory on the same day, and when Easterbrook was shot down on November 3 during the First Army's final assault, he became an ace in that battle. Erwin and Baucom were also shot down in spectacular fashion after strafing German troops on November 5, but information obtained from their reconnaissance missions nevertheless set the stage for the First Army divisions' final assault to establish bridgeheads over the Meuse River, terminate the war, and complete the victory.

William P. Erwin, Byrne V. Baucom, and Château-Thierry Offensive Operations, July 1918

William Portwood Erwin

The son of Reverend William Albert and Lula Portwood (maiden name) Erwin, William (Bill) Portwood Erwin was born on October 18, 1895, in Ryan, Oklahoma, just 2 miles north of the Red River (the Texas border) and the intersection of federal and state highways US 81 and SH-32. Reverend W. A. Erwin was pastor of the Presbyterian Church in Ryan, then found at the intersection of Lincoln Avenue and 7th Street. He was also president of the Ryan Cumberland Presbyterian College, then situated at the intersection of Washington Avenue and 13th Street. Lula was musical director of both the church and the college. Under his mother's guidance, Bill began studying music at the age of four—playing piano, violin, and pipe organ, and singing in the church choir. At six he began playing violin in Sunday school and church.[1]

Although Bill later recalled that he was 12 years old when his family moved to Amarillo, Texas, Reverend Erwin was in Amarillo at least as early as December 1905, and Lula at least from July 1906. From August 17 to September 28, 1906, Mrs Erwin advertised in Amarillo's *Twice-a-Week Herald* that, "Mrs. W. A. Erwin will begin her Music Class at her residence, 1308 Polk, Next house to the Public School Building, Monday, Sept. 3, 1906." Although their house technically should have been across the street from the Polk Street School, located at 1210 South Polk, since West 13th Street was not then open or cut through to South Polk, they were indeed the first house south of the school. Lula Erwin's postgraduate teachers' course in music at the Klindworth Conservatory in Atlanta, Georgia, from April–May 1907, highlights her qualifications as a music teacher. Her instructor was the great German artist, Herr Kurt Mueheller. Professor Mueheller was then the greatest exponent in America of the Leschetizsky method of piano technique. After she returned on May 10, she had many advanced pupils in Amarillo, including Bill, preparing for their annual recital at the end of June.[2]

Reverend Erwin was pastor of the First Presbyterian Church, a member of the Southern Presbyterian denomination, then built at 406 South Fillmore, but the Cumberland Presbyterian Church (denomination) was only two blocks south at 610 South Fillmore. By 1908, his old Presbyterian Church had been completely torn down and rebuilt at 600 South Fillmore, the same block as the Cumberland church, which had been popularly known as the "Fillmore Street Presbyterian Church." However, in 1909, after making plans to construct a new red brick building at 1000 South Taylor Street, it renamed itself "Central Presbyterian Church." The church moved into the new building in June 1910 with 191 people on its education rolls, its size taking up two lots and being about twice as large as the First Presbyterian Church on Fillmore.[3]

Called "Will" when he attended Amarillo High School, then at 506 South Johnson, moving to Amarillo allowed him to expand his musical studies. His violin solo at the Presbyterian Church on January 10, 1912, and piano solo at the high school in mid-February 1912 were commonplace performances, yet he still found time to play tennis and was on his high school football team. His parents had encouraged him to make music his life in high school and become a professional musician. Reverend Erwin often preached in surrounding towns, and his reported stays were typically a week or more. With Bill graduating from high school, his trip to Pawhuska, Oklahoma—57 miles north-northwest of Tulsa and about 21 miles south of the Kansas state line—shows insight on Bill's inclusiveness in his ever-expanding evangelism. In May 1912, Reverend Erwin evangelized in Pawhuska on the Sundays of May 5, 12, and 19. The *Osage Journal* proclaimed, "Rev. Erwin is a great leader of song, his son is a wonder on the piano and violin."[4]

By the time Bill graduated from high school in 1912, he was already a proficient piano player and had composed some church music. His parents encouraged him to enroll in two conservatories of music: in New York City, where he learned professional basics, before going on to the Chicago Musical College at 430 South Michigan Avenue, across the street from Grant Park, for advanced studies. After graduation in Chicago, Bill was selected to tour America as a concert pianist. The constant exposure of meeting people in so many different places and being the subject of so much public adulation developed into a way of life, supplying excitement and satisfaction that he learned to crave. At the conclusion of the first tour, the tour directors were impressed with his musical abilities and favorable public acclaim received after his concerts.

This resulted in a second countrywide tour in 1916, just as the war in Europe was intensifying. Local newspapers published front-page stories of the indiscriminate sinking of American ships, and Bill could see that American citizens were preparing for war. The turning point in his musical career occurred in Atlanta, Georgia, the first week of April 1917. Once America declared war on April 6, religious revival meeting attendance dropped alarmingly. People had only one goal for the next two years—to help in the war effort. Bill prepared to enlist in the U.S. Army.[5]

Orders were issued on April 17, 1917, for establishing an officers' training camp at Fort Logan H. Roots, the military post in North Little Rock, Arkansas, where Bill enlisted as a member of their first class. Officer candidates, after careful screening, were given three months of intensive training. Graduation from Fort Roots would make him a second lieutenant in the infantry, but Erwin was more interested in aviation. This enticed him to apply after graduation and instead enlist as a private first class in the Aviation Section of the Signal Corps at Austin, Texas, reporting in mid-July 1917. He completed his ground school course at the School of Military Aeronautics in early September 1917.[6]

As a new cadet, he was given 10 days of leave and one last opportunity to return home. Upon his return, he discovered that he was chosen as one of 17 cadets ordered to France without preliminary flight training in America. This was a great honor. Erwin sailed aboard the White Star liner SS *Megantic*, leaving at 9:15 a.m. from Hoboken, New Jersey, on October 10. Amongst the other 124 Aviation Section, Signal Enlisted Reserve Corps cadets on board were the later famous author Norman Archibald and one future 27th Aero Squadron pilot, Oliver T. Beauchamp, who protected him in battle almost 10 months later and paid the ultimate sacrifice on August 1, 1918. They arrived safely in Liverpool on October 17, 1917, and went on to a rest camp on the outskirts of Southampton. Several days later they crossed the English Channel to reach Le Havre in northern France.[7]

From there, Cadet Erwin was one of 125 cadet aviators who arrived by truck with two officers, Major H. C. Davidson, Commanding, and 1st Lieutenant R. Benson, at the 3rd AIC (Aviation Instruction Center), Issoudun, on November 2. With only three barracks erected when they arrived, they spent the first month helping to build the camp—digging ditches and constructing roads and a miniature railroad. Then on November 30, Erwin and the 16 other cadets who had sailed with him were told that all preliminary flying fields in France were filled to capacity. Since the 3rd AIC was intended to provide advanced and pursuit training for pilots, no endeavor was made to give a preliminary course there at that time.[8]

As a result of a phone call on December 22, Erwin was one of 76 cadets, members of the Fourth Foreign Detachment (Air Service)—who had

Due to severe overcrowding at the 3rd AIC, Issoudun, many cadets were transferred to other venues for preliminary flight training, such as the 2nd AIC, Tours. Cadet Private First Class Bill Erwin, third from left, appears to have been involved in a mishap with Caudron G-3 D.2, C.6250, an 80hp Le Rhone rotary engine, dual control trainer, known to have flown from the 2nd AIC on May 3, 1918. The man on Erwin's right was probably his French *moniteur* (flight instructor). (Courtesy of San Diego Air and Space Museum)

graduated from ground schools in America during the first two weeks in September and then sailed overseas on October 9 under the command of Maj. H. C. Davidson—who then transferred to the French Aviation School at Châteauroux, 27 km southwest of Issoudun. The transfer was made on motor trucks and the cadets were set up at Châteauroux in three French barracks. The Ecole d'Aviation Francaise was at first used only as a means of instruction for some of the many American cadets awaiting preliminary training in France. It was destined to become an important item on the training schedule of the American Air Service, since instruction continued there long after the American detachments had been withdrawn from most of the other French flying centers.

The cadets there were divided into 10 squads of eight men each (four other men, former members of the American Field Ambulance Service, were also part of the detachment), with each squad assigned a French *moniteur* (flight instructor). Only four of the 10 *moniteurs* spoke English, so French-speaking cadets were distributed among the remaining squads as interpreters. The French *moniteurs* spent the first three days registering, photographing, and examining the students. December 29, one of only three good flying days in

France since the middle of the month, was when they first marched the cadets to the flying field for their first double-control flights.

About 75 days was the initial length of time required to complete the entire training period, dependent on available winter flying weather days. Although the cold weather hampered progress during the winter, lectures on technical subjects in machine shops and hangars, and discussions on flying with the instructors, kept the cadets occupied on days unsuitable for flying. Erwin's letters home do not specify his flying dates there. The students first flew Caudron G-3s with Anzani motors. After attaining some familiarity with the air, they were transferred to finishing *moniteurs* who flew them in Caudron G-3s with Le Rhone rotary motors. At that stage they continued until considered ready to fly alone, taking their first solo flights with Le Rhones, and upon attaining reasonable proficiency with this type, they went into the Anzani solo class. A student had to take between 20 and 40 solo flights, a considerable part of them in spiral work, before being permitted to undertake the Brevet test, the requirements for which were as follows:

(a) Spiral: cut the motor at 600 meters and land within 50 meters of the spot directly beneath the point where the motor was cut.

(b) Two straight-line voyages of 60 km each: Châteauroux–Civray and back twice.

(c) Two triangles of 200 km each: Châteauroux–Avord–Romorantin–Châteauroux, and Châteauroux–Romorantin–Avord–Châteauroux.

(d) Altitude: remain for one hour above 2,000 meters. It was permissible to make the altitude test upon one leg of a triangle. If made separately, it was permissible to go above 2,000 meters and remain for 15 minutes, land and repeat.

To secure the *Brevet Militaire* badge, the student had to successfully pass the Brevet tests and a technical examination prescribed by the French. He must have had 25 hours in the air (double-control time included) and have made 50 solo landings. The Brevet tests required from 10–15 hours of flying time which could be made in from one-and-a-half to three days, depending on the student and the weather. Erwin passed his *Brevet Militaire*, returned to Issoudun about March 9 for advanced flight training, and started his course of instruction there about April 9, 1918.[9]

When students first entered flight training at Issoudun, they were assigned numbers, lesser numbers representing how many students had preceded them. But if they transferred, were killed, or otherwise left the program, those numbers were removed from the records. If they returned later, they were then

Another view of Caudron G-3 D.2, C.6250, a dual control trainer, loaded aboard a trailer, apparently after Cadet Bill Erwin (left) nosed it over upon landing and broke the propeller at the 2nd AIC, Tours, probably in April 1918. The man on his left with goggles and trench coat was most likely his French *moniteur*. (Courtesy of San Diego Air and Space Museum)

assigned new numbers. Records show him returning to Issoudun for advanced flight training, as student number 667. Of two cadets whom he sailed with aboard SS *Megantic*, Beauchamp's student number was 249 and Archibald was number 262. Between that sequence of numbers, 250, 251, 255, and 261 are missing. As Erwin was initially in the same group with them, he likely represents one of the missing numbers. Since he transferred to Châteauroux for preliminary flight training, they apparently removed his original number and then reissued him with number 667 upon returning to Issoudun to complete his training. What is also notable is that it took Archibald and Beauchamp about four months to complete their advanced training course at Issoudun, while by the time Erwin returned to the 3rd AIC, the course had since been shortened to 59 days. This included 33 days of ground training and 26 days of flying training. He complained there were 200 flyers on the waiting list ahead of him, and that he had to wait five more weeks to be reassigned to flying duty once he returned, although part of that time was taken up with ground training. After Cadet Erwin's first flight at Issoudun, he kept brief notes:[10]

> **April 20**—Started flying. Nieuport 23 double control. *Moniteur* Lt. Farnum—good *moniteur*. 5 hops, fair landings. Am rusty. [A total of 110 minutes flying instruction was required on the 80hp Nieuport 23 double-control before he could move to the 80hp Nieuport 23 solo.]

April 26—Was placed on active duty per S.O. 110, G.H., S., A.E.F. Glad to put on my bars and belt. Had 30 minutes' air work. Very tricky ship.

May 16—Did figure 8s twice. Good 8s, but second bunch too near the ground. Was taken off flying for three days.

May 22—Vrilles [nose spins]. Very interesting.

May 23—More aerobatics. Like them immensely. Spirals, *renversements* [reversals], *virages* [turns], sideslips, etc. Lt. Col. Kilner, in command, plays violin very well. Major Spatz, in charge of training, plays the ukulele and likes ragtime. Play a good deal with them at their quarters. Bum piano.

May 26—*Laches* [promoted] to Field 7 with grade of A.

June 3—Four trick formations. One altitude record, 6100 meters [about 20,000 feet]. One of best records ever made by American student on the field, much higher than any record so far made in America. *Laches* to Field 8 with grade of A.

June 4—Best field in school. Most wonderful combat aerobatic field in world. Ships braced for any strain. Took pictures of fixed target with camera.

June 6—Combat work with camera gun. Very, very interesting. Got some excellent pictures.

June 7—Sent to Cazaux Aerial Gunnery School.[11]

They did cross-country, altitude, and aerobatics training at Field Six, Field Four, and Field Five, while flying 15-meter Nieuport 17s. On May 18, 1918, he also flew his cross-country and altitude test from Field Five at Issoudun on a Nieuport 17. He flew from Field Seven for formation flying on June 3 and Field Eight for combat flying on June 6. He was photographed in uniform on a beach in Arcachon, or surrounding Arcachon Bay, about 16 km north of the French aerial gunnery school at Cazaux, probably the weekend of June 8–9. After taking a train via Paris and Bordeaux to Arcachon, a scheduled truck service took them to that flying field, located at Lake Cazaux, for the required 20-day course in aerial gunnery training. He should have returned to Issoudun about July 1 and graduated as a 1st lieutenant among a class of 220 students who graduated from the 3rd AIC on July 9.[12]

He was then temporarily assigned to the American Aviation Acceptance Park No. 1 at Orly aerodrome, situated on the Fountainbleau road, 12 km southeast of the center of Paris and 1.5 km northwest of the town of Orly. It was situated there because nearly all the French aviation factories were in the suburbs of Paris, and it was also within easy flying distance of London and the English aviation factories. This was also the central distribution point for American airplanes to their squadrons. Pilots assigned to that post as ferry pilots were ordered there from the American training school at Issoudun because they had but few hours in the air, or they had shown by their flying that with more time they would make good *chasse* pilots. Assigned to the Dispatching Division, which averaged over 150 pilots on hand to ferry planes after they had been first equipped and inspected, Erwin logged five more hours in his

Cadet William P. Erwin (left), with his Junior Military Aviator badge, is lined up with three other cadets, all with Military Aviator badges, from secondary flight training at Issoudun, probably along Arcachon Bay in mid-May 1918. They were likely in Arcachon to attend the French aerial gunnery school at Cazaux, accessible by truck 10 miles south of Arcachon. (Courtesy of San Diego Air and Space Museum)

pilot's logbook before July 14, Bastille Day, commemorating the beginning of the French Revolution. He spent the French national holiday on a 24-hour leave in Paris, watching the parades and celebrating with Parisians.[13]

He was posted to the 1st Aero Squadron on July 19, along with four other pilots who had been assigned as ferry pilots at Orly aerodrome: Lieutenants Raymond F. Fox, James M. Richardson, Arthur J. Butler, and Edward Groteclose, Jr. There were five new Salmson 2A2s dispatched from Orly aerodrome to Francheville aerodrome during the third week of July. Lieutenant Walter B. Miller had been posted on the 15th and ferried in one of the Salmsons, while Lt. Ernest G. Wold had been posted on the 20th, the same dates that the 1st Aero Squadron received new Salmsons. The first four Salmsons were dispatched without any inspection, showing that their primary mission was to deliver pilots, rather than fully equipped and inspected airplanes. The five new pilots most likely thus arrived aboard three new Salmsons.

He had assured his parents in a letter home that he would be a *chasse* pilot: "I will fly the small one-seat fighters. We will protect the bombing and observation planes while they do their assigned work. Our duty is only to scrap, and, of course, do reconnaissance work. I am raring to get my first Boche. Think after I get about fifty maybe I'll retire."[14] Although trained as a *chasse*

Next to an early 1st Aero Squadron Salmson, 1st Lieutenant Bill Erwin stands in oily flight clothes with helmet ready. (Courtesy of San Diego Air and Space Museum)

pilot, he was assigned to where the Air Service needed him most. But after telling his parents what he really wanted to do, he joined his squadron with a fighter pilot's mentality. Only a combination of luck and divine intervention could keep him alive thereafter.

Château-Thierry Offensive Operations

The 1st Aero Squadron arrived at Saints on June 30 and began operating over the front on July 1. They were then equipped with Salmson 2A2s, which at first caused some difficulty due to unfamiliarity with the mechanics of the motor. On July 5, the squadron moved to the flying field near Francheville. It acted as the Army Corps squadron of the First Army Corps, doing reconnaissance, photography, and artillery surveillance work. Infantry contact work was minimal. The Germans had concentrated many aircraft over this sector to counter a similar number of British aircraft previously operating there prior to the 1st Aero Squadron's arrival. Combats with enemy planes were thus frequent, resulting in heavy squadron casualties. Three Salmsons made forced landings on July 5, while a fourth Salmson caught fire on landing behind Allied lines. Another Salmson had a forced landing on July 6, while they lost another Salmson wrecked in a forced landing on July 7, as well as an old Dorand AR2 wrecked on landing that they still had on hand. They listed no operational casualties though.[15]

When 1st Lt. Bill Erwin arrived at the 1st Aero Squadron, the third and last phase of the Marne campaign had only recently begun on July 18 with the battle of Soissons, the Allied counteroffensive between Soissons and Château-Thierry. Marshal Ferdinand Foch, the Allied Commander-in-Chief, had moved several French and American divisions to the vicinity of Soissons, the dormant northern flank of an enemy salient. To mislead German aerial observers, he sent troops during daylight hours in the direction of Reims to simulate reinforcements being rushed there and to divert attention to the concentrations sent to the opposite flank.[16]

All observation operations of the American I Corps Air Service were based at Francheville aerodrome, a temporary wartime airfield located 8 km north-northwest of Coulommiers in the Seine-et-Marne department of the Île-de-France region in north-central France, and part of the I Corps Observation Group. The 1st Pursuit Group, consisting of the 27th, 94th, 95th, and 147th Aero Squadrons, based at Touquin, normally supplied protection for I Corps Observation Group missions. During operations in this sector, the 1st Aero Squadron's work consisted of reconnaissance, photography, and artillery surveillance. It acted as the Army Corps squadron of the American I Corps, and as such did little infantry contact work. With many German airplanes concentrated on this front, the squadron suffered heavy casualties. Despite this handicap, the squadron did excellent work and flew in all kinds of weather to obtain information that was of great value. Erwin and Baucom were ultimately two of six pilots and observers who bore the brunt of the work in this operation, although not yet together that often.

The French Tenth Army, near Soissons, was chosen to deliver the main counteroffensive attack. The spearhead of that army was the French XX Corps, which was to capture the high ground south of Soissons. It consisted of the American 1st and 2nd Divisions and the French 1st Moroccan Division. Its direction of attack would be eastward over the plateau just south of Soissons and across the main railroad and highway leading south from Soissons. The composition of the corps was such that four-fifths of its numerical strength was American.[17]

The concentration of troops was carried out with the utmost secrecy, with the 1st and 2nd Divisions going into the line only at the last minute. Some units of the 2nd Division marched all night and then double-timed over muddy roads in the dark so they could jump off with the barrage. On July 18, they launched the assault at 4:35 a.m. without any prior artillery preparation and took the German troops completely by surprise. The units of the 1st and 2nd Divisions, with those of the 1st Moroccan Division between them, advanced with characteristic dash and vigor. After much hard fighting and staggering losses, by 5:30 p.m. forward elements of the 1st Division had advanced nearly 6 km, captured 1,500 prisoners, 30 guns and howitzers, and many machine guns, but had no reinforcements to draw upon.[18]

The 1st Division's objective for July 20 was the line from Berzy-le-Sec to Buzancy, their goal being to capture and cut off the highway between Château-Thierry and Soissons. At noon, all 1st Division heavy artillery began firing to destroy Berzy-le-Sec until 2:00 p.m., when their 75mm cannon began a rolling barrage in front of the advancing infantry. Opposed by the German 11th Bavarian Division and the 28th, 34th, and 42nd Divisions on this date, the 1st Division captured Ploisy, 1.6 km west of Berzy-le-Sec, but in the process all their tanks going in with the assault units were disabled. Despite this, the right (southern) part of the division advanced another 0.8 km east, crossing the main railroad tracks leading south from Soissons. Darkness and frequent bursts of fire caused confusion, making it difficult to find units and maintain liaison, so 1st Division's commander, Major General Charles P. Summerall, ordered the 1st Aero Squadron to locate the position of their front lines.[19]

The 1st Aero Squadron had only been issued Salmson 2A2 airplanes in abundance since July 1, considerable motor trouble initially being experienced due to their mechanics' lack of familiarity with Salmson motors. Much better results were obtained within a short time, however, after which squadron members held their Salmsons in high esteem. Erwin was assigned serial number 3204 (fuselage number 8). Enemy airplane concentrations on this front attacked advancing troops and caused many squadron casualties while flying their first missions over the French Tenth Army/1st Division sector from dawn to dark. They assigned the requested infantry contact patrol to 1st Lieutenant Erwin, along with observer 1st Lt. Herman St. John "Benny" Boldt, transferred from the infantry and a popular squadron member who was also worshiped by the local French village children.[20]

However, low clouds and approaching darkness made it necessary to fly very low, making the Salmson an easy target for German machine gunners.

1st Aero Squadron Salmson 2A2 3204 "8," received July 1, 1918, assigned to 1st Lieutenant Erwin on July 19, 1918. (Courtesy of Greg VanWyngarden)

Upon reaching the front lines, Erwin later reported calling Lieutenant Boldt through the speaking tube connecting the pilot and observer cockpits. After getting no response, Erwin immediately started for home to his flying field. Upon landing, they determined that German machine gunners had killed Boldt with ground fire, the observer becoming the squadron's first casualty.[21]

The 1st Division captured Berzy-le-Sec on July 21 and then crossed the Soissons–Château-Thierry highway that was one of the goals of the French Tenth Army attack. Upon reaching Buzancy, just east of the highway, they effectively cut off the most important road of the German communication system within the salient. They were relieved from the line on the night of July 22/23 by the 15th Scottish Division. Boldt's sacrifice was just one of the 7,083 casualties of officers and men sustained by the 1st Division. Three-quarters of all the division's infantry field officers were either killed or wounded. In five days of continuous fighting (the artillery fought for six or seven days) along their north–south 3.2 km-wide lane, the division gained 11 km across the enemy's rear. They cut the railroad and the high road from Soissons, upon which the enemy mainly depended for his supplies. They met and overcame elements from seven German divisions, capturing 125 officers, 3,375 men, 75 field guns and howitzers, 50 trench mortars, 500 machine guns, and vast quantities of ammunition and stores.[22]

Byrne Virchow Baucom

On July 25, the 1st Aero Squadron teamed up Erwin with observer 2nd Lt. Byrne V. Baucom, a fortunate pairing for both of their careers and an asset to the squadron. Baucom was born in Milford, Ellis County, Texas, on June 19, 1892. He graduated from Milford High School in 1915 and enrolled in Arts and Sciences at the University of Texas from August 1915 until May 1917. Prior to entering military service, Baucom worked as a newspaper reporter and linotype operator in central Texas. His reports, as shown below, supply a sense of accuracy because he approached this duty in the same manner as that of a newspaper reporter.[23]

From May 8 to August 15, 1917, Baucom attended the first student-officers' training camp on the Leon Springs Military Reservation, north of San Antonio, Texas, and was commissioned at Camp Funston as a 2nd lieutenant of the 15th Provisional Division, 343rd Field Artillery Regiment, Third Battalion, Company B. After returning from leave on August 29, he reported back to the officers' training camp at Leon Springs. He then attended the School of Equitation at Camp Travis, San Antonio, where his instructor, Maj. George Grunert of the 360th Infantry Regiment, was based. (Both the 343rd and 360th Regiments were later attached to the 90th Division.) Grunert graded his officer-students at the end of the course and ranked them according to their overall practice of horsemanship and riding. Of the 32 students, 2nd Lieutenant Baucom ranked last. After transferring to the Air Service, Baucom first trained at Kelly Field, San Antonio, and then as an observer at Post Field, Fort Sill, Oklahoma. He received orders in April 1918 to continue overseas, where he further trained at Issoudun in France. On June 11, he was posted to the French *Escadrille* Sop. 5, which then became Sal. 5 in July after equipping with and flying Salmson 2A2s not long before his transfer to the 1st Aero Squadron on July 16 as a 2nd lieutenant.[24]

As a former journalist, Baucom wrote much of the 1st Aero Squadron's history. He begins here by reflecting on his first flights with his new squadron:

> Lieut. Erwin, Pilot, and Lieut. Baucom, Observer, is here given not to portray their individual deeds but by portraying them to illustrate the work of the entire organization. Both joined the Squadron at the beginning of the Château-Thierry offensive and here they began their long list of brilliant exploits, writing day by day until operations ceased one of the brightest pages in American history. Lieut. Baucom's story of [one of] his first flights with the squadron is given below:[25]
>
> About July 11th, Lieut. D'Amour and I, after having spent five very prosperous and happy weeks with a French squadron, *Escadrille* Sal. 5, got orders to proceed to Coulommiers,

Seine-et-Marne, about 40 kilometers southwest of Château-Thierry, where we were assigned to the First Aero Squadron, First Corps Observation Group. We arrived at the squadron July 14th. The squadron was then camped at the little town of Francheville. We got there just in time to be participants in the second battle of the Marne, which started July 18th.[26]

I had several trips over the lines and several flights. Then late in the afternoon of July 25th, Lieut. Erwin, Pilot, and I had our first "hop" together. Our adventures and lucky career immediately set in. He was a stranger to me and I a stranger to him. I did know one thing though: and that only a few days before, he had brought home a dead Observer in the rear cockpit. I had seen the precious blood all over the floor of the cockpit and splattered over the outside of the fuselage. The mechanics had washed it off as best they could and put a coat of dark blue paint over the floor of the cockpit. On this present trip I was sitting in that selfsame cockpit. I never was very superstitious, but I must confess that I didn't feel any too comfortable. I tried to "kid" myself into believing that two people couldn't die in the same place, and therefore the chances were in my favor. Since I had never heard of two people dying in the same place, I gradually began to believe my own doctrine.

Anyway, I was in the ship, and we were whizzing through space faster than 100 miles per hour towards the lines, and about 2000 meters high. Therefore, I had to make my philosophy fit the occasion. It was ship No. 8, a machine that was destined to take us thru so much excitement and so many narrow escapes that I don't hesitate to say that we always had a third passenger—and that was God.

We had a load of propaganda on board that we were going to drop, among other things that we intended to do. We were just reaching the lines when we saw a "dogfight" taking place over in a corner of the sky, about over Beuvardes, between 6 or 8 Boche *chasse* and 5 or 6 Americans. It was a battle royal, and our brave and fearless, though inexperienced, American flyers were giving a good account of themselves against their more experienced adversaries. I almost jumped down in the fuselage and clapped my hands with patriotic glee. Everybody was busy trying to entertain the other fellow. It seemed that everybody was trying to make everybody welcomed. On second glance we saw the Boche had the Americans slightly outnumbered, and we couldn't stand for that, so we didn't do a thing but go crashing madly over to them with our bristles up like a wild and angry boar. We didn't propose to see our American brothers overpowered by an enemy in both numbers and experience. We had no more than thrown ourselves into the fracas when two of the damn Boche got on our tail and began giving us the warmest reception either of us had ever received. Their tracer bullets were going through every part of our machine, but I was not idle. I had a pair of twin Lewis machine guns that were beauties. They were working like a streak of greased lightning; and I had both wide open, sending a double stream of fire into one of the devils that was trying so desperately to get us. One of the American *chasse* pilots dove on the other Boche and began entertaining him. Presently my adversary went down in a steep glide toward his own lines.

But I didn't have time to see if he later went out of control, or whether I had put his motor on the bum and caused him to make a forced landing. About that time, we saw a Boche bi-place (two-seater) observation machine 1500 meters below us going around and around with one of our bi-places that was doing an infantry liaison. So, we immediately started down after the brute. We were then about 2000 meters altitude, but the Boche saw us coming down upon him like the wrath of God from heaven, which he knew was due him, and immediately beat it for home.

This was the same fight, I think, in which one of the *chasse* men (of the First Pursuit Group) brought down a Boche Captain, that is, forced him to land on our side of the lines, and having a bullet through his own motor, he landed beside the Boche machine, and the conqueror and conquered got in an automobile and rode back to headquarters together.

Erwin and I climbed back up to about 2000 meters and went over into "Germany" five or six kilometers east of Fère-en-Tardenois and dropped our propaganda.[27]

Then we spied a Boche observation balloon a few kilometers west of Fère-en-Tardenois and it looked like a mighty nice thing to shoot at. We didn't have any incendiary bullets and knew that as far as material damage was concerned, we might as well be shooting at it with a "bean flipper." But it would at least be good target practice. So, Erwin "peaked" on it with his front gun when we were about over Fère-en-Tardenois, and while he was shooting at the balloon, I had my twin Lewises playing a tune into the town itself.

After having a continual round of pleasure for a couple of hours, we went limping back to the airdrome, with our machine in pretty bad condition. There were 10 or 12 bullets in it; a flying wire and a drift wire were shot into; and, a 3-inch antiaircraft shell had gone through the upper wing, not more than two feet from our heads, without exploding.

Leutnant Karl Menckhoff, *Jasta* 72 commander, shown wearing his *Pour le Mérite*, Royal House Order of Hohenzollern, and Iron Cross First Class awards. (Courtesy of Lance Bronnenkant)

Leutnant Karl Menckhoff holding his dog prior to a mission while standing in front of his Fokker D.VII, which had a white "M" insignia on both fuselage sides and top wing. (Courtesy of Lance Bronnenkant)

> Otherwise, we were none the worse off for having made the trip. And within a day or two our wonderful bunch of fine mechanics had her all fixed up and ready again for the skies.[28]

After returning, Erwin and Baucom found eight bullet holes in their ship, two flying wires cut by bullets, and an antiaircraft shell had passed through the upper right wing's fabric without bursting. They had apparently intervened in an aerial engagement between Spads of the 95th Aero Squadron and Fokker D.VIIs of Royal Saxon *Jasta* 72 north of Château-Thierry at about 6:45 p.m. The "Boche Captain" forced down was *Jasta* 72 commander and 39-victory ace *Ltn.* Karl Menckhoff, his adversary 1st Lt. Walter L. Avery's lucky shot having destroyed Menckhoff's intake manifold. It was Avery's first patrol over the front lines. However, Baucom's recollection that Avery and Menckhoff rode back to Headquarters in an automobile together was somewhat inaccurate. According to the 95th Aero Squadron's history, "Lieut. Avery did land and saw the pilot go by in an automobile."[29]

On July 27, the 1st Aero Squadron moved to Ferme de Moras aerodrome, a temporary wartime airfield located 3.1 km east of the commune of La Ferté-sous-Jouarre, also known as Moras Farm.[30]

Three days later, Lieutenant Erwin flew a reconnaissance mission with his observer, 2nd Lt. Stewart Bird. Returning 45 minutes later, their attempt was unsuccessful, with stations covering a wide area north, south, east, and west of Château-Thierry all later reporting very hazy conditions with very poor visibility in the morning, although the skies cleared by that afternoon.[31]

On July 31, flying Salmson 2A2 3204 "8," Lieutenant Erwin performed another reconnaissance mission with Lieutenant Bird. Cumulus clouds were building up at 1,200 meters over Fismes, 42 km north of Château-Thierry, so they maintained an altitude of 1,000 meters to complete their mission and returned safely after an hour and 40 minutes. Also on this date, Lieutenant Baucom flew a mission with pilot 1st Lt. David A. McDonald, who had to make a forced landing at May-en-Multien, wrecking Salmson 2A2 3672 in doing so. Although Baucom was not injured, McDonald later became sick, was hospitalized on August 8, and thereafter was discharged from the squadron.[32]

CHAPTER 2

Black Thursday—1st Aero Squadron and 1st Pursuit Group's Worst Day

During these first two weeks of the offensive, troop movements were so rapid that it became impossible to photograph all the territory in the line of advance. The unstable nature of the front made it imperative to secure frequent photographs of the enemy front-line positions. Great difficulty was experienced in carrying out these missions due to frequent and persistent attacks of hostile pursuit patrols. The missions on this date were neither the first nor last attempt to use accompanying pursuit patrols as protection, although these were seldom completely successful. The low-speed, low-altitude protection assignments placed pursuit pilots at a great disadvantage during enemy attacks.

Any enemy pursuit airplane having the advantage of speed gained solely from altitude could dive through the protection patrol and destroy the observation airplane they were assigned to protect before they could react. Speed obtained by altitude was often the deciding factor in aerial combat that the protection patrol lacked. Their own airplanes were practically at the mercy of hostile pursuit patrols attacking from above unless they left the formation. If attacked, they at once ceased to be of value as direct protection for the observation teams occupied with taking photographs. During aerial encounters, they could not turn and fight to the rear without deserting the airplane they were sent to protect. The protection patrol's speed also made it difficult to give individual protection to their much slower observation airplanes, while their smaller fuel capacity sometimes limited how long they could maintain protective cover.[1]

These differences were exemplified in the difficulties imposed by the aerial battles of August 1. The Nieuport 28s had a top speed of 122 mph, only 6 mph faster than the Salmson 2A2s they were protecting. Furthermore, their endurance was only 90 minutes, as opposed to the three-and-a-half hours the Salmsons could stay in the air. The difference was much greater for the protecting Spads: 130.4 mph at the 3,800 meters altitude the Salmsons were flying in early morning, along with two hours' duration. This meant that the Nieuports were better at maintaining formation with the Salmsons, which indeed proved to be the case, while the Spads were faced with either flying much higher to lower their speed, or else flying in curves around the formation. Because the aerial photographs had to be taken at a relatively low altitude, even with the protective Nieuport and Spad formations flying above the two Salmsons, this still automatically gave the enemy the advantage of altitude.[2]

The squadron's change from Nieuport 28 to Spad XIII airplanes was not yet complete, so the pilots still flew a mixture of both. While the Spads were better than the Nieuports, they were more difficult to keep in commission, and both pilots and mechanics had to adapt to them. Granted that they were both built for speed and maneuver in combat, not for protective work, a greater factor was that they had little understanding of the inherent dangers they faced on the morning of August 1. German aerial opposition was decidedly strong and aggressive, and they always had superior numbers of pursuit planes. The French Intelligence Service estimated the aerial odds favored the Germans by four to one at one point. Nevertheless, ground commanders desperately needed such photographs, which were an invaluable tool in planning advances. The question then became to what extent the Air Service could learn from these first hard lessons that close protection was costly, and whether they were willing to pay this price on an ongoing basis, change their tactics, or whether they could it afford only when the gains justified the losses.[3]

On the morning of August 1, two Salmsons—Lieutenant Erwin and his observer, 2nd Lieutenant Baucom, in Salmson 2A2 "6," and 2nd Lt. Walter B. Miller, with observer 2nd Lt. James J. Sykes, in Salmson 2A2 792 "18"— were ordered to photograph German artillery and machine-gun positions that might hinder the advance of the 42nd (National Guard) Division. The 42nd Division was at that moment fighting 3.2 km east of there in Seringes-et-Nesles. Their goal on the following day was to advance northward and capture Mareuil-en-Dôle, another 3.2 km to the northeast (but almost 8 km by road). Erwin said, "The pictures had to be taken … just above Fère-en-Tardenois." The arrangements to have escorts accompany the Salmsons were made, as Lieutenant Erwin stated, "by telephone for a Spad squadron of a neighboring Pursuit Group to act as protection." The 27th Aero Squadron supplied the necessary 12 Spad XIIIs and six Nieuport 28s. Mareuil-en-Dôle is assumed to be the area where the aerial battle took place that day.[4]

Reports by the 1st Aero Squadron hereafter portray the essential need for those photographs, embodied by their pilots' and crews' determination to obtain them through their sense of duty, mission, and bravery. Their reports cast new light on earlier assumptions, while portions of B-Flight reports portray how they influenced overall events. The second photography mission later that morning has never previously been documented, Erwin and Baucom having returned from the first mission with only 10 good photos. Erwin left on the second mission with 1st Lt. Karl B. Spencer as his observer. A second Salmson 2A2, serial 1011, was piloted by 1st Lt. Ernest C. Wold, with observer 2nd Lt. James C. Wooten. Twelve 95th Aero Squadron Spads initially protected this second mission.[5]

The 18 27th Aero Squadron planes left at 7:05 a.m. on August 1 to rendezvous with the two Salmsons over Moras Farm aerodrome at 3,000 meters and then travel over the front lines together. Some B-Flight members met up with the 1st Aero Salmsons at 7:40 a.m., while others arrived at 7:50 a.m. Lieutenant Baucom noted, "After circling around for a few minutes to give them time to get back in formation and get their positions, we started for Hunland." Between Erwin's and Baucom's accounts, these included six Nieuports and eight Spads. The Spads comprised B-Flight, plus C-Flight pilots Wehner and Rucker.[6]

Within the next 20 minutes, the formations crossed the front lines and rose to 3,800 meters. Erwin reported that two C-Flight Spads dropped out

Nieuport N.6161 "1" of the 27th Aero Squadron's A-Flight. Lieutenant Arthur L. Whiton, who joined the squadron on July 25, was flying this ship when brought down in German lines on August 1, 1918. Before that time, it is thought to have been the machine of Lieutenant Alfred A. Grant. Behind it is another A-Flight machine, N.6162 or N.6187, still bearing the numeral "6" in the format of its former 95th Aero Squadron incarnation. The civilian's presence is unexplained. (George H. Williams photo GHW.1/T8804-5 via Alan D. Toelle)

Lieutenant Clifford A. McElvain poses by his Nieuport 28 N.6214 "5," the machine he was flying on August 1, 1918, when *Leutnant* Fleischer of *Jasta* 17 brought him down. This is the third plane in the A-Flight lineup photo. Note the Masonic emblem painted below the Vickers gun. On November 3, McElvain was photographed with a group of 24 fellow Freemasons interned at Villingen prison, Germany. (National Museum USAF, FCD8513-21)

due to motor trouble before they reached the front lines; Rucker was certainly one of these two. Lieutenant Wehner either initially dove to follow Rucker as his wingman, or somehow momentarily lost his concentration and the rest of the formation but did not return due to motor trouble. He later reported that at 8:05 a.m., he was just passing Château-Thierry, following in their direction but somehow more than 22.5 km south of the main formation. This left separate Spad and Nieuport formations of six planes to protect each individual Salmson.[7]

The A-Flight Nieuports' chief tactic in flying this type of photographic mission was to have flight leader McElvain (in Nieuport 6214 "5") fly 200–300 meters over and a little to the rear of Miller and Sykes (in Salmson 792 "18"). The other five Nieuports flew behind in a V-shape, it being harder to be surprised by Fokkers if they were tiered above the Salmson. They seemed to be in the proper position, as confirmed by Baucom: "With these six little Nieuports hovering above us, like fighting falcons protecting their mother bird, I didn't bother much about looking for Boche." Little was accomplished, however, because they had barely arrived when the Fokkers attacked, as Baucom

Table 1: 1st Aero and 27th Aero Squadron Personnel, Airplanes, and Casualties, August 1, 1918.

1st Aero, Salmson 2A2	Serial #	Fuselage #	Results	Status
1st Lt. William Erwin	Unknown	6	Baucom took 10	Returned
2nd Lt. Byrne Baucom			photos; protected by	Returned
			B-Flight	
2nd Lt. Walter B. Miller,	792	18	Miller flew into	KIA
2nd Lt. James J. Sykes			railroad overpass bridge	KIA
			2.4 km WSW of	
			Mareuil-en-Dôle	
1st Lt. Ernest C. Wold	1011	Unknown	Made three attempts to	WIA-DOW
2nd Lt. James C. Wooten			take photos; attacked	KIA
			by five Fokkers; crashed	
			into American battery	
			position	
1st Lt. William Erwin	3204	8	Twelve 95th Aero	Returned
1st Lt. Karl B. Spencer			Squadron Spad XIIIs	WIA
			fly protection; Spencer	
			wounded, evacuated to	
			hospital, left squadron	
			August 18	
A-Flight, Nieuport 28				
1st Lt. Clifford A.	6214	5	Separated from flight,	POW
McElvain, flight leader			flew wrong direction	
			to Saints; wounded	
			Ltn. Schuster, *Jasta* 17,	
			then FTL by *Ltn. d. R.*	
			Fleischer, *Jasta* 17	
1st Lt. Arthur L. Whiton	6161	1	Chased Fokker at	POW
			least 5 km north into	
			enemy lines; credit	
			Ltn. Gisbert-Wilhelm	
			Groos, *Jasta* 11	
1st Lt. Richard C. Martin	6301	16	Tracer bullet thru hand,	WIA/POW
			explosive bullet thru	
			shoulder; credit *Vzfw.*	
			Franz Hemer, *Jasta* 6	
1st Lt. Jason S. Hunt	6259	4	Exploded at 2,000	KIA 8:30 a.m.
			meters, 2nd combat;	
			credit *Ltn.* Koepsch,	
			Jasta 4	
1st Lt. Leo H. Dawson	Unknown	2	Probably participated	9:05 a.m.
			in two combats with	
			Hunt, retuned low	
			on gas	

(Continued)

Table 1: 1st Aero and 27th Aero Squadron Personnel, Airplanes, and Casualties, August 1, 1918. *(Continued)*

	Serial #	Fuselage #	Results	Status
A-Flight, Nieuport 28				
1st Lt. Charles B. Sands	6275	17	Shot down in flames by *Ltn. d. R.* Richard Wenzl, *Jasta* 6, vicinity German 24th Res. Div.	KIA 8:15 a.m.
B-Flight, Spad XIII				
1st Lt. Jerry C. Vasconcells, flight leader	Unknown	12	Shared confirmation— Fère-en-Tardenois— unclear whether for Fokker or Rumpler with Hudson	9:05 a.m.
1st Lt. Oliver T. Beauchamp	15143	5	Battled-damaged, spun in and crashed upon landing back at Saints, credited to *Ltn.* Lothar von Richthofen, *Jasta* 11	KIA
1st Lt. Robert W. Donaldson	Unknown	Unknown	Account details suspiciously contrast with other flight members; returned to Saints	9:05 a.m.
1st Lt. Donald Hudson	Unknown	Unknown	Shared one Fokker confirmation over Fère-en-Tardenois with Vasconcells and Nevius, later received two victory confirmations over Rumplers at Saponay, one shared with Roberts; awarded DSC for this action.	9:05 a.m.
1st Lt. Ruliff V. Nevius	15107	18	Fired at *Jasta* 6 Fokker, one gun jammed, shared a confirmed Fokker victory with Hudson and Vasconcells	9:05 a.m.
2nd Lt. Ivan A. Roberts	15156	23	Shared Rumpler victory confirmation with Hudson	9:05 a.m.

(Continued)

Table 1: 1st Aero and 27th Aero Squadron Personnel, Airplanes, and Casualties, August 1, 1918. *(Continued)*

	Serial #	Fuselage #	Results	Status
C-Flight, Spad XIII				
1st Lt. Alfred A. Grant, flight leader	Unknown	Unknown	Motor problem, aborted and returned early	Returned early
1st Lt. L. N. Polk	Unknown	Unknown	Motor problem, aborted and returned early	Returned early
1st Lt. E. W. Rucker	Unknown	Unknown	Dropped out due to motor trouble before reaching Château-Thierry and front lines	Returned early
1st Lt. Joseph H. Wehner	15310	21	Lost formation, no combat participation but reported on other aerial engagements	9:05 a.m.
2nd Lt. Kenneth S. Clapp	15295	22	Motor problem, aborted and returned early	Returned early
2nd Lt. Frank Luke, Jr.	15155	26	Motor problem, aborted and returned early	Returned early

colorfully recalled: "We had just reached our objective, and I had taken one picture and shifted the magazine and snapped the second when Holy high rolling billows of the Dead Sea"![8]

The table below shows all participating 1st Aero Squadron Salmsons, the 18 27th Aero Squadron Spad XIIIs and Nieuport 28s, their respective personnel, and casualties sustained on August 1. Records showing all the 95th Aero Squadron Spad XIIIs that protected the second photographic mission that day are unavailable. The caveats here are: 1) not all these Nieuport pilots were permanently assigned to A-Flight, but all were assigned to protect just one Salmson; 2) Lieutenant Roberts was a C-Flight member but appears to have left with B-Flight on August 1; 3) previous researchers have assumed a B-Flight mixture of Nieuports and Spads, which is unrealistic, given their different flight characteristics; 4) flight assignments kept Spads and Nieuports separated, such that they were assigned to protect their respective Salmson; and 5) *Jagdgeschwader* Nr 1 records overlap and conflict in some cases with those of *Jasta* 11 previously published in *Over the Front*, making it ambiguous which German pilot was credited in each case. The 27th Aero Squadron had suffered engine problems ever since recently receiving their Spads, so were not yet combat ready, while the Nieuport 28s did not match up well against Fokker D.VIIs flown by veteran pilots with many hours of combat experience.[9]

The first air battle started at 8:10 a.m., the time Hudson, Roberts, and Vasconcells all reported being attacked by eight Fokkers, a mere 20 minutes after their first rendezvous with the Salmsons. Based 50 km to the southwest at their Puisieux Farm aerodrome, as many as 12 Fokker D.VIIs of *Jastas* 6 and 10 initially approached head-on from above, then turned from behind and dove into the A-Flight and B-Flight Nieuports and Salmsons. Baucom only referred to the Nieuports in his report, while Erwin only mentioned the B-Flight Spads: "I was paying very strict attention to my course so that the pictures would be the best possible when I saw the leader of the Spads dive around my wing, which was the prearranged signal that the Huns were in the air and about to attack." This indicates that the Salmsons were not close enough to provide mutual protection for each other, further verifying that each flight protected one Salmson. From Erwin's and Donaldson's reports, B-Flight's formation was like that of the Nieuports—200 meters higher (at 4,000 meters).[10]

Lieutenant Nevius reported that B-Flight was, "Northeast of Fère-en-Tardenois [when] we were attacked by Fokkers of checkerboard squadron." Of the three B-Flight members reported as being attacked by eight Fokkers, two of them—Lieutenants Roberts and Nevius—said the attackers were the "Checkerboard Squadron." Their comments were consistent with how *Jasta* 6 marked their Fokkers with black and white stripes on the tailplane, the motor cowling and wheel discs, while each plane also bore a personal marking on the fuselage. *Jasta* 10 Fokker markings consisted of a yellow nose, struts, and wheel covers.[11]

A-Flight Summary

Lieut. Martin made the following [postwar] statement:

1. On August 1st the 27th Aero Squadron furnished six Nieuport "28" machines for a protective mission to protect an American Salmson which was to take photographs behind the German lines. I was in one of the Nieuport machines during the mission.
2. We were attacked by a superior number of German Fokker machines and in the ensuing combat, I received a tracer bullet thru the hand and a minute or so later an explosive bullet thru the shoulder. I was forced to break off from the combat immediately and attempted to get back to our lines flying at a low altitude. On account of dizziness and approaching fainting,

I prepared to land. I was taken to a dressing station and before regaining consciousness, my flying kit, watch and purse were taken from me.[12]

This was the first half of Lieutenant Martin's postwar repatriation statement relating to his captivity and internment. Martin's most likely victor was *Vizefeldwebel* Hemer of *Jasta* 6, who claimed and was credited for his 17th victory, over a Nieuport 28 at 8:10 a.m.[13]

Lieutenant Whiton's postwar repatriation from captivity and internment statement about the air battle is confounding. It seems that he exaggerated how far behind the lines his formation was as an excuse for his later downing there. Writing in the third person, he said:

> Shortly before seven o'clock on the morning of the first day of August, Lieutenant Whiton was one of the formation of seven machines which left the Saints Aerodrome to protect photographic machines. About twenty kilometers behind the lines they were attacked by a large Fokker formation. A general fight ensued, during which Lieutenant Whiton succeeded in putting down one Hun. He followed him down to make sure he crashed.
>
> He then started back to his own lines as there was no formation for him to join as all but one of the machines, including a Bi-place had been put down. He was attacked at long range by two Fokkers. A chance bullet pierced his gasoline tank and the motor stopped. He glided towards the lines, but he did not have sufficient altitude to reach them and he got no further than the German 3rd Line. Here he deliberately crashed his machine, being thrown out unhurt. He was made prisoner by infantry and artillery soldiers before he could burn his plane.
>
> He was marched nine kilometers to Braine and after a short rest marched twenty-five kilometers more to Beaurieux.[14]

It is bewildering to understand Whiton following a Fokker that led him at least 5 km further north into German lines, leaving his squadron mates surrounded by Fokkers north-northeast of Mareuil-en-Dôle if he remained within the 42nd Division sector. Their pilots had been warned that "the Hun 'Archie' [antiaircraft fire] was most accurate, and very active," and that "the Fokkers would hang above us waiting to pick off the stragglers of our formation." Yet here Whiton had flown alone as far north as the German third line before being shot down. The *Jasta* 11 Fokkers patrolling that sector were faster than Whiton's Nieuport 28. His probable victor was *Ltn.* Gisbert-Wilhelm Groos, who claimed and was credited with his seventh victory, a Nieuport 28 at 8:40 a.m. on August 1. The 4th Division line of advance did not extend that far north until August 3, when they secured the road connecting Chéry-Chartreuve and Mont-Notre-Dame, through the Bois de Dôle.[15]

Lieutenant McElvain—according to *Out of Control*, the newspaper published by the 1st Pursuit Group—unexpectedly showed up back at the 27th Aero Squadron on December 10, 1918, after his return from prison at

Villingen in Hesse, Germany. Here is the immediate postwar story of his last fight over the lines near Mareuil-en-Dôle:

> At 7:00 a.m. on the morning of August 1st, this officer, leading a formation of six machines, set out on a mission to protect a reconnaissance machine over the enemy lines. Despite the fact that he was kept waiting forty minutes with his patrol, thus diminishing his supply of gasoline, this officer realized the importance of the mission, remained with the reconnaissance machine and pushed over into enemy territory in full sight of several enemy formations of Fokkers.
>
> The reconnaissance machine led him and his patrol into close proximity of two formations of enemy Fokkers, totaling twenty machines. This officer without fear or hesitation attacked one of these formations as the latter was about to destroy the reconnaissance machine. By his good judgment and determination, the photographic machine was enabled to get back to our lines, but a terrific encounter ensued in which it has been estimated that between thirty and fifty machines engaged Lieut. McElvain's patrol.
>
> Lieut. McElvain fought bravely and determinedly five enemy machines by himself, using up all his ammunition in a combat lasting twenty minutes. He succeeded in shooting down two Fokkers, but finally had his engine so badly shot up by machine gun fire that he was forced to land in enemy territory, destroying his machine in so doing. As an indication of the enemy's appreciation of this officer's extraordinary heroism he was complimented by the enemy patrol leader on his work and informed of the fact that he had destroyed two Fokkers in his effort.
>
> It was due to this officer's ability and determination, coupled with extraordinary heroism that some important photographs were obtained that morning on that particular mission.[16]

Many years later, however, McElvain told a completely contradictory version of this story and admitted that he separated from A-Flight. "I had had enough for one day and I headed home," he said. "As I flew, I discovered too late that I was on a collision course with a flight of five Fokker D.VIIs, coming at them out of the sun, and they apparently did not see me." These *Jasta* 17 Fokkers appear to have been flying southeast, while McElvain was mistakenly headed northwest. Making the most of it, he fired at the lead Fokker. "The three others simply got out of the way and circled," McElvain continued, "leaving one man to deal with me by himself."[17]

The German who dealt with McElvain was *Ltn. d. R.* Alfred Fleischer. After checking behind to ensure there were no other American pursuit planes nearby, Fleischer rushed to aid his *Staffelführer*, already in a smoking descent. "I was very light in both fuel and ammunition," McElvain recalled, "so my Nieuport was especially agile. Fleischer's Fokker D.VII was faster and could out-climb me, but even so our aeroplanes were pretty well matched."[18]

Fleischer fired and McElvain went into a steep climb, which would have worked against most German fighters, but not the D.VII, which climbed even faster. McElvain evaded Fleischer's next burst with a wingover to the left. The

Lieutenant Jason M. Hunt, 27th Aero Squadron, seated in a Nieuport 28, possibly N.6259 "4." He was killed in action on August 1, 1918. (John Eggleston album, Robert Erickson collection via Alan D. Toelle)

two opponents circled for some time, neither gaining an altitude advantage and neither able to get off more than a few poorly aimed shots at the other. Fleischer later recalled what happened next.

> At an altitude of approximately 1000–1500 ft., I successfully placed several well directed shots after having first completed a reverse ascending curve. Soon thereafter, McElvain exposed himself in a manner at first entirely incomprehensible to me. I was able to gain a position 120–150 ft. behind him, and I already aimed my machine gun upon him, ready to pull the trigger in the fever of the chase. There I beheld, thank God, in the last moment that the propeller of my adversary stood still and that the aeroplane, totally out of control, prepared to land.[19]

McElvain emerged unhurt from his crash and waved to the victor. Fleischer landed nearby and the two enemies shook hands, conversed for a time, and exchanged addresses, before McElvain was led off to prison. This was the aerial engagement with "five enemy machines" that McElvain had previously referred to, but it was near Soissons, deeper in German-controlled territory and about 22.5 km northwest of where the first aerial engagement was, while Saints aerodrome was almost 63 km south-southwest of the first aerial engagement.

Lieutenants Hunt and Dawson were yet to be accounted for, although Lieutenant Wehner's combat report, generally disregarded because he was so far away from the air battle, still offers two important clues here: "About 8h 20 I noticed a lot of archies about over Sergy and in the midst of the puffs a formation of Americans were engaged in a combat with Huns. One ship exploded at an altitude of 2,000 meters and fell to the ground. Fight lasted 2 or 3 minutes, the ships then scattered in all directions." Sergy is about 6.4 km south of Mareuil-en-Dôle.

This presents the question whether Hunt lasted 10 minutes in such a dogfight, perhaps accompanied by Dawson and Miller/Sykes. If this was Hunt's Nieuport exploding at 2,000 meters, the probable victor would have been *Jasta* 4 pilot *Ltn.* Egon Koepsch, who claimed and was credited with his fifth victory, a Nieuport 28 at 8:30 a.m. on August 1, 1918. Squadron records list Hunt as "Killed" on August 1, while another page tells a different story: "It is very doubtful as to what happened to Lieutenant Hunt, but it is quite possible that he was forced to land in Germany because of lack of gasoline, the fight having started very late in the patrol."[20]

Lieutenant Sykes's squadron obituary reports that he and Miller were protected by six Nieuports, and that the entire formation was wiped out. Their Salmson "fell on the railroad only a few kilometers north of Fère-en-Tardenois. I think it was near an overhead crossing where the railroad went through a cut. It was an awful crash; and the bodies of our comrades were in a terribly mutilated condition."[21] Only Lieutenant Dawson remained of A-Flight, and he returned to Saints safely.

After studying the detailed map of American Operations in the Aisne–Marne Region, May 31–October 12, 1918, and then comparing it to a Google Earth search of this area, the roads, railroad overpass stone bridge, and railroad tracks remain in the same positions they were 100 years ago. The bridge is located 2.4 km west-southwest of Mareuil-en-Dôle, following the Rue du Château (D967) west for the first 1.6 km, and then turning west onto route D21 for the last 0.8 km until reaching the single-lane stone overpass bridge that crosses the double set of railroad tracks, just as described above. The railroad tracks are elevated by 8 meters from just north of this overpass bridge, south to where they enter Fère-en-Tardenois, while cutting through the farmland plateau and the woods along their way. The location where Miller flew into this bridge is still identifiable via Google Earth Street View. Lieutenant Wehner also seems to have corroborated sighting Miller and Sykes in his combat report: "Noticed a Salmson toward Fère-en-Tardenois on *reglage* patrol so I played around about 10 minutes when it headed southwest."[22]

Lieutenant Oliver Beauchamp poses by a Blériot-built Spad XIII with the red wheel-disc and "5" of A-Flight. Although flying a Spad during the August 1 battle, he was not a member of A-Flight. This therefore brings into question whether the machine in this photo was really the one he was flying on that day. If machine "5" was serviceable, one would expect it to have been flown by Lieutenant McElvain, although McElvain and all of A-Flight were flying Nieuports. (Charles Wooley via Greg VanWyngarden)

B-Flight Summary

Lieutenant J. C. Vasconcells reported:

> Protection patrol for Salmson in the region of Fère-en-Tardenois. Picked up Salmson at 7h 40. Were attacked by 8 E.A. [enemy aircraft] in the region of Fère-en-Tardenois at 8h 10. After firing burst at E.A. which attacked Salmson, several E.A. continued to circle around. I observed 2 E.A. on Lt. Beauchamp's tail and I turned to the left and fired a burst at long range. One E.A. turned sharply to the left and dived, the other continued firing. I observed Lt. Beauchamp turn over and go down on his back. I then crossed above the Salmson and got in a burst at one E.A. on the tail of another Spad. This burst was at about 40 yards. The E.A. turned and spun and the Spad continued south.

Although Beauchamp brought his bullet-riddled Spad back from his run-in with *Jasta* 6, he fatally crashed upon landing. Major Harold Hartney, 27th Aero Squadron commander, recalled, "Directly over our field his ship went into a spin, and he was killed almost at our feet."[23]

Lieutenant Donald Hudson later stated:

> Were attacked by 8 Fokker biplane *chasse* machines east of Fère-en-Tardenois at 8h 10. I tried to bank left and fell into a spin; when I came out of the spin there were 4 E.A. on my tail. I tried to turn again but fell into another spin; I was followed by the 4 E.A. down to 1000 meters. As I was coming out of the spin, a machine was headed straight at me. I fired and he turned to the left; I turned a little to the left and turned back again. Being right on his tail, I fired about 20 rounds into him. He fell off slowly on his right wing and went into a spin. I turned on the other machines and went into a spin; when I came out the other machines were climbing up. Just as the fight began, I saw an EP [enemy plane/pilot] fall off on his right wing and spin in exactly the same manner as the machine I shot down. I saw something else fall in flames. A Spad passed within 20 feet of my right wing falling on its back. My engine was boiling, and I could not climb as my Nourrice [fuel tank] was empty, and by using the hand pump I could just keep going. When northeast of the railroad between Fère-en-Tardenois and Saponay, I encountered a Rumpler bi-place at between 100 and 200 meters. He passed me on the right and banked up to give his observer a good shot at me. I turned and got on his tail and followed him in a circle, firing right into the cockpit. Suddenly his right wing came off and he crashed. I was being fired at by machine guns on the ground and was essing [weaving back and forth, evasive maneuvers to avoid antiaircraft fire] when I noticed another Rumpler under me to my left. I turned down and fired at the observer. He disappeared, and the machine crashed just beside the railroad embankment. I circled the machine once to see if either the pilot or the observer got out, but they did not. Confirmation for three (3) requested."[24]

Hudson's Spad experienced a loss of pressure in the main fuel tank. Hudson then used the hand pump to restore and maintain air pressure to force the gasoline to the Nourrice tank in the upper wing center section and hence to the carburetor. On February 8, 1919, Hudson was awarded the Distinguished Service Cross (DSC) for this action, the citation for which read as follows:

> First Lieut. Donald Hudson, Aviation Section, 27th Aero Squadron. For extraordinary heroism in action near Fère-en-Tardenois, France, in August 1918. A protection patrol of which Lieut. Hudson was a member was attacked by a large formation of enemy planes. He was separated from the formation, forced to low altitude by four enemy planes (Fokker type). He shot down one, drove off the other three, and started to our lines with the damaged machine, but was attacked by two planes. He shot down both of these planes and by great perseverance and determination, succeeded in reaching our lines.[25]

Lieutenant R. Nevius reported the following about the day's events:

> Protecting Salmsons on Reconnaissance Northeast of Fère-en-Tardenois, we were attacked by Fokkers of checkerboard squadron. Seeing one attacking a Spad, I zoomed at him, firing

Lieutenant Ernest W. Hewitt, in the cockpit, and Tom Applegate, a mechanic, pose with Nieuport 28 N.6275 "17." This was the ship flown by Lieutenant Sands when he was shot down in flames and killed by *Leutnant* Lothar von Richthofen of *Jasta* 11 on August 1, 1918. This was certainly Hewitt's plane, as he was later associated with Spad "17." (Walter S. Williams scrapbook, National Museum USAF via Alan D. Toelle)

both guns, one jammed but the other continued. I zoomed away when less than two fuselage lengths from him and lost him, do not know the result of my bursts. A few minutes later, I saw [a] Fokker crash into woods below, wing down. Seeing [a] Salmson and two Spads heading for home, I tried to catch up with them, but motor [was] working badly and failed to do so. Early in fight a plane went down in flames. Confirmation requested."[26]

This was Lieutenant Sands, who *Ltn. d. R.* Richard Wenzl shot down in flames in the vicinity of the German 24th Reserve Division for his fifth confirmed victory at 8:15 a.m. From this report it is little wonder that Sands's body was never found. Supposedly, seeing a Fokker crash into the woods below prompted Nevius to request a victory confirmation, which the squadron later accepted. It was Erwin's Salmson that he saw with two other Spads headed home that he tried to catch up with but could not because of motor problems.[27]

Lieutenant I. A. Roberts's account of proceedings was as follows:

Escorted Salmsons over Fère-en-Tardenois and were attacked by 8 enemy aircraft at 8h 10 (Checkerboard Squadron Fokkers). One machine dove at me from the side and succeeded in getting a few shots in my fuselage. I zoomed to get above him, and he zoomed at the same time, bringing us up at about the same level. I *viraged* [turned] around to a position on his tail and gave him a burst of about 20 shots. He succeeded in getting a few more shots in my plane, none of which were serious. Then as he banked to the left behind me and at a distance of about 40 or 50 meters, [I] shot a burst at him head on. He zoomed up and fell on his back and went down in a loose spin. I was prevented from watching him crash by another E.A., which came at me from the side. I *viraged* around and gave him a good burst, but he did not go down. By this time, I was well separated from the formation, so I climbed to get height. Just then I saw 2 Spads and a Salmson going south, so I followed.[28]

Lieutenant Donaldson reported:

One got on my tail and I dived, and he followed at about 2000 meters. I fell with a spin and he left me. We were about 4000 meters when the fight started. After shaking the Hun, I looked around but could see none of the rest of the formation so came back over the lines. Came back at altitude of 1000 meters and was archied with black archie for about 4 or 5 minutes ... The Huns came upon us at about 200 meters above us and to our left about that far, coming straight toward us head on. They turned and dove on our tails. I first pulled up and fired at them, so they went by, but when the one got on my tail, I dove, and he followed. One gun jammed and I could not fix it at all.

Not all this report is quoted because the rest provides conflicting information regarding how much was accomplished prior to the initial attack, when it first occurred, and being attacked by only seven Fokkers. Unfortunately, the 27th Aero Squadron apparently restated some of this misinformation in their Gorrell's published history, on the "Operations on the Château-Thierry Sector" page.[29] Below are Erwin's and Baucom's original accounts, which are intertwined, each section preceded by the narrator's name, to show how they compare—or conflict:

Baucom: Erwin and I had the first mission that morning. We left the field shortly before sunrise and went over to see if we could find some Boche batteries in action, but it was a very misty morning and observation was almost impossible. We stuck around for about an hour, then came home. When we got back there was a photo mission already due to leave, but the pilot and observer had not yet shown up. They were due to be at 3000 meters over the field within twenty minutes, where it had been prearranged to meet a *chasse* formation from the First Pursuit Group, who were to give them protection while they took the pictures. Lt. Tytus (now Capt. Tytus), who was in charge of the field that day, asked Erwin and me if we would take the mission. We were glad of the opportunity but were sorry that we didn't have time to change the camera to our old faithful ship No. 8.[30]

Erwin: After having come down from an early morning reconnaissance, my observer Lieut. Baucom (Battling Baucom we called him) and I started out at 7:00 A.M., August 1st for pictures just above Fère-en-Tardenois in the Château-Thierry sector. The pictures had to be taken regardless of everything, as our troops were to advance over that ground in the next day or two, and the camera would save many lives by uncovering new battery positions and machine gun emplacements and the like. Arrangements were made by telephone for a Spad squadron of a neighboring Pursuit Group to act as protection, (for the Germans had an overwhelming concentration of air forces on our sector at that time and [were] sending out patrols of as many as forty and fifty machines echeloned in three formations but all working together).[31]

Baucom: However, the camera (52-centimeter focal length) had already been put in the other machine, which had been well gassed, oiled and groomed, and set like a fine racehorse ready for the finals. We hopped in; the mechanics gave the propeller a twist and we were off in a cloud of dust. Erwin stuck her nose up and made her climb as she had never climbed before. They were just about now at the place of rendezvous, and not finding us there might think that we had gone on towards the lines, and try to find us up that way, thereby causing them to miss us entirely. We must meet them at the appointed place at the appointed time. It had to be done. Erwin pulled the throttle wide open and pulled her nose high into the air. The motor was running fine. She climbed and climbed, despite the excess load she carried—the heavy camera and two or three extra magazines of plates. We soon reached 3,000 meters, and there the *chasses* were sitting up there waiting for us.[32]

Erwin: Attaining our altitude, we were met by eight Spads and started out for the lines. Before reaching the lines, two of the Spads developed motor trouble and lost the formation. When we reached the place we were to photograph, we were at an altitude of about 3800 meters and the coast seeming clear, Lieut. Baucom started in. I was paying very strict attention to my course so that the pictures would be the best possible when I saw the leader of the Spads dive around my wing, which was the prearranged signal that the Huns were in the air and about to attack. I yelled thru the speaking tube to Baucom, but he was already on the job. (I think he can smell a Hun—I know one never caught him napping.)[33]

Baucom: After circling around for a few minutes to give them time to get back in formation and get their positions, we started for Hunland. As I had already been over once this morning and didn't see any Boche planes, I really didn't think we would meet any on this trip. And with these six little Nieuports hovering above us, like fighting falcons protecting their mother bird, I didn't bother much about looking for Boche. We had just reached our objective, and I had taken one picture and shifted the magazine and snapped the second when Holy high rolling billows of the Dead Sea! It seemed that somebody had knocked the floor out of an airdrome in heaven and let all the machines come tumbling down upon us! I almost threw up my hands to ward off one from falling on my head. It was ten or twelve of the famous von Richthofen bunch who had suddenly and unceremoniously dropped into our midst. Their machines painted in gay and gaudy colors were unmistakable. It was really the only time I was ever taken by surprise, and ever afterwards I kept my eyes open, no matter how many *chasses* I had for protection.[34]

Erwin: Pulling up into a chandelle [climbing turn], I saw the party had already commenced. Eleven Fokkers had dived out of the sun on the seven of us and a dogfight had commenced in earnest. One Spad climbed on a Fokker's tail and started down, whereupon apparently from nowhere a Fokker started pouring lead into this Spad. I whipped my nose around and started my Vickers pumping a stream of tracers into this German. He dropped off into a kind of a half-spin and disappeared under my wing, but my bullets came too late—this chap he was shooting at fell out of control and crashed horribly 12,000 feet below. I learned afterwards that he was Lieut. Beauchamp, a chap who came over from the states with me and we all went thru our training together.[35]

Baucom: It was one of the quickest and snappiest fights I ever saw. Erwin and I tried to get our big Salmson machine out of the way. As we were getting out of the mix-up, I saw a Boche crowding one of our boys pretty closely, and I opened up on him; but one of my guns jammed without ever firing a shot. About that time another Boche got on our tail and began riding us. Then I blazed away at him, and I don't think I fired more than three shots before the other gun jammed. There we were, with a Boche on our tail, not seventy-five meters away, and both guns jammed. I could plainly hear the Boche's machine gun going tat-tat-tat-tat-tat-tat. I didn't know what the hell to do. I knew what I wasn't going to do; I wasn't going to let that damn Boche see me fixing my guns, for the devil never would have pulled off of us. I yelled to Erwin through the speaking tube that both guns were out of commission. Then I thought I would try a big American bluff. I pointed my guns straight at Mr. Boche and held them there as if they were working fine. I felt like a fool pointing a pair of dead guns at a man who was firing seven hundred shots a minute at me. I was beginning to wish that his blame gun would jam also—not that I wished him any bad luck at all. Presently Lieut. White [this was Lieutenant McElvain actually] of the First Pursuit Group, who was flight commander of our *chasse* formation, interrogated the scamp and drove him away.

During the fight I saw one of our American comrades meet flyers death and go down in a "vrille" and crash into woods a mile and a half below us. But I also saw one of the enemy go tumbling down. The American fell in woods a few kilometers east and a little south of Fère-en-Tardenois.[36]

Erwin: Almost at this moment I heard the rat-tat-tat—the song of the Fokker on my own tail, and another stream of tracers seemed to be coming from under my right wing. I dived down into this fellow with my own gun; meanwhile Lieut. Baucom was giving the glad hand to the one on our tail. I thought "good old Lewis guns" when one of his guns cut out. Then horror of horrors, both Baucom's guns jammed and [with] that Fokker in the immediate vicinity of our tail and intent on murder. I can assure you it is not a pleasant sensation to see the tracers passing by and wondering if he's going to lean on the gun and puncture you with the next one. I really believe that Baucom and I would be pushing up daisies over here now except that at about the time that Hun was mentally adding up his list of victims, Lieutenant now Captain Vasconcells, seeing our plight, pulled up into the Fokker and gave him a tremendous burst from both guns. Luck combined with Vasconcells's skill was with us—his first shots sent the Fokker to earth in flames. This being the third one sent down in the scuffle, the others retired. We limped on back home pretty badly shot up, but immensely satisfied to be living and able to think up some new method or manner of "damning the Boche."[37]

When Erwin returned to Moras Farm aerodrome, among the scattered bullet holes in Salmson "6," one had shot through one of its longerons (the long main timbers of the fuselage). Salmson 3204 "8" was ready to go, so they switched the camera over to that ship, and 1st Lt. Karl B. Spencer was assigned as his observer to return to the same area for a late-morning photography mission. Seven 95th Aero Squadron Spad XIIIs, led by 1st Lt. Harold Buckley, and accompanied by 1st Lt. Norman S. Archibald (Spad XIII 15036 "12"), protected Erwin on this second mission. Archibald's later book

Heaven High—Hell Deep also describes these mission details, which outline the events that led to this second battle. While Erwin claimed that their initial protection was provided by 12 Spads, it appears that five of these, including 1st Lt. Lansing C. "Denny" Holden (Spad XIII 15123 "22"), were actually protecting Lieutenants Wold and Wooten in the other Salmson, and that Erwin and Wold were not flying together to provide mutual protection.[38]

Lieutenants Buckley, Archibald, and five others in 95th Aero Squadron Spads met Erwin at 2,000 feet above their aerodrome at the agreed upon time. Buckley was positioned above and to the left, Archibald flew above and to the right, while the other five Spads hovered above. Archibald counted eight planes in all. Just before reaching the front lines, the five Spads above rapidly climbed and headed northeast. They supposedly were climbing to ward off an attack, although none was imminent at that moment. They soon disappeared, leaving just the two Spads to protect Erwin's Salmson as they crossed the lines at an altitude of 9,000 feet.

Suddenly, eight Fokkers dove on them from 2,000 feet above. Buckley and Archibald did their duty in staying close to protect the Salmson, as the three ships turned back towards the front lines. The Fokkers, not wanting to engage directly over the front lines, climbed towards their former altitude and circled. They would wait and see, their job being to keep the observation plane from taking its photographs. But then Erwin did the inexplicable. He suddenly turned his Salmson around and headed into what Buckley and Archibald thought was a deathtrap. Erwin's following account documents his second attempt at taking photographs on this second mission:[39]

> Lieut. Baucom and I only got about 10 pictures, whereas our strip of ground required at least thirty-six. So, at eleven o'clock I started out again with Lieut. Spencer as my observer. This time we were met at 2500 meters by twelve Spads, of whom we lost all but two before reaching our lines. At 3500 meters we started taking our pictures. The Germans put up a terrific antiaircraft barrage all around us, some of which I thought would surely blow us to atoms, but the pictures had to be taken so we continued on our course.[40]
>
> I sighted ten Fokkers over in the distance but decided to keep on after the photos. We did until they cut us off from the rear. At this point we had taken about one magazine (12 plates) of very valuable pictures. Starting back, I saw we waited too long and was in for a fight with the ten Fokkers in order to regain our own lines. So, I gave my machine all the power it had, put the nose down and tried to make it as near to our lines as possible before the mêlée began. They picked us up, however, about five kilometers from the line, [and] one Fokker got on one of the Spad's tail and forced him to "dive for it," which he did and managed to get away.
>
> The other Spad, piloted by Capt. Buckley, and my own machine started for the center of the Fokker formation. The leader of the formation peaked straightaway on me and I pulled up into him, both of us opening fire at about 200 meters. He was firing in bursts,

whereas I simply squeezed the trigger and poured it into him all the time, praying that the gun wouldn't jam. We came together like that at terrific speed, both of us shooting, and I knew one of us would have to fall, so I just unconsciously prayed: "Oh Lord, if you can't help me, for God's sake help that Fokker."

As we neared, I could see my tracers apparently going into the body of the machine. I also heard his, as they crackled by, as one tore thru one front strut of my right wing and others as they were puncturing spars and ripping fabric. Those thin threads of smoke from his two guns seemed both lined on my head, but they missed though some not so far, four puncturing the fabric just above my head. We were only about thirty meters apart and coming hellbent for election at each other when one of my bullets took effect. He seemed to fall over on the stick, for he dropped off to the left in an almost vertical nosedive, and about 100 meters farther down started into a spin and slipped and fell out of control till he crashed into the forest below.[41]

Don't think, however, the other Huns were merely watching us. Of course, this all took only three seconds, but the others were shooting at us from all sides. We were making it for our lines and fighting them off the best we could, but with tracer bullets pouring in from all sides, I knew it was only a question of time till they would get us. Then a bullet cut my rudder controls and I could no longer maneuver, so I threw the ship over on her back and let her drop into a spinning nosedive. This bit of strategy apparently fooled the Huns, as they only followed us down a little way, evidently thinking we were done for. I let the machine spin for perhaps 600 meters, then started to bring it out very "*doucement*." [gently] When we came out, as luck would have it, we were headed for our own lines. I could not put on the motor at first, as the torque of the propeller would tend to turn me around in a circle, but finally by cocking the machine on the side with the ailerons and flying with the motor throttled, we "tacked" our way home. When we arrived, we found our nice magazine of pictures all shot full of holes, several wires cut thru, our spar shot thru in two places and forty-two other bullet holes in the plane, including one thru Lieut. Spencer's side. He had bravely manned his guns and shot the Hun off till we escaped, though wounded.

Four brave men from this squadron, Lieut. Miller and Sykes, and Lieut. Wooten and Wold made the supreme sacrifice that day, trying to get these pictures in order that our boys on the ground might advance with less cost of their own lives, not to speak of the two pursuit men who were lost that morning in the seven A.M. fight, and the five who went down helping Lieut. Miller and Sykes, and both of these times that I have related today, it seems but the intervention of a kind providence saved the lives of Lieut. Baucom and I, and later Lieut. Spencer and myself when by all the rules of the game the Huns should have had us both times. In this last fight I knocked down my first Hun plane, [but] as to the sensation, frankly I can't say I had any. I was too scared the other nine were going to bump me off to feel any elation over any initial success.[42]

Lieutenants Buckley and Archibald felt lucky to make it back alive. Erwin angered Capt. David Peterson, the 95th Aero Squadron CO, for risking their lives in what he thought was a hideous travesty, particularly after he found out the mission did not result in any good photographs, and that Erwin had later boasted that he would have gone back a third time over the front lines except for his disabled rudder. Although Erwin later wrote that his airplane had, "many wires cut and some forty-two bullet holes in the plane," the official inspection report counted only the rudder control wire cut and 12 holes, but did not include the other structural damage: on the lower right wing, a bullet through the front strut at the end of wing, one hole through a spar near the end, and one through a spar about the center of wing that nearly tore the spar completely through; on the lower left wing, one hole near the fuselage and one hole through the lower aileron; four bullets through the fuselage body, one of which went through the observer's seat, tearing his flying suit, while others cut the rudder control and the observer's safety belt; on the upper right wing there was one hole near the fuselage; and two holes in the center section above the gasoline tank.

Erwin also said, "My observer, Lieutenant Spencer, was wounded in the side. Was taken to hospital—will be well again soon." However, Lieutenant Spencer's wounding caused him to leave the squadron and transfer to a hospital on August 18, adding one more permanent squadron casualty. Erwin later wrote that he was "recommended for the DSC and *Croix de Guerre* for the incident" himself, but that was not a credible statement. Archibald reported that Erwin was "severely criticized for the maniacal combat he forced us into." Meanwhile, Commandant Gerard of the VI Armée Aeronautique congratulated Buckley and Archibald for the efficiency of the protection they provided during this mission.[43]

The scene of 1st Lieutenant Oliver Beauchamp's crash of Spad XIII S.15143 "5" after he spun in when landing at Saints aerodrome on August 1, 1918. "Beauchamp joined the 27th Squadron on July 23, 1918 ... His total elapsed time at the Front was exactly 9 days. He was a good flier and a likeable, personable and unpretentious chap ... Well—that's the way war goes. Here today—gone tomorrow. A guy cracks up, his bones put away and he is lucky he carried government insurance. More flags are waved, more Liberty bonds are sold, brass horns in hometown bands get more polish, and all a poor soldier gets out of the deal is a Purple Heart and kindly remembered by folks he left behind."—J. Broz. (From the files of Alan D. Toelle)

First Lieutenant Norman S. Archibald, 95th Aero Squadron, beside his Spad XIII 15036 "12." (*National Museum USAF via Alan D. Toelle*)

First Lieutenant Norman Archibald points to a bullet hole patch in the fuselage of Spad XIII 15036 "12" after returning from the August 1 patrol. (National Museum USAF via Alan D. Toelle)

Lieutenant Wold's and Wooten's obituaries show a final desperate struggle to obtain the needed photographs while fighting off Fokkers. Starting out with 95th Aero Squadron Spads providing protection, Wold and Wooten were driven back twice over the front lines by an overwhelming number of Fokkers. Then they decided to make a third attempt alone to take more photographs but were attacked by five Fokkers. Single-handed, pilot Wold engaged them with some brilliant fighting, while Wooten held them off with his rear guns. They fought their way back over the front lines, but Wold was so seriously wounded that he lost consciousness and crashed into one of the American battery positions from a height of 100 meters. Still alive, Wold was evacuated to Evacuation Hospital No. 4 at La Ferté-sous-Jouarre, where he died and was initially buried. Lieutenant Wooten was initially buried in Coincy.[44]

Lieutenants Miller and Sykes were both initially buried near Soissons. The 27th Aero Squadron fared the worst in the early-morning mission. First Lieutenants Oliver T. Beauchamp, Charles B. Sands, and Jason S. Hunt were killed, while 1st Lieutenants Richard C. Martin, Clifford A. McElvain, and Arthur L. Whiton were taken prisoner after being brought down.[45]

The 27th Aero Squadron's "Combats and Victories" sheet seemingly takes credit for five squadron victories, although later researchers determined that all but one confirmation was shared. Lieutenant Hudson's Fokker D.VII confirmation was shared with Lieutenants Vasconcells and Nevius, his first Rumpler confirmation was shared with Lieutenant Roberts, and his second Rumpler confirmation was his fifth "victory" and thus made him an ace. Erwin's August 1 victory claim remains unconfirmed in squadron records, although he personally claimed it and later had his mechanics paint a German victory cross symbolizing it on his next Salmson "8" ship. Nevertheless, the possible known corresponding German casualties were: *Ltn. d. R.* Walter Lehmann of *Jasta* 10, shot down and taken prisoner; *Jasta* 6 commander Paul Wenzl, wounded in the right arm, although he remained with his *Staffel*; *Feldflieger* Köhler and *Leutnant* Holland, a two-seater crew from *Fl. Abt.* 29 wounded west of Soissons; and McElvain did not learn until later that he had wounded *Ltn. d. R.* Günther Schuster, a six-victory ace and commander of *Jasta* 17, who came down near Soissons.[46]

Despite these two squadrons' worst day for losses in the entire war, confidence was inspired by the presence of pursuit escorts during photographic missions, and pursuit protection was not entirely abandoned. Although pursuit escorts were arranged to accompany the photographic airplanes as frequently as possible, a new policy recognized the liabilities involved, but not until just prior to the Meuse–Argonne offensive in late September. This involved sending out

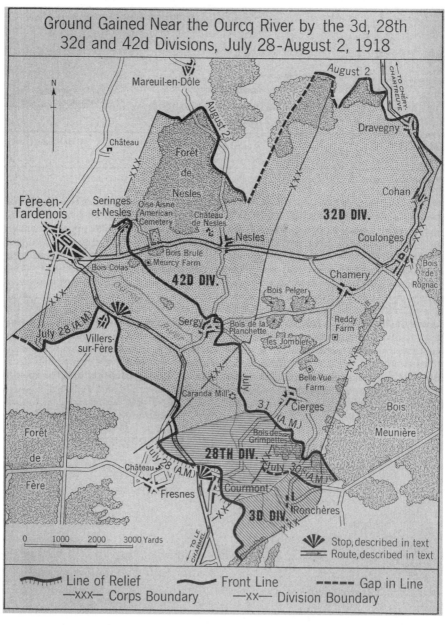

Ground gained near the Ourcq River by the 3rd, 28th, 32nd, and 42nd Divisions, July 28–August 2, 1918

Château-Thierry July and August operations

a few observation airplanes together, the lead plane of the formation carrying a camera, while one or more other gunships surrounded it to protect it. Erwin was later protected by up to four of these gunships on photographic missions, and although Fokker D.VIIs routinely attacked such formations, alert gunners usually drove them off with concentrated fire. This policy seems to have worked well, as no more than four 1st Aero Squadron Salmsons were shot down by Fokkers after August 1. Several others were shot down by antiaircraft fire or ground fire, and several others were so severely damaged by ground fire or aerial attacks that they had to be discarded. At the same time, 1st Aero Squadron pilots and observers claimed 13 confirmed victories.[47]

The 42nd Division was successful nevertheless, finally capturing Meurcy Farm, a kilometer south-southeast of Seringes-et-Nesles, on August 1. This placed the 42nd Division's line of advance in control of the heights north of the Ourcq River and advancing northward towards Mareuil-en-Dôle. They captured this town on August 2 after a battle with German machine-gun units but then retired, voluntarily abandoning it the same day. This nevertheless prompted the Germans to withdraw during the night of August 2 to their next prepared "Blücher" withdrawal position, 16 km north-northeast and extending all along the north side of the Vesle River. The 4th Division then relieved the 42nd and reoccupied Mareuil-en-Dôle on August 3.[48]

First Aero Squadron, First Army Air Service, and other *Gorrell's History* records are incomplete for the Château-Thierry offensive operations on August 4, leaving Erwin's previously published letters and logbook entries as the only insight into 1st Aero Squadron missions flown between July 29 and August 12, 1918. One of these was a reconnaissance mission on this date with Lieutenant Baucom as his observer in Salmson 2A2 3204 "8," with Erwin noting they had a "Good trip."[49]

On August 5, the 1st Aero Squadron moved to Coincy aerodrome, which a French Sixth Army division had only recaptured on July 24. Many officers received 24-hour passes, which they used to visit Paris.

Lieutenant Erwin flew another reconnaissance mission the next day with Lieutenant Baucom, this time in Salmson 2A2 3190 "2," with Erwin noting it was a "Successful mission."

Erwin flew a protection mission with 2nd Lt. Austin F. Hanscom in Salmson 2A2 3204 "8" on August 7 and reported: "Six Boches dived out of a cloud on us and [the] plane we were protecting. We drove them off of [the] other plane until it escaped, then made good our own getaway. Only received two bullets in our plane."[50]

On August 8, Erwin flew a photographic mission with 2nd Lt. Fred E. D'Amour as his observer between Fismes and Bazoches-sur-Vesles: "Successful mission. Not much fighting."[51]

Lieutenant Erwin recounts that he was transferred to Rocourt on August 9, even though the squadron history does not confirm this, so it is unclear whether this might have been just his flight rather than the entire squadron:

> Transfer to Rocourt. Damn nasty place. Our camp right in middle of battlefield—woods full of unburied Huns and quite a few Frenchmen and Americans. The burial squads will probably arrive when we move. One big dead German in our back yard rotting. Lots of hand grenades and German fireworks left around. We do quite a bit of experimenting. Only the luck of fools saves someone from being bumped off. A hospital is across the way—Evacuation 4, with some interesting girls and doctors. Have promised to take the Colonel up for a ride tomorrow. I'll give that old bird the thrill of his young life.[52]

The following day, holding good on his promise, Erwin "Gave the Colonel his ride. He was a good sport and seemed to enjoy everything I did." Erwin later left Coincy on a photo mission in very good weather with 2nd Lieutenant D'Amour as his observer at 6:00 p.m. They were protected by two flights of 94th Aero Squadron Spads, led by patrol leader 1st Lt. Eddie Rickenbacker, verified by Rickenbacker's August 10 reconnaissance report reflecting a protection patrol for the 1st Aero Squadron on that date.[53]

Erwin reported: "Photo mission. D'Amour. Eddie Rickenbacker and his squadron went along as protection. Got all our pictures. Had a good fight. Didn't get any, however." At 6:30 p.m. they saw 11 enemy planes, which shortly thereafter engaged in combat with a French patrol west of Fismes at 3,000 meters. When three Fokkers from that group started diving on the Salmsons below, Rickenbacker also dove to intercede. Erwin's letter home of August 11 described his version of the action:

> Had a nice free-for-all yesterday—was out with Eddie Rickenbacker's patrol from the [94th Aero] squadron … when eight Boche dived right out of the sun on us. There were seven of us. We started a Lufbery circus, i.e., all going around sitting on each other's tail till some poor devil gets overeager and enticed into our center or until we could make out the strength of the attack. Then the leader breaks the circus and hops on the Boche in the most advantageous position, and each in turn separates his and the dogfight begins. But yesterday they had another layer above them of six or eight planes which we saw, so as soon as possible broke off the fight. We had the best of the fight. I didn't get a single bullet in my plane, but I got two good bursts at my Boche. Would have undoubtedly got some but for having to break off the fight—with those others sitting up there in the sun, waiting to dive down on us, it would have been foolish to continue. We all returned safely and the Boches beat it back farther into Germany.[54]

According to the reconnaissance reports written by Rickenbacker and the other 94th Aero Squadron patrol leader, 1st Lt. Reed Chambers, what Erwin described was a dogfight involving a French patrol above them. Erwin's pilot's logbook notation specifically disagrees with the Reconnaissance Report narrative written by Chambers, the lower flight leader. Chambers wrote that he led the 1st Aero Squadron Salmsons back to the American balloon line and that they were not themselves attacked that day, declaring, "Protection accomplished." Rickenbacker was the only one who engaged the attacking Fokkers after the Salmsons withdrew. He regained altitude to join what he thought was a dogfight between his upper flight and the other Fokkers, which turned out to be only the French patrol that was engaged. Rickenbacker attacked one Fokker, but the results were inconclusive.[55]

Erwin flew a successful photographic mission on August 12 with 2nd Lieutenant D'Amour as his observer.[56]

On August 20, the squadron went to Chailly-en-Brie for three days' repose. Thereafter, on August 22, it moved with 18 airplanes from Chailly-en-Brie to Croix de Metz aerodrome, 1.6 km northeast of Toul, to take part in American operations in the St. Mihiel region. Four squadrons of the 2nd Pursuit Group and the 12th Aero Squadron of the I Corps Observation Group also then used this same airfield.[57]

CHAPTER 3

St. Mihiel Operations and Easterbrook's Arrival

Initially assigned to the French 62nd Division, the 1st Aero Squadron's responsibilities included visual reconnaissance, surveillance, infantry contact patrols, artillery adjustment, alert planes for special missions, and all photographic missions required by the American I Corps. In the Order of Battle for this offensive, planned for September 12, the I Corps Observation Group kept the 1st Aero, 12th Aero, and 50th Aero Squadrons and added two French *Escadrilles*, Sal. 208 and Sal. 214. The pilots and observers soon began practicing army liaison coordination with the French 62nd Division. Then they were reassigned to work with the American 5th Division, practice work with them going well. However, two days before the first attack, they were once again reassigned to support the American 2nd Division, which included Baucom's brother, Sgt. Wirt L. Baucom of the 5th Marine Regiment, and five former schoolmates, but it was too late to have any more practice work since everything was moving into position. The 1st Aero Squadron began operations on August 26. Lieutenant Erwin worked with a variety of observers on practice missions, including one practice photo mission on August 27 with newly arrived observer 1st Lt. Arthur E. Easterbrook, who had only been with the squadron since August 20. Having learned the trade from the back seat of a Royal Air Force (RAF) reconnaissance/artillery spotting two-seater on the British fronts during the Château-Thierry operation, Easterbrook was no stranger to danger. A close bond soon formed.[1]

Arthur Edmund Easterbrook

Born on November 4, 1893, in Amsterdam, New York, Arthur was only five when his father, Edmund Easterbrook, a chaplain in the 2nd New York Volunteer Infantry, went to war in Cuba in 1898. Edmund apparently afterwards transferred to Fort Flagler, Washington, a U.S. Army Coast Artillery fort. In 1914, Arthur attended the nearby University of Washington (UW) in Seattle, about a 56-mile drive and ferry ride away. He majored in mechanical engineering, was a member of Sigma Chi Fraternity, and enjoyed wrestling and track athletics. After America declared war in April 1917, he joined the new Army ROTC (Reserve Officer Training Corps) program, offered in cooperation with UW. He was one of 1,104 UW students and faculty members who served in World War I.[2]

Full-length studio portrait of Arthur E. Easterbrook in uniform, 1919. (The Arthur E. Easterbrook Collection/The Museum of Flight, Seattle (2004-09-15), Box 1, Folder 1)

At ROTC graduation that summer of 1917, he was commissioned as a 2nd lieutenant and assigned as a gunnery officer to the 20th Field Artillery Regiment (which served in France with the 5th Division) in Leon Springs, Texas. In January 1918, Easterbrook was transferred to Camp Greene, North Carolina, with the 23rd Infantry Regiment (which served in France with the 2nd Division), where he was an aide to Major General George H. Cameron, commanding officer of the new 4th Infantry Division. This new National Army division was filling with draftees, it was in the middle of winter, and the U.S. Army School for Aerial Observers at Post Field, Fort Sill, Oklahoma, had just been established that same month. Cameron sent him there for training, where he logged nine hours and 40 minutes at Post Field, most likely while flying in Curtiss R-4 airplanes.[3]

The 4th Division embarked for France in April 1918, but upon arrival was generally unprepared for trench warfare on the Western Front until mid-July, so Easterbrook's skills were parceled out to British allies. The 4th Division was the only American combat force to serve with both the French and British in their respective sectors. Easterbrook was temporarily assigned to 9th Squadron RAF on May 30, a corps observation squadron. Perhaps they thought this would be similar work to what they needed later in July, when the 4th Division was attached to the French Sixth Army and its II and VII Corps during the combined French–American counteroffensive of July 18.

He flew on R.E.8s, an obsolescent airplane compared to the 1st Aero Squadron's Salmson 2A2s. Although 13 of his first 14 combat sorties were bombing missions between June 15 and July 2, at least they luckily met no enemy aerial opposition. His most noteworthy sortie occurred on July 4, for which his logbook described trench strafing with their two-gun R.E.8, whose crews were successfully dropping 83,000 rounds of ammunition to Australian troops in the vicinity of Hamel. The squadron was surprised how shredded their R.E.8 became, yet it brought its crew back intact to the airdrome. Easterbrook recalled:

> Australian push. Zero hour 3:10 A.M. Leader of formation of three machines. Went over and did trench strafing. About 400 infantry in trees on river bank K33a [map reference]. Bombs dropped on them and fired one drum at same. Three and one-half drums fired at small parties. Nest of machine guns K31c, men in ravine K22a, men in wood K8d. Towns of Sailly, Hamel and Morcourt burning. Battery located in Cerisy. Clouds at 2,000 meters. MG fire very heavy, machine hit several times. Returned for more bombs. Hostile battery located on last trip, bombed with four 20-lb. Two seen to burst on house, others 20 yards from crossroads. One drum fired into same, fired three drums at various trench junctions where several small parties were seen. MG fire very active, our machine so badly hit that it was unfit for further use. Dropped eleven 20-lb. bombs.[4]

Later that same day, Easterbrook and his pilot, Captain Hilton, "went to Depot for new machine to replace the one damaged during the push." His last logbook entry with 9th Squadron shows a three-hour, 55-minute artillery shoot on July 19. By that point, he had flown 27 missions and logged over 50 hours in the rear cockpit of R.E.8s. When the 4th Division needed his services the most coincided with his being relieved from duty with 9th Squadron after that last mission. Elements of the 4th Division attacked eastward as part of two French divisions in the Sixth Army on July 18 in the Noroy-sur-Ourcq and Chevillon area, until the 26th Division relieved them on July 21. Thereafter, they were attached to the American I Corps, although still part of the French Sixth Army. The 4th Division fought their next battles, from August 3–6, in the general vicinity of Mareuil-en-Dôle and St. Thibaut, then entirely in the St. Thibaut sector from August 7–12. Thus, it was the I Corps "Order of Battle" attachment to the 1st Observation Group that led to Easterbrook being assigned to the 1st Aero Squadron.[5]

Practice Photography.
August 26th, Northwest St. Mihiel, 15:50–17:00, Pilot Lieut. Erwin, Observer Lieut. Kerr, 22 photos taken, 20 of which were good.
Reconnaissance.
August 27th, Pont-à-Mousson, Éply, 17:30–18:35, Altitude 800 to 10,000 meters, Visibility good, Pilot Lieut. Pitts, Observer Lieut. Baucom.
Practice Photo Mission.
Villers-en-Haye, 14:25–16:35, Altitude 100 meters, Visibility good, Pilot Lieut. Erwin, Observer Lieut. Easterbrook, 24 photos taken. [This was the first mission that Erwin flew with Easterbrook, during which an antiaircraft shell passed through the top of the left fuselage side of Salmson 2A2 3204 "8" about two feet behind Easterbrook's cockpit, leaving a gaping hole but without exploding.]
Reconnaissance.
August 28th, Foret du Bois le Prêtre, Cornay, 8:25–10:20, Altitude 2000 [meters], Visibility good, Pilot Lieut. Erwin, Observer Lieut. Duckstein, Fired at by hostile machine guns at point 72.5–43.7.
Photography.
August 28, Lesménils, Clémery, 14:10–15:15, Altitude 1000 meters, Visibility good, Pilot Lieut. DeCastro, Observer Lieut. Easterbrook, 20 oblique photos, all of which were good.
Reconnaissance.
August 30, Pont-à-Mousson, Éply, 17:00–18:30, Altitude 1200 meters, Visibility poor, Pilot Lieut. Erwin, Observer Lieut. Yates.[6]
Photography.
August 30th, Marbache, Saizerais, 9:00–10:20, Altitude 3000 meters, Visibility good, cloudy, Pilot Lieut. Erwin, Observer Lieut. D'Amour, 30 photos taken. Mission partially successful.
Photography.
August 30th, Éply, Lesménils, 15:10–15:55, Altitude 1000 meters, Visibility fair, Pilot Lieut. DeCastro, Observer Lieut. Easterbrook, 10 oblique photos taken.

Photography.

August 30th, Cheminot, Pont-à-Mousson, 15:10–15:55, Altitude 1100 meters, Visibility fair, Pilot Lieut. Fox, Observer Lieut. Baucom, 13 oblique photos taken.

Reconnaissance.

August 31st, Pont-à-Mousson, 10:00–11:05, Altitude 1400 meters, Visibility good, Pilot Lieut. DeCastro, Observer Lieut. Easterbrook.

Reconnaissance.

September 2nd, Éply, Fey-en-Haye, 10:15–11:55, Altitude 800 to 3600 meters, Visibility fair, Pilot Lieut. Erwin, Observer Lieut. Baucom, One hostile plane bi-place seen over Fey-en-Haye at 11:00.

Photography.

September 2nd, Éply, Lesménils, 8:50–9:55, Altitude 100 meters, Visibility fair, Pilot Lieut. DeCastro, Observer Lieut. Easterbrook. 20 oblique photos taken all of which were good. One plane from First Aero Squadron furnished protection.[7]

Erwin, Baucom, and Easterbrook apparently took a break from the action between September 3 and September 5. On September 6, the 1st Aero Squadron recorded, "Visibility poor throughout the day," without showing whether any missions were flown. While Erwin confirmed the weather report, he also recorded one mission in his personal diary that is not otherwise confirmed in squadron records. One possibility for this is that Erwin and

Lieutenant Easterbrook (rear) has just returned from his first mission with Lieutenant Erwin (front), an August 27, 1918, practice photo mission, during which they took 24 photos in good visibility in preparation for the St. Mihiel offensive. Note the German cross bullet hole patches on the fuselage and the gaping hole caused by an antiaircraft shell passing through without exploding. (Easterbrook Collection, National Museum USAF via Alan D. Toelle)

Baucom volunteered rather than being assigned for the mission, and they did not want to report this much activity when all other air operations were grounded, just prior to the beginning of the St. Mihiel offensive.

> **Sept. 6**, Reconnaissance—Lieutenant Baucom. Good trip. It rained while we were up and Baucom got quite wet. In the shadows caused by the clouds we picked up the flashes of the Archie who was annoying us. By careful maneuvering threw him off range and literally slid down his barrel on him. Looking down in his gun we'd see a flash, then behind or perhaps in front of us the shell would go "Pam!" and we'd see the little black puff of smoke. Some high explosive fragment and shrapnel entered the machine, but none hit us. At about 500 or 600 meters they stopped the Archie and began plugging with machine guns and tracers. But I was diving at a speed of perhaps 200 miles an hour and opened up my own gun. About 100 meters or less over them I pulled out and, spiraling, gave Baucom a chance with his Lewis guns. We forced them to leave their guns, killing or wounding a few of them. My plane was hit several times, but not seriously damaged.[8]

> Photography
> **September 7**th, Pagny-sur-Moselle, *Bois du Trou de la Maie* [just north of Tautecourt, the southern edge of these woods marking the front lines of the 5th Division's sector on September 16], 11:50–13:30, Altitude 4000 meters, Visibility good, Pilot Lieut. DeCastro, Observer Lieut. Easterbrook, 7 photos taken all of which were good, Mission was not completed owing to the fact that a patrol of enemy planes was in the vicinity, 4 planes from the 2nd Pursuit Group furnished protection.[9]

The area they were trying to photograph was a 15 km strip, 8 km inside of German lines. Easterbrook's later letter to a friend, who provided this information to the *Seattle Daily Times*, held details of the 1st Aero Squadron Commanding Officer's memo to the Commanding General, American I Corps, complaining that 15 of what turned out to be 13th Aero Squadron Spads were available as protection, but that they undertook their mission with only four. A review of 2nd Pursuit Group's records for September 7 reveals that only the 13th Aero Squadron ordered a patrol matching the same time and altitude as 2nd Lt. R. E. DeCastro's and Easterbrook's mission, from 11:30 a.m. to 1:15 p.m., at 3,500–5,500 meters. Flying Order No. 31 scheduled five separate reconnaissance patrols on September 7, of five Spads each. Flying Order No. 32 listed their protection patrol of Easterbrook's Salmson as just one part of their regular patrol, which is the reason the 13th Aero Squadron started with only five Spads, rather than 15, on September 7.[10]

The 13th Aero Squadron's Reconnaissance Report says that they saw a total of 11 enemy planes. They encountered six Fokkers over Lironville at 12:55 p.m. at 6,000 meters, but after firing 200 rounds at one of them, the Fokkers returned to their own lines. They saw another three Fokkers northeast of Pont-à-Mousson at 1:05 p.m. before returning to Croix de Metz aerodrome

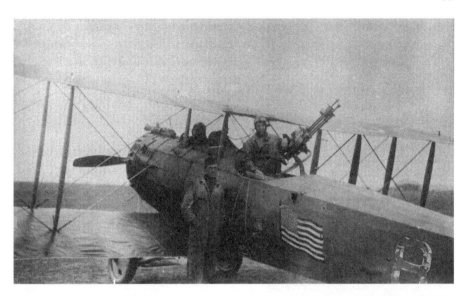

An extended view shows Easterbrook resting an arm on his twin Lewis guns of Salmson 2A2 3204 "8," with much of the "8" by then worn off. An unknown mechanic stands alongside. (Easterbrook Collection, National Museum USAF via Alan D. Toelle)

at 1:20 p.m. DeCastro was likely frustrated that the Spads were not staying close enough to protect them, prompting him to turn back early with their mission only partially completed. Although Easterbrook's letter to his friend said that "one pursuit machine of his protection was brought down," 13th Aero Squadron's September 7 Reconnaissance Report denies any such loss. This, however, does not rule out the possibility that one or two Spads developed motor trouble and returned early, despite their Reconnaissance Report not listing them as such. Things should have been different the following day, moreover, since Flying Order No. 32 also said that, starting September 8, half of all available planes had to be ready to start on a protection patrol that morning. This order emphasized the protection aspect, rather than reconnaissance, and should have afforded at least a dozen Spads as protection.[11]

First Aero Squadron records for September 9 show that only Lieutenants Richardson and Hanscom attempted a reconnaissance mission, which they did not complete due to adverse weather conditions. However, Erwin's flight logbook shows that he successfully completed a photographic mission above Thiaucourt, taking 46 photographs. A ground mist obscured much of the landscape, so they had to work slowly and carefully. "We got all the pictures," he wrote in his logbook. "Had a fight with a Halberstadt, knocking him down out of control, but could not see whether he crashed or not on account of the haze."

MERICAN OBSERVER IN PLANE

First Lieutenant Arthur Easterbrook, shown here behind his guns before a mission, also won a DSC for his heroic actions on September 12, 1918. (Charles Wooley via Greg VanWyngarden)

Even though Erwin later found a couple of infantry officers who corroborated a Halberstadt crashing that morning at that location, the squadron never filed a victory claim for the Halberstadt, and it remains unconfirmed.[12]

The American I Corps held a 19 km sector from Limey to Port-sur-Seille, with five divisions at its disposal, on September 11. The 82nd Division held the sector from Port-sur-Seille to the Forêt du Bois le Prêtre, and the 90th Division from the eastern edge of Bois le Prêtre to Mamey. The front line to the corps boundary at Limey was held by detachments of the 90th Division. The 5th and 2nd Divisions were deposited in depth behind these detachments, the 5th Division from Mamey to Remenauville and the 2nd Division from Remenauville to Limey. The 78th Division was concentrated in the rear as corps reserve.

On September 12, the 1st Aero Squadron was assigned to the 2nd Division. They and the I Corps Observation Group commander and staff, along with the 12th Aero Squadron, were based at Toul, while the 50th Aero Squadron and French *Escadrilles* Sal. 208 and Sal. 214 were based at Bicqueley. The 12th Aero Squadron was assigned to the 5th Division and the 50th Aero Squadron to both the 90th and 82nd Divisions for all aviation duties, which included visual reconnaissance, surveillance, infantry contact patrols, artillery adjustment, alert planes for special missions, and all photographic missions required by the American I Corps. *Escadrilles* Sal. 208 and Sal. 214 were assigned to Corps Heavy Artillery for all adjustments, counter battery work, control of fire, surveillance of enemy artillery, and alert planes for the corps artillery commander. Their advanced landing field, with no hangars, was at Saizerais.[13]

Rain and poor visibility had not allowed flying on September 10 and 11, and no one had previously experienced what was to follow—the 2:00 a.m.

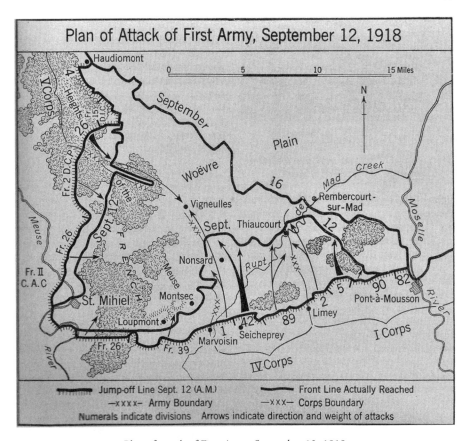

Plan of attack of First Army, September 12, 1918.

artillery bombardment that shook the aerodrome buildings as if by earthquake. Lieutenant Baucom, the designated "star" observer of the squadron, also wrote much of its history. Below are most of his comments about his and Lieutenant Erwin's final preparations for the St. Mihiel offensive, the squadron's "lead-off" men to fly into battle on September 12:

Erwin and I had been groomed, trained, and coached for the hell-busting infantry liaison. Lt. Hartigan, then Operations Officer of the Squadron, had picked us for the job. We were to fly the first infantry liaison of the First Aero Squadron, First Observation Group, with the First Army Corps, in the first offensive of the First American Army. We were to work with the famous Second Division, the Division with the Marine Brigade in it. I had a brother and five or six old school mates in the Marines. I had visited them while they were in reserve. Then they started moving into position. I bade them farewell and a hearty God's speed. It is a peculiar sensation to tell a brother goodbye on the eve of battle. I told them I would be with them when they went over the top and to keep their eyes open for a white-nose Salmson No. 8, carrying the American flag on the side of the fuselage as our squadron insignia.

The day dawned; the day that was to decide ... the fate of the Boche in the St. Mihiel sector. We had waited patiently for "D" day and "H" hour. On the night of September 11th, we received notice that the next morning, September 12th, at 5 o'clock, things would jar loose. I didn't sleep much that night. I was restless. I knew not what the next day would bring, nor what it held in store for us. Erwin and I were to take the first mission. We were "lead-off" men.

There was a standing order out that an infantry liaison plane would fly no lower than 600 meters, as it was almost sure to be shot down by ground machine gun fire, but we intended to fly a good deal lower than that. We intended to fly through our own barrage. We intended to fly anywhere from 50 to 400 meters. Our comrade doughboys were going over the top, and we intended to follow them through hell if necessary. We intended to tell the Boche machine gunners to go straight to purgatory. We were going to stick with our doughboys through thick and thin. I had a brother and five or six former schoolmates in the Second Division, and Erwin and I were going to stay with them till the cows came home.

About two o'clock in the morning of September 12, our artillery opened up and such an opening! I didn't know there was so much artillery in the world. We must have had guns piled on top of each other. The buildings on our aviation field trembled as if by earthquake. I didn't sleep any more that night.

Shortly after daylight we were all set. Old No. 8 had been rolled out of the hangar and was standing on the starting line, with her nose in the air as if scenting the sky for weather conditions. The mechanics put a little more gas in the tank to make sure that it was full and patted her affectionately on the cheeks as they gave her a final inspection. I checked up my very pistol ammunition [pyrotechnic signals]; looked over my map boards and code cards; and tested the tension on the mainsprings of my guns.[14] One of the radio men had put a special wireless reel in the ship and connected up everything so that I had the strongest radio set of any airplane in that sector. Lt. Erwin warmed up the motor, tested the magnetos, and air, and reported everything in his end of the ship O.K.

We were off. The sun came up before we got to the lines, but soon disappeared behind the clouds, which were at four or five hundred meters. Beneath the clouds the visibility was fairly good. There was no ground mist. Our divisional sector was a little less than three kilometers in width, extending from Remenauville to Regniéville-en-Haye, with the axis of advance towards Thiaucourt. When we arrived at the lines, our infantry had just crossed the Boche first line of trenches and were advancing towards the woods beyond.

The rolling barrage was to advance at the rate of 100 meters every four minutes. The first thing I saw was a battalion panel saying artillery fire was falling short. I quickly pinpointed its location on my map and sent down the information to the division headquarters. In order to make doubly sure, we also flew back to the division panel and dropped a message to that effect, giving too, the location of the troops. We kept it up for three hours. About the time our troops got to the southern edge of the Bois d'Heiche [located on the north side of the highway to Regniéville, 2 miles southeast of Thiaucourt], a battery of Boche artillerymen on the eastern side of the woods, at coordinates 8295, saw that their only salvation was hasty retreat. They deserted their guns and took to their heels. The officers were on horses, but Erwin and I saw them, and we immediately pounced upon them. Erwin would give them hell with his front gun, and then I would blast loose with mine. We knocked one of the officers off his horse and drove the whole bunch into the woods and made them stay there until our infantry came along and escorted them back to our prisoners' camp.

A few minutes later we found three wagons on the road on the west side of this same woods. They had stopped in a cut in the road to take shelter of our artillery fire. The drivers were sitting on their horses. We began strafing them also and drove them into some dugouts beside the road. Our infantry was only a couple of hundred meters away, so we made the Boche stay under cover until our infantry came up. The last we saw, some of our doughboys were driving the wagons back to headquarters and the Boche were walking along beside them.

We stayed over our troops that morning for three hours. When we left them, they were almost ready to enter Thiaucourt. Our ship was supposed to carry only three and a half hours gasoline, and we were three hours and twenty minutes from ground to ground. It was a cloudy day, and the air was very rough and bumpy. And as we were flying so low, there was so much artillery banging away, it was still worst. When I got down, I was almost sick and didn't feel well for the remainder of the day. But our troops had made a good advance that morning; and every time they took a step there were a cocarde of an American plane hovering above them, not only to protect them from any lurking Boche that might happen along, but also to help point out the way and help them in every manner possible.[15]

Lieutenant Byrne Baucom had, in fact, spent an entire evening with his brother, Sgt. Wirt Baucom of the 5th Marines, 2nd Division, the previous week. For this opening mission of the St. Mihiel drive, he and Lieutenant Erwin apparently conducted two separate functions within the same mission. They first flew a "Reconnaissance" between Limey-Remenauville, within Allied lines, found along the *Grande Rue* (Great Street) highway, and Thiaucourt-Regniéville at the recommended altitude of 600 meters in poor visibility, between 6:20 a.m. and 7:10 a.m. But rather than landing, they instead continued onto their "Infantry Contact Patrol." Their second report showed they flew at an altitude of 200 meters in good visibility, between 6:10 a.m. and 9:25 a.m. This would imply that it took them 10 minutes to fly from their Croix de Metz aerodrome to Limey. The only other new information not already included in Baucom's comment summary is their chasing a German two-seater from Thiaucourt to Pont-à-Mousson, before losing it in the clouds.[16]

Lieutenant Easterbrook left at 9:35 a.m. in fair visibility with his pilot, 2nd Lt. R. E. DeCastro, to take photographs in the area between Vilcey-sur-Trey, Villers-sous-Prény, and Norroy-lès-Pont-à-Mousson. The 90th and 82nd Divisions desperately needed those photos to support their attack the following morning. They were looking for roads, trench systems, artillery emplacements, machine-gun pits, ammunition stores, bunkers, and buildings in those villages serving as part of the German defenses. Marshal Philippe Petain, Commander-in-Chief of the French Army, regarded Hill 327 in the Forêt du Bois le Prêtre as invulnerable. The Germans had held it for four years, the fighting in this wood having cost the French 123,000 casualties, 18,000 of whom were killed. It had since become a no-man's land strewn with more barbed wire entanglements than perhaps existed on any other sector of the

The usual off-hours occupation was the game of craps, universal throughout the AEF. Pilot Ralph De Castro observed that, "Craps should be a game of chance, not skill; somebody would usually end up each game with all the money." Left to right: Lieutenants James W. Corley, unidentified, James C. Wooten, Paul D. Meyers, Bradley Saunders Jr., George L. Hammann, Henry H. Perry, and William G. McNaulty. Half of these observers were gone by the second week of September, as Saunders left to join the 135th Aero Squadron on July 31, Wooten was KIA on August 1, Perry was transferred to the I Corps Air Service headquarters on September 2, and McNaulty got sick and left the squadron for hospital on September 8. (Courtesy of San Diego Air and Space Museum)

Western Front, as well as scattered limestone quarry pits to the right front that afforded a plentiful supply of building materials. Although the 90th Division was already encircling the forest from the south on September 12, the hill's imposing 380-meter maximum elevation initially protected Villers-sous-Prény (elevation 210 meters) north of the forest.[17]

To reach these villages, DeCastro and Easterbrook penetrated 4 km into the German lines at an altitude of 600 meters without any 1st Aero Squadron gunship protection or 2nd Pursuit Group escort. While engaged in photographing at an altitude of 400 meters, they were attacked by four enemy airplanes but succeeded in completing their mission after successfully exposing eight plates and fighting off the attack. Nine of their 10 total photos taken were good, and they returned at 10:50 a.m. Although these aerial photographs are now unavailable, 90th Division infantry photographs show what those defense systems looked like soon after they captured Bois le Prêtre, Vilcey-sur-Trey, and Norroy-lès-Pont-à-Mousson on September 13, as well as Villers-sous-Prény on September 15.

Baucom's assessment of the cloud layer being at 400 or 500 meters and visibility being good beneath it had been correct, prompting Easterbrook to similarly engage in a low-level flight. The mission request appears to have been spontaneous rather than planned well in advance and the timing had them leaving one hour after the 13th Aero Squadron's available and ordered protection patrol at 8:30 a.m. The 50th Aero Squadron flew reconnaissance missions that left at 7:53 a.m. and 7:55 a.m., and the 12th Aero Squadron flew an infantry contact patrol at 7:35 a.m. It thus appears that the 13th Aero Squadron's protection patrol would have been available with just a little advance notice. It is unknown whether that patrol even left the ground, since they never filed a reconnaissance report for it.[18]

Lieutenant Erwin, along with his Observer Lieutenant Baucom, tried another reconnaissance mission on September 13, starting at 9:25 a.m. Two 1st Aero Squadron Salmsons had already left at 9:05 a.m. to supply protection. However, rain and low clouds prevented them from carrying out their mission, and once their two gunships left them, Erwin decided to return to Croix de Metz aerodrome five minutes later, arriving back at 10:00 a.m.[19]

Erwin flew four missions on September 15, three with his observer Lieutenant Baucom. The first one involved Erwin and Baucom, flying Salmson 2A2 "5," taking photographs in good visibility from 9:00–10:45 a.m., while protected by 10 22nd Aero Squadron Spads, led by 1st Lt. John A. Sperry. The other patrol members were Capt. Ray C. Bridgman, 1st Lt. John G. Agar, Jr., 1st Lt. James D. Beane, 1st Lt. Henry B. Hudson, 1st Lt. Arthur C. Kimber, 2nd Lt. Watson W. LaForce, 2nd Lt. Raymond J. Little, 1st Lt. Murray E. Tucker, and 1st Lt. Frank B. Tyndall. Their actual course route started at Toul, then went 27.4k m north-northeast to Pont-à-Mousson, 8.8 km east to Éply, 4.8 km north to Louvigny, 8 km northwest to Lorry-Mardigny, 6.4 km west-southwest to Prény, and finally 33.8 km back at Toul. Sperry said in his report that they saw 20 Fokkers in the area between Lorry and Prény but did not encounter any. He also said that while some Fokkers, black and grey with white stripes, were chasing them, Erwin made a sudden turn and they lost him, but since they knew his mission route, they patrolled it until 11:15 a.m. Baucom took 34 photos at 2,600 meters, all of which were good, while the Spads were patrolling at altitudes between 5,000 and 5,200 meters.[20]

The 22nd Aero Squadron Spads all returned safely at 11:30 a.m., but the main reason their mission was uncontested was that nine 13th Aero Squadron Spads engaged the same number of Fokkers near Vaux at 10:10 a.m., 11.3 km north of Lorry. Then at 10:30 a.m., these same 13th Aero Spads encountered five more Fokkers near Corny-sur-Moselle, still about 5 km north of the 22nd Aero Squadron's patrol line. Major Carl Spatz of 13th Aero Squadron—who went on to command U.S. Strategic Air Forces in both Europe and the Pacific in World War II—was later credited with the destruction of a Fokker over Vaux at 5,000 meters at 10:10 a.m. Three Fokkers were confirmed destroyed over Corny at 5,000 meters at 10:30 a.m., one being credited to 1st Lt. W. H. Stovall (his third confirmed victory), another to 1st Lt. Leighton Brewer, and the third one shared between 1st Lt. Murray K. Guthrie and 2nd Lt. Frank K. Hays (Guthrie's third and Hays's fourth confirmed victories). This kept the Fokkers in that area otherwise engaged and allowed Erwin and Baucom to complete their mission unmolested.[21]

Pilot 2nd Lt. James M. Richardson and observer 1st Lt. Arthur W. Duckstein then left at 11:55 a.m. on an infantry contact patrol in good visibility for the 2nd Division, between Rembercourt and Charey. Lieutenant Erwin had teamed up with 1st Lt. Homer W. Dahringer in a Salmson to fly mission protection. Meanwhile, the 11th Balloon Company (Army) near Mamey sighted a Fokker at 12:25 p.m. approaching from the southwest. It first attacked a balloon on their right, southeast side of Mamey, but that balloon was hauled down rapidly, and a barrage was put up by French antiaircraft guns headquartered at Ansoncourt Farm. The Fokker then flew low over a hill from the southeast and made a slight dip to attack the 11th Balloon Company's balloon. The German pilot opened fire, putting 16 holes in its fins, nine through the gas bag, and nine more through the ballonet, but since the balloon did not burn, the observer received no order to jump, and he remained in his basket. The Fokker then banked to the left flank of the balloon, heading southwest, setting fire to the balloons of the 1st Balloon Company (Divisional) and 2nd Balloon Company (Corps), the next two balloons in line.

Charey is 15.3 km north-northwest of Mamey, and as Richardson and Erwin approached the balloon lines, which were at least 6.4 km behind the front lines, they saw flames suddenly burst from balloons No. 1 and No. 2, tethered over the woods of the Bois des Hayes and Bois de la Lampe, respectively, southwest of Mamey. Erwin spotted the Fokker retreating north, but Richardson was already chasing and firing at it from 250 meters behind. Erwin was closer and high enough to dive on it, gaining sufficient speed to close to a short range and fire before the Fokker could pull away. It continued only another 500 yards before falling into a spin and crashing into Allied lines. The fast-moving battle had ended quickly, with the Boche being downed in sight of the two balloons he had just sent down in flames. First Army, Balloon Wing and 11th Balloon Company reports for September 15 confirm the loss of the two balloons. Headquarters, First Army Air Service, confirmed this victory on October 8, via General Orders Number 14, crediting 1st Lieutenants Erwin, Dahringer, and Duckstein and 2nd Lieutenant Richardson for the destruction of an enemy airplane at 12:30 p.m. on September 15.[22]

Erwin had just returned from that mission at 2:04 p.m., but then turned around and left with Baucom at 3:10 p.m. on another photographic mission, covering the same area as their morning mission. Flying at an altitude of 3,000 meters in fair visibility, they took 34 photos, none of which were good. The 1st Aero Squadron Salmson gunship protecting them did not dissuade a German two-seater from attacking them at 4:30 p.m. over the woods of the Bois de Grande Fontaine. Even returning safely at 5:30 p.m. did not mean their day was over though. After the 2nd Division repulsed several counterattacks by the German 31st Division that day, it continued trying to advance its line and needed reconnaissance. They sent Erwin and Baucom back out on such a mission at 6:15 p.m., which they flew between Haumont-lès-Lachaussée and Villecey-sur-Mad at 700 meters. However, with poor visibility and approaching darkness cutting their mission short, they returned at 7:10 p.m.[23]

Although plans were not generally executed to extend American operations northward beyond Vandières in the eastern St. Mihiel region between September 12 and November 11, 1918, Prény became the objective of frequent raids by the 7th and 90th Divisions. Many hand-to-hand fights took place near this picturesque town, situated on a long ridge in the Hindenburg Line, the last fully prepared German position. The other villages photographed were also slightly north of this boundary, which the U.S. Army VI Corps (Brigadier General Charles T. Menoher commanding) liberated post-armistice. While Erwin's later DSC citation mentions an observation balloon and driving off enemy planes, it does not actually credit him for his victory on September 15. The 78th Division relieved the 2nd Division on the night of September 15, after which it left its sector, along with its artillery. The 1st Aero Squadron was then assigned to work with the 78th Division for all aviation duties after 10:00 a.m. on September 16.[24]

Pilot Lieutenant DeCastro and observer Lieutenant Easterbrook left at 1:40 p.m. on September 16 on a photography mission for the 78th Division, flying at 1,000 meters in good visibility between Xammes and Vandières. Suddenly, one of their two 1st Aero Squadron protection planes dove on them from above, forcing them to dive into the German lines to avoid a collision. Under intense antiaircraft ground fire, they regained their altitude and exposed 17 more plates of the territory behind the lines of the German observation balloons, thus gaining pictorial information of immense value. After having taken 20 oblique photos, they returned at 2:30 p.m.[25]

The following day, pilot 1st Lt. John E. Michener and observer Lieutenant Easterbrook were sent out on a photography mission between Vandières and Rembercourt-sur-Mad at 3:00 p.m. in fair visibility, with one protecting 1st Aero Squadron Salmson. They took 19 oblique photos from 1,000 meters, four of which were good, and returned at 4:05 p.m.[26]

The squadron finished its work in the St. Mihiel sector with a reconnaissance mission on September 18. Probably no other period in aerial warfare was as productive of learning as these last seven days of the St. Mihiel drive for the First Army and 1st Aero Squadron. The squadron had several requirements they had to follow: keep two planes constantly on alert through the hours of daylight; keep a liaison officer at Division Headquarters; planes returning from all missions had to drop reports at the division and corps P.C. (command post, the place from which the commander directed the operations of his unit); keep a surveillance constantly over their sector throughout the hours of daylight; and send out a contact patrol plane whenever ordered by the division commander. Trying to attain such requirements, however, also uncovered serious deficiencies.

Given that it was most difficult to fly at low altitudes in extremely poor weather, it was their task to go up and find the front lines and get this information back to division commanders. After infantry contact patrols, pilot/observer teams returned to Toul to report that the division identity panels had not been laid out by troops to mark the forward progress of the troops. Planes that did artillery fire adjustment carried radios to communicate and needed those panels to make sure that they did not fire on friendly troops. But radio calls for panels were ignored, artillery *reglage* calls went unanswered, radio response from forward posts did not exist, and their low-flying Salmsons were fired upon by rifles and machine guns. The photographic missions were more relied upon by the infantry. The corps and army headquarters' need for daily reports was to plot movements of enemy units, and they studied each picture carefully for locations of artillery and machine-gun nests.[27]

Headquarters of the First Army Air Service finally resolved the issue about how to protect observation airplanes on missions on September 20, their inherent problems having been shown at the beginning of Chapter Two. Their one-page study discussed the fallacies of single-seat pursuit airplanes, versus the attributes of two-seater airplanes in protection work. Their first recommendation was that single-seat pursuit planes no longer be assigned for the individual protection of observation airplanes. Justifications not previously discussed included that pursuit planes could not fire to the rear, and that a two-seater had approximately the same speed as the observation airplane and could fire to the rear, making it a more suitable type. According to this study, the best way pursuit planes could offer protection was when they were free to attack whenever an enemy plane was sighted. However, when later put into practice during protection missions for the 1st Day Bombardment Group, it also sometimes left DH-4 and Bréguet 14B2 bombers vulnerable to attack and losses, while the enemy planes being chased simply retreated.

This concept had worked well on September 15, when a large patrol of 13th Aero Squadron Spads kept German *Jastas* occupied 4.8 km north of the 1st Aero Squadron's photography mission route, leaving them and their 22nd Aero Squadron escorts unmolested. Times where things did not go well included September 7, when DeCastro and Easterbrook had to return early because their 13th Aero Squadron escorts wandered too far away to be of any help if they were attacked; and even the second mission on August 1, when five of the seven escorting Spads suddenly left the formation before they even reached the front lines, essentially dooming the outcome before it started. During the Meuse–Argonne offensive, the 1st and 2nd Pursuit Groups, which had escorted 1st Aero Squadron Salmsons during the Château-Thierry and St. Mihiel operations, then became part of the 1st Pursuit Wing, assigned to gain air superiority in designated sectors prior to important photography and reconnaissance missions. The American I Corps commander called the 1st Pursuit Wing commander to marshal all forces necessary to meet any sudden concentration of enemy airplanes. Yet from that point on, the observation squadrons were bringing along extra two-seaters on missions, acting as gunships, and relying upon their rear guns for protection, the pursuit airplanes being deployed as that shown in the next chapter on September 26.

On September 21, the 1st Observation Group was ordered to move to Remicourt aerodrome, located 2 km west of Remicourt, in the Marne department in northeastern France.[28]

The next day, 1st Aero Squadron ferried 17 Salmsons from Croix de Metz aerodrome to Remicourt aerodrome in preparation for the upcoming Meuse–Argonne offensive, along with the 648th Aero Supply Squadron and the 1st Photo Section. The 12th Aero Squadron similarly ferried 18 Salmsons to Remicourt on September 22. Due to severe weather, the 50th Aero Squadron was not able to ferry its DH-4 Liberty planes to Remicourt until

September 24. It is unknown how many Liberty planes, the only American-built airplane flown into combat in World War I by American crews, they ferried to Remicourt that day. However, the 50th Aero Squadron had 14 such DH-4s available for mission duty on September 26. The 1st Aero Squadron had compiled statistics on hours flown by both pilots and observers over the front for the St. Mihiel operations between August 26 and September 22. What really stood out was Lieutenant Erwin's 34 hours 45 minutes of flight time over the front. Only one other pilot had even 60 percent as much flight time, and Erwin more than doubled and even tripled all the other pilots' flight times over the front during that time. He even had 10 more hours' flight time than 2nd Lieutenant Baucom and 20 more than 1st Lieutenant Easterbrook. In addition, Baucom's 24 hours 45 minutes of flight time over the front was not only the second most among all squadron observers, but also more than all squadron pilots other than Erwin.[29]

CHAPTER 4

Meuse–Argonne Offensive Operations

On September 23, under Operations Order No. 5, 1st Aero Squadron was assigned to the 35th Division from September 24 to October 2 for all aviation duties, including visual reconnaissance, surveillance of enemy artillery activity and fugitive targets, infantry contact patrols, adjustment and control of fire of division artillery, alert planes for special missions for division or corps commanders, and photographic missions required by the American I Corps. The French *Escadrille* BR 211 was assigned to Corps Heavy Artillery for control of fire, surveillance of enemy artillery activity, counter battery, adjustment, and alert planes at disposal of the corps artillery commander, but they were based at Sommeilles, 8 km southeast of Remicourt. The 12th Aero Squadron was similarly assigned to the 28th Division, and the 50th Aero Squadron was assigned to the 77th Division.[1]

Under Operations Order No. 7, all observers who had not previously been sent out over the front lines in the 35th Division's sector were dispatched in French planes with French pilots on September 25. The 1st, 12th, and 50th Aero Squadrons were ordered to paint the insignia of their assigned infantry division as large and clearly as possible on the underside of both lower wings of all planes likely to be called upon to carry out infantry contract patrols. The order for the 1st Aero Squadron was rescinded later that day, "owing to the danger of its being mistaken for a camouflaged black cross." Referred to as the "Santa Fe Division," its symbol was a crosshair, its various units having different quadrant colors and border colors. Most units had olive drab crosses, which in poor light could have been mistaken for black German crosses, and then subsequently fired upon by friendly troops. The American I Corps then held an 11 km front between La Harazée and Vauquois with three divisions in line: 77th Division on the left, 28th Division in the center, and 35th Division on the right. In the region of Clermont-en-Argonne, 92nd Division was held in corps reserve and 82nd Division as army reserve.[2]

Artillery preparation for the attack began in full force at 2:30 a.m. the following day. First Army's 2,700 guns kept up an intense bombardment of German positions until 5:30 a.m., at which time the assaulting infantry jumped off, protected by a rolling barrage. The dense fog during the morning, the networks of wire, myriads of shell craters, deep ravines, and thick woods presented great difficulties to those making the attack. On First Army's left, I Corps made a deep penetration along the Aire River, its left flank fighting its way forward about 1.6 km in the Argonne Forest. The 1st Aero Squadron was ordered to keep reconnaissance and surveillance over the 35th Division sector throughout the hours of daylight and to locate the front lines as early as possible. Just as they did in the St. Mihiel offensive, they chose Lieutenants Erwin and Baucom as "lead-off" men.[3]

Erwin and Baucom left at 6:40 a.m., with one 1st Aero Squadron Salmson providing protection, to fly an infantry contact patrol at an altitude varying between 200 and 1,500 meters. Their starting point was the 35th Division Headquarters at Boureuilles and the main road heading north-northwest towards Cheppy, Charpentry, and Exermont. From there they flew as far north as Exermont, the 35th Division's ultimate September 26 goal. About 7:00 a.m. they checked in with a division panel and read it's message "understood." So, they flew back to the division headquarters, dropped a message, and found a panel that read, "Where are my advanced elements"? Baucom acknowledged it several times but did not receive an "understood" panel in response. The 35th Division called for the front line, but it was impossible for Erwin and Baucom to find them, because of heavy clouds and mist over the valley through which the division was advancing. So, they returned to the division HQ, dropped a message to tell them they could not locate their front-line troops, and returned to their aerodrome.

The 1st Pursuit Wing covered the entire First Army sector, from La Harazée in the west to Beaumont-en-Verdunois in the east. Their first patrol mission included a two-hour offensive sweep at 6:30 a.m. to clear the air of enemy aviation at intermediate and high altitudes. If a favorable opportunity presented itself to attack a *Luftstreitkräfte* (German Air Service) observation airplane or pursuit formation, they could deviate from their assigned patrol route. The 1st, 2nd, and 3rd Pursuit Groups, and their respective squadrons, were then assigned individual missions to create an area 10 km in front of advancing Allied troops where it was safe for their observation planes to work. The individual pursuit groups were also assigned to attack enemy balloons within their assigned sectors and prevent all enemy planes from crossing Allied lines. The 1st Pursuit Group focused on destroying enemy observation balloons all day. The 13th, 22nd, 49th, and 139th Aero Squadrons of the 2nd Pursuit Group all flew three patrols of six planes each at different times that afternoon. Their orders were to sweep either 5–7 km or 6–9 km in advance of the line of battle. Some patrols flew at assigned altitudes of 2,500–3,500 meters, with others at 3,500–5,500 meters.[4]

The 3rd Pursuit Group maintained protective patrols from dawn to 1:00 p.m. to help Army Corps observation airplanes and were assigned to attack enemy reconnaissance planes. Their patrols consisted of seven Spads flying at 3,500 meters in the eastern half of the 1st Pursuit Wing's sector. In the western half they flew 14-Spad patrols, arranged in two seven-plane flights. One flight flew at 3,500 meters and the other at 4,000 meters, while keeping close contact with each other throughout their patrol. The schedules of the 28th, 93rd, 103rd, and 213th Aero Squadrons were arranged such that all four squadrons flew patrols in both the western and eastern sectors within the same morning. One such mission called for the 3rd Pursuit Group to send all available Spads to protect eight DH-4s of the 11th Aero Squadron and six of the 20th Aero Squadron, 1st Day Bombardment Group, which left at 3:35 p.m.

Led by Flight Commander 1st Lt. Cyrus J. Gatton and observer 2nd Lt. Lawrence Ward in DH-4 "1," the eight 11th Aero Squadron DH-4s flew northward in good visibility to Bar-le-Duc and then northeast to Etain. They then dropped 16 50-kg 155-mm bombs on the rail center at Etain from an altitude of 13,000 feet without interference by the enemy. They saw bombs burst in the center of the town before all teams returned safely at 4:40 p.m. All six 20th Aero Squadron DH-4s also reached their objective and bombed the railroad tracks at the entrance to the railyards with 24 50-kg 155-mm demolition shells from 13,000 feet. Antiaircraft fire damaged two of the DH-4s during their return at 5:20 p.m. They only saw five enemy airplanes at a distance, encountered none, but did observe aerial combats between enemy and 3rd Pursuit Group pursuit planes. While the 3rd Pursuit Group history for this date claimed four enemy planes were either destroyed or forced down out of control, only one victory was later confirmed for an enemy plane destroyed on this afternoon mission, by 28th Aero Squadron pilot Lt. Martinus Stenseth, in the area between Grimaucourt-en-Woëvre and Hautecourt-lès-Broville. Although this exemplified a successful protection mission—using overwhelming force with four pursuit squadrons, a morale booster with no personnel losses—11th and 20th Aero Squadron raid reports showed unawareness of this protection.[5]

The 35th Division captured Varennes-en-Argonne on the left side of their sector, as well as Cheppy in the middle of the sector along Ruanthe Creek. Despite their call for the front-line location, heavy clouds and mist over the Ruanthe Creek valley made it impossible to find the troops advancing through the valley. Nevertheless, at the end of the day they had advanced two-thirds of the way northward between Cheppy and Charpentry, which was a little more than halfway between their 5:30 a.m. starting point and Exermont.

Once the weather improved somewhat by late afternoon, Erwin and Baucom left on a photography mission at 4:30 p.m. in Salmson 2A2 3204 "8." Three DH-4 Liberty planes from the 50th Aero Squadron escorted them as gunship protection. Their crews comprised the following pilots and observers: 2nd Lt. David C. Beebe and 1st Lt. Milton K. "Micky" Lockwood in DH-4 "4"; 1st Lt. Robert M. Anderson and 2nd Lt. Mitchell H. "Mitch" Brown in DH-4 "16" "Shy-Ann"; and Lieutenants Russell E. Evans and Daniel P. Brill in DH-4 "15." Observer Micky Lockwood later recorded details of their mission in his diary:[6]

> In the afternoon they sent me up as protection for a Photo plane from the 1st Squadron. There were three of us Libertys protecting the photo Salmson. Flew a diamond. The Photo plane at the peak, Beebe and I on the left. Anderson and Brown on the right and Evans and Brill at the rear, all at different heights. Very pretty formation and as close as we were flying almost impregnable as we had no "blind spots." We went quite a ways into Hunland and got into the hottest Archie barrage I have ever seen. They were near enough to hear, and one was close enough to shake the plane. But such a side slipping and ducking as we went thru, all five [sic] of us tumbling around but right on into Germany. There were many planes in the air, and a bunch of six that Beebe and I went to look over promptly peaked, so Beebe threw her tail around to give me a good field of fire and then the pretty work started. One would peak and I would give him a burst and away we would go back into Germany, and then another would try. All six took their turns at us and all six left and I could see my tracers going right into the engine as they peaked down. At this same time Anderson and Brown were engaged with a circus of several others but didn't get scratched. Our formation was pretty well smashed up and the photo plane was gone, and we could not find him. Hung around over the front for 45 minutes but couldn't find him and headed south and got lost and landed at a French field about 30 kilometers south of here. Showed the Froggies how a Liberty takes off and came home, landing at the same time as our photo plane, who had accomplished a successful mission.[7]

The six attacking German fighters withdrew after a short combat. Baucom only mentioned two of the three DH-4s being attacked by Fokkers, so it is assumed that Evans and Brill in DH-4 "15," as well as two French Spads that joined them northwest of Boureuilles before they reached Montblainville, supplied adequate protection for the rest of the mission. Baucom then took 25 aerial vertical photographs along a 5 km route parallel to the front lines

Lieutenant Robert Anderson's DH-4 "16" "Shy-Ann" encountered enemy fighters while providing gunship protection on Erwin and Baucom's September 26, 1918, photo mission. This aircraft did not yet display the unique 50th Aero "Dutch Girl" insignia, since, as per existing regulations, the squadron had not yet served a month at the front or been cited for distinguished service. On October 7, Anderson and observer Lieutenant Woodville J. Rogers finally established the position of the "Lost Battalion" in the Argonne Forest, flying "Shy-Ann," now proudly displaying its "Dutch Girl" insignia. (Milton K. Lockwood Album, National Museum USAF Archives via Steve Ruffin)

between Montblainville and Eclisfontaine, both then only 1 km northwest of the front lines, from an altitude of 1,100 meters in hazy visibility. The main road heading southwest from Eclisfontaine pointed straight at Montblainville, making the route easy to follow and transecting the entire 35th Division sector. The resulting 10 good photographs provided an estimate of the terrain they needed to capture on September 27. Erwin returned to Remicourt at 6:25 p.m.[8]

The American I Corps ordered Erwin and Baucom to find the 35th Division's front lines as early as possible on September 27 and to continue reconnaissance and surveillance over their sector. Carrying a wireless radio, they left at 5:05 p.m. with two protecting 1st Aero Squadron gunships in fair visibility. Flying between 50 and 400 meters, they received a call for help at 6:10 p.m. The 35th Division units needing front-line spotting had advanced up the Ruanthe Creek valley northward towards Charpentry, and then fanned out northeastward, following the tributary creek that paralleled the main road running northeast between Charpentry and Eclisfontaine. Baucom's following intelligence report was filed with the I Corps Observation Group:

Divisional panel requested front line. Got front lines at 18h.10. Line outpost in trench at 05.4–78.2, probably company there. 1 or 2 platoons at 05.4–78.9 in shell holes. The rest of the division seemed to be in the valley S. of the road Charpentry–Eclisfontaine, ½ km. from the road, mostly between the points 04.4–77.1 and 05.5–77.9. About a platoon N. of the road at 05.2–78.4.

Division asked for the location of their P.C.s. Fired several rockets, but no P.C. panels displayed.

At 05.7–77.0 the infantry sent up one white and one green rocket indicating that heavy artillery was falling short.

At 18h.10 the barrage was at 08.9–77.8 and 04.7–77.9. 1 Company of Boche in the bend of the road at 03.9–78.9 S. of the woods. Another Company came into the same woods from the N. I fired my machine guns at them at an altitude of 50m. The road was cut from 5 or 6 ft. and had dugouts on either side.

Two tanks just S. of Cote des Houleaux. These tanks were coming back from direction of our line, they had apparently advanced beyond our infantry, and were coming back for protection.

At 18h.50 two tanks in the open at 04.5–78.3. Saw a train at Gesnes [-en-Argonne]. Barracks at 05.6–83.5 were also 05.4–85.5 in the woods and would hold about 2 Battalions each. Woods were full of barracks. Fired on battery of artillery at 03.4–84.3 going SW on the road. Saw convoy parked S. of the woods at 02.3–84.5: fired at a convoy in the woods at 01.4–84.2. Fired on Boche troops in Fléville. There were more than a Battalion of enemy troops in this town.

The lights at Division P.C. (35th Div.) were very conspicuous. Troops massed around them would afford an excellent target.

Was fired at by Boche biplane. Two other enemy planes over Divisional sector.

No message dropped at Corps Headquarters because of darkness.[9]

With approaching darkness, Erwin and Baucom returned to Remicourt at 7:05 p.m. After the group commander filed this report with the 1st Army, Corps Observation Wing, Major M. A. Hall noted that the report was "an example of the work being done by observers in this Corps. The accuracy of the information reported has since been confirmed in several ways ... Although this report is exceptional in length and detail, there are many other observers doing equally good work." The report was then forwarded to First Army Headquarters with another note from Major L. H. Brereton, who further endorsed Baucom in saying, "This observer has shown remarkable skill and courage in his work consistently since joining the First Aero Squadron."[10]

Lieutenant Erwin attained his second, and Baucom his first, confirmed victory during an infantry contact patrol on September 29, their orders being to locate the 35th Division's front lines as early as possible. Flying at altitudes between 150 and 600 meters, they engaged a German Rumpler two-seater 3.2 km north of the infantry front lines, exchanged gunfire, and shot it down between Fléville and Sommerance. The Rumpler crew also caused damage, however, firing bullets into the Salmson's radiator and engine that compelled

Erwin to return south and make a forced landing at their advanced field at Remicourt at 4:00 p.m. Their Salmson 2A2 3204 "8" was later salvaged at the 1st Air Depot at Colombey-les-Belles. Another 1st Aero Squadron Salmson had supplied gunship protection on the mission. On October 27, 1918, Headquarters, First Army Air Service, issued General Orders Number 21, confirming their victory and the destruction of a German Rumpler at 4:55 p.m.[11]

Easterbrook and his pilot, 1st Lt. Arthur J. Coyle, were on another infantry contact patrol at about the same time, between Fléville and Gesnes-en-Argonne. They left at 4:05 p.m. and flew at altitudes ranging between 50 and 500 meters in fair visibility. They fired on one hostile plane at 4:35 p.m., before Easterbrook sent a message asking where the front lines were. Easterbrook located 35th Division troops at map reference 01.3–80.3 to 06.4–81.3 at 4:50 p.m., then he pinpointed the opposing enemy battery locations at 97.5–82.6, 91.4–82.4, 99.6–82.5, and 03.4–84.4 at 5:00 p.m. On his way back, he strafed an enemy convoy on the road leading out of Fléville at 5:05 p.m. He then spotted enemy machine guns at 01.5–81.5 firing on 35th Division troops, so he fired 150 rounds at them from a height of 50 meters. Easterbrook then showed the American troops where he found the enemy at 5:10 p.m.,

Squadron commanding officer and pilot 1st Lieutenant Arthur J. Coyle, who had one aerial victory, and his observer, 2nd Lieutenant James W. Corley, who had three victories (two on October 1 and one on October 2), in Salmson 2A2 1161 "24," ready to take off during the Meuse–Argonne offensive. (George H. Williams via Greg VanWyngarden)

collected his information in messages, and dropped them on the P.C.s of both 35th Division and American I Corps. One 1st Aero Squadron Salmson flew gunship protection for him.[12]

The pursuit protection issue of two-seaters and how it was supposed to function was further blurred when 16 Spads of the 13th Aero Squadron and 12 Spads of the 22nd Aero Squadron, 2nd Pursuit Group, all laden with bombs, accompanied nine DH-4s of the 11th Aero Squadron and six of the 20th Aero Squadron for an afternoon raid over Grandpré. Although this mission was touted as the pinnacle of success in pursuit protection, the 2nd Pursuit Group labeled it as a "bombing raid" rather than pursuit protection. Moreover, the first time the 22nd Aero Spads spotted Fokkers, they dropped their bombs to chase them further into their own lines, which meant fewer bombs dropped on target. The antiaircraft fire was light but accurate, with two DH-4s damaged, although the two-seaters did not encounter any aerial opposition, which was not surprising considering the Spads outnumbered them by almost two to one. Five 96th Aero Squadron Bréguet 14B2 bombers had initially accompanied the raid but did not reach the target after they were called back when orders were received changing their objective to Etain.[13]

The squadron received Salmson 1286 as Erwin's replacement ship on September 30. The squadron's artist was kept busy painting the American flag insignia and number "8" on the fuselage sides, while the nose ring and engine cowl were painted white.

The 1st Division relieved the 35th Division in the line on October 1, with command of the sector passing to them at 4:00 a.m. With their operational orders being to photograph the entire I Corps front to a depth of 5 km, Erwin flew this mission with observer Lieutenant Easterbrook. This covered all 1st Division ground gained on the Romagne Heights, from Apremont 8 km northward to Sommerance. They flew their route at an altitude of 1,200 meters in fair visibility, taking 24 photographs, all of which were good. The highway connecting Apremont north-northwest to Saint-Juvin formed the western border of the 1st Division and 28th Division sectors. One 1st Aero Squadron Salmson and a single 50th Aero Squadron DH-4 flew as gunship protection. The pilot of the DH-4 was 1st Lt. Floyd M. Pickrell, who supplied specific details about this event through interviews conducted via written correspondence exchanged with Steve Ruffin from the late 1970s until the early 1990s:[14]

> One time I had to fly a protection mission for the 1st Aero Squadron. They had Salmsons and were doing photographic work, and they were short some planes. They wanted somebody to fly protection, so they came to our squadron. The captain asked me if I wanted to go, and I said I would. So, Lt. Erwin … was the man I flew protection for that day. We went

12 kilometers over the German lines. There were patches of cumulus clouds that day and they were 2500 feet high. We had to fly under the clouds in a straight line, and the archies just gave us hell all the way over there and back. I had a chunk of shrapnel stuck in my plane, and I wore it as a weight on a watch for a while. But that day we knew what antiaircraft sounded like. We had just a continual stream of smoke over and back—archies after us …

Well, we made it—there were three planes—we got hit and my propeller was chipped; some of it stuck in the plane. Nothing you could do but fly straight and hope they don't hit you. Lt. Erwin was flying a Salmson at this time and they were slower than our DH-4s and we had to throttle down. I was flying the only DH-4 [32517 "6" with his observer, Lieut. Alfred C. George] in that formation.[15]

Lieutenant Baucom was appointed as the squadron's ground liaison officer on October 2, spending his entire time in that role at the 1st Division Headquarters. While Baucom was unavailable, Erwin continued working with Lieutenant Easterbrook as his observer. The 1st Aero Squadron was ordered to take photographs between Exermont and Fléville at 3,500 meters. Erwin left with Easterbrook on this photographic mission at 11:15 a.m., but due to low clouds and poor visibility it was impossible to take pictures. They spotted a formation of five Fokkers over Exermont, but with the odds stacked against him, Erwin dropped into the fog and rain. *Jasta* 13 Fokkers then controlled the air space in that sector and the previous day their commander, *Ltn.* Franz Büchner, had just shot down 1st Aero Squadron Salmson 2A2 867 "1" in flames over Fléville, killing 1st Lt. Raymond F. Fox and 1st Lt. Walter A. Phillips for Büchner's 38th victory. With discretion being the better part of valor, Erwin dove over the front lines at 12:30 p.m. for Easterbrook to gather bits of information as they went along, before returning at 12:50 p.m.[16]

On October 3, the 1st Division requested infantry contact patrols to locate their front lines at 6:20 a.m., 6:50 a.m., and 10:30 a.m. the following morning. In preparation for the offensive to resume, Erwin and Easterbrook left on an early evening reconnaissance patrol for them a little before 5:00 p.m., with one 1st Aero Squadron Salmson furnishing protection. Easterbrook began rapidly picking up enemy battery locations, flashing them back to headquarters with his wireless as they went along: "Enemy batteries K-6, J-8, B-3, Z-8. Machine gun emplacements H-5, W-7. Fired effectively on our plane. Fired forty rounds at them. Two guns, B-7, N-3, moving into Exermont. Fired forty rounds at same. Lot of traffic movement in St. Juvin and a little in Sommerance. Recommend shelling crossroads H-2 and E-9."

Suddenly, a Fokker appeared northward, prompting Erwin to start closing with it, but just as he got within range, the Fokker spotted him and turned

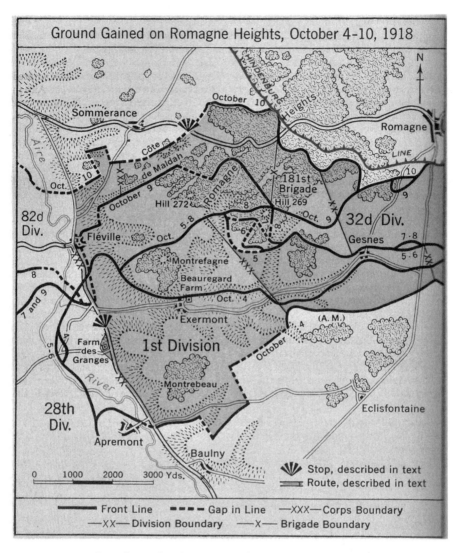

Ground gained on Romagne Heights, October 4–10, 1918.

back into Germany. Erwin fired his Vickers gun anyway, but without success. As he did so, Easterbrook yelled a warning through the tube, and they looked up eastward to see seven more Fokkers above them, swarming to the defense of the lone Fokker.

Erwin dropped into a vrille and eluded them, but as he leveled off a few hundred feet from the ground, machine-gun bullets snapped about his ears. The next moment there came the click of a bullet upon metal and the engine coughed. As he glided back into the comparative safety of American territory and swept along seeking a place to touch down, his motor gave a final cough and stopped entirely. Fortunately, he had barely made it to the advanced landing field at Remicourt. Nosing downward, the ground below still littered with scattered trees, he swept low over the field, his motor silenced by a bullet. With his controls still operable, he managed to lift the heavy ship over one obstacle after another until he finally let it pancake near the 1st Corps Observation Group P.C. The landing was well done: a wheel snapped off and the ship swung around upon the dragging hub, striking its wing against a tree and splintering it, but the damage was not irreparable and neither Erwin nor Easterbrook was injured.[17]

Erwin was ordered to conduct an infantry contact patrol with Easterbrook in the late afternoon of October 4. The battle on the ground had already begun early that morning at 5:25 a.m., 1st Division's first obstacle being a large, isolated wooded area called Montrebeau. Supported by 47 tanks and artillery fire, their vigorous advance suffered great losses but Montrebeau, Fermes des Granges, Exermont and the line Beauregard Farm–La Neuville-le-Comte Farm (now known as Fermes de la Neuve Forge). As a result of the day's fighting, the 16th Infantry Regiment, on the left, had advanced more than 4 km and 2 Brigade some 2 km. The gap between these extremes was filled by the 18th Infantry Regiment, which faced northeast with its center clinging to the difficult and strongly held Montrefagne. While flying over

On October 4, 1918, 1st Lieutenant Edward Groteclose, Jr., was flying Salmson 2A2 3171 "9" on an infantry contact patrol when he was forced to land at Varennes by machine-gun fire from the ground at about 8:50 a.m., and his observer, 1st Lieutenant Charles A. Henry, was wounded in the resulting crash. Shown here is Groteclose's replacement ship, 3376 "9," received by the 1st Aero Squadron on October 5, 1918. (Alan D. Toelle)

Landres, Easterbrook called to Erwin through the speaking tube and pointed down to a road where an artillery convoy was moving. Erwin nosed down in a wide spiral, and just then the engine stopped dead. He somehow managed to glide at least 27 km westward to safety. "Landed two kilos north of Cheppy in a shell hole," Easterbrook's report read, concluding: "Enemy battery 01.3, 84.4. 5:15 p.m. Walked into Cheppy and reported to G.H.Q., First Division."

When they reached 1st Division Headquarters in Cheppy that evening, they found not only Baucom, but another 1st Aero Squadron Salmson crew forced to land with motor trouble that day. After landing near Véry earlier that morning during an infantry contact patrol that left at 8:50 a.m., pilot 1st Lt. Irving S. Morange and observer 1st Lt. Joseph H. Farnham walked the 2.5 km south along the road connecting the two towns to the 1st Division GHQ. Morange and Farnham flew the protection plane for pilot 1st Lt. Edward Groteclose, Jr., and observer 1st Lt. Charles A. Henry, who were forced to land by ground fire at Varennes, 1.8 km west of Cheppy, Henry being wounded in that landing.[18]

Erwin and Easterbrook took off in poor visibility at 5:15 p.m. on October 5 for an infantry contact patrol. Flying at altitudes varying between 100 and 800 meters while the battle raged below them on the wooded and hilly terrain between Exermont, Fléville, Sommerance, and Imécourt, they spotted two German infantry contact planes that had just fired rockets calling for their infantry to reveal their front lines. Erwin and Easterbrook first attacked and drove them away, and then when the German infantry displayed flares, they noted their locations before returning to Remicourt at 7:00 p.m. Easterbrook reported as follows:

> Located German lines K-2 to J-4. Two Rumplers fired rockets when we came to lines. Dived on them and they returned to Germany, but German infantry displayed their flares 6:05 p.m. Enemy batteries A-7, E-9. Enemy convoy of six guns going into Imécourt at Y-9, T-2. Fired forty rounds at same. Turned over two guns. Troops and trucks in Imécourt. Pilot and I shot up the town (200 rounds). Convoy drawing northeast out of St. Juvin; fired sixty rounds. Enemy troops and mg emplacements at Martincourt Farm. Dugout at A-7, E-3. Fired eighty rounds at a battery K-4, E-6, and made them stop firing. Three Fokkers over Bois de Romagne. Large fire at Beffu de Morthomme. All enemy convoys moving north. Advise shelling Imécourt. Plane badly hit by mg fire from ground. Hit twice by burning onions [flare or tracer ammunition fired by antiaircraft gun], burning our plane. One missed me by eight inches. Did not leave for home until after dark.[19]

The 1st Division's advance was successful in capturing Ariétal Farm, extending their front line from Fléville into the Bois de Moncy, but they had sustained nearly 3,500 casualties since the attack had begun the previous day.[20]

The 1st Aero Squadron was reassigned to Army Corps work from October 6–24. Erwin again had a successful mission on the 6th, teaming up with

Easterbrook for his third confirmed victory and Easterbrook's first. They left at 6:30 a.m. in fair visibility as gunship protection on an infantry contact patrol for 2nd Lieutenant Richardson and his observer, 1st Lt. Gordon Kibbs. Although they were flying within the Exermont–Fléville–Sommerance triangular area, Saint-Juvin is only 4.8 km west-northwest of Fléville and Sommerance, and Erwin spotted a German two-seater near Saint-Juvin, flying below them at 500 meters.

Erwin and Easterbrook had been planning a new maneuver for a couple of days, and here was their opportunity to try it. Erwin left Richardson temporarily and headed for the enemy observation plane. He dove straight downward on it and pulled the trigger of his Vickers machine gun once he got within range. Then, when directly above it, he pulled into a chandelle, or climbing turn. Just as both speed and wind resistance dropped to a minimum—the very moment when the enemy ship was clearly exposed to Easterbrook's view—Easterbrook fired 80 rounds from his twin Lewis guns into the German's gasoline tank and crew compartments. As they pulled away, the German ship burst into flames and fell. The enemy had only managed to register one burst of shots in defense before its death spiral.

Soon thereafter they saw it in flames on the ground near Saint-Juvin. Easterbrook's logbook tersely describes the encounter: "Shot down an enemy bi-place from 500 meters at 96.2 [map location]. Time 7:15. Pilot fired 120 rounds; I, 80, on which plane went down in flames. Our plane had 28 holes through one side." Richardson, flying between 300 and 500 meters, was wounded in the foot by machine-gun ground fire, so they had to return early to Remicourt after being out for little more than an hour. On November 2, Headquarters of First Army Air Service confirmed their victory north of Saint-Juvin at 7:15 a.m. in General Orders Number 22.[21]

The squadron was ordered to have one infantry contact plane and one counterattack plane continuously between Cornay, Fléville, and Sommerance, and to fire on enemy troops at every opportunity. At 4:00 p.m. on October 8, the 1st Battalion, 1st Engineers, assisted by a detachment of the 26th Infantry Regiment, attacked and captured Hill 269, about 0.8 km west-northwest of Gesnes-en-Argonne. Lieutenants Erwin and Easterbrook left at 3:40 p.m. to conduct their patrol between 100 and 2,000 meters, during which the duo scored one of the only two double victories during the same flight ever scored by a 1st Aero Squadron flight crew during the war, a summary of which by Easterbrook follows:[22]

> Troops showed panels at, S2-C5, W1-X0, W9-X4, O5-X7. Troops seen at M4-X4. Convoy of wagons going south, C2-U4. Hostile balloon seen NW of St. Juvin and Sommerance, in vicinity of Landres-et-Saint Georges, and another farther east.

Saw one plane doing *reglage* at 1800 meters at about over Exermont. We fired at him and he went into Germany, but continually returned. Saw three planes immediately north of Varennes at about 900 meters. We attacked and split their formation in all directions. We believe to have crashed one, a bi-place, which was seen to go down out of control. This was about 4:25 and confirmation is requested. Then we attacked two more enemy planes and drove them into Germany. We then, again, attacked a large enemy bi-place machine immediately after he had fired rockets for the front line. (Rocket was a large star which split into many smaller ones.) This combat took place in the rain at about 600 meters and took place just south of Sommerance. After about three minutes maneuvering, the pilot Lieut. Erwin shot and either killed or severely wounded the enemy observer. Continuing the combat, the pilot fired about fifty rounds into the German from about fifty meters and from the fact that none of these shots seemed to have taken effect, believes this plane to have been armored. He then pulled up into a chandelle over the enemy and I fired a drum in two bursts, my tracers apparently entering the pilot's cockpit. After the second burst the machine crashed to the ground, from fifty meters altitude.

After forcing this machine to the ground, we returned and picked up the lines, after which we had a brief combat with an enemy Halberstadt, which however was without results.

I, the observer, was shot thru the thumb by machine gun fire from the ground, and during one of the combats a bullet had entered our motor so that we had to return to the airdrome.[23]

On October 10, 1918, Headquarters, First Army Air Service cited Erwin and Easterbrook via General Orders Number 15 for their courageous actions on this date, but with no medals awarded, as follows:

1. The Chief of Air Service, First Army, desired to record in General Orders the splendid courage of Lieutenants Erwin and Easterbrook of the 1st Aero Squadron, who, on October 8th, 1918, while attempting to locate our infantry, encountered an enemy plane conducting an adjustment over Exermont. They attacked and forced the enemy plane to retire. Shortly after they encountered three enemy planes over Varennes and broke up the formation. Again, they encountered two enemy planes engaged in Infantry liaison and forced them to retire. Shortly after this they encountered an enemy bi-place south of Sommerance, in which combat Lieutenant Erwin wounded or killed the hostile observer. Following up this advantage, they closed on the enemy plane and drove it to the ground where it crashed. In spite of all these combats, these officers returned to complete their mission and after finishing this, they encountered an enemy Halberstadt, which combat was without result.
2. These officers showed a courage and devotion to duty which all the Air Service can well emulate.
3. This order will be read to all units at their next formation.

By command of Brigadier General Mitchell:
T. DeW. Milling,
Colonel, A.S., U.S.A.,
Chief of Staff[24]

Erwin returned at 5:40 p.m. after a two-hour flight. On October 27, General Orders Number 21 confirmed the first victory at 4:30 p.m. and the second at 5:15 p.m. Erwin dispatched his first two-seater after executing an Immelmann maneuver, diving headlong with his Vickers gun wide open towards the

Junkers J.I 586/18 fits the description of the type downed by Lieutenant Erwin for his fifth and Lieutenant Easterbrook's third confirmed victories on October 8, 1918. Junkers designed this first all-metal military airplane in quantity service to be as impervious as possible to gunfire, integrating armor plate to protect the crew and engine part of the fuselage. The only fabric covering was on the fuselage between the rear cockpit and tail, the fabric removed between "Junk J.I" and "586/18" here exposing its steel airframe. Junkers J.I 802/17 shows how formidable it would have looked that day, here with its observer manning a reliable Madsen machine gun with telescopic sight. Junkers built 221 J.Is in 1917–18. (Courtesy of Colin Owers)

middle ship of the formation of three, and then rising into a chandelle to let Easterbrook's Lewis guns bear on the target. The unfortunate German ship slipped sideways and went down, as the other two-seaters swung wide in opposite directions and sped away. What surprised Erwin the most about his second victim was that it held its ground. He could only down this larger, but slower and less maneuverable ship by first either killing or incapacitating the observer, so that he could rise above it in a chandelle maneuver to allow Easterbrook to kill the pilot with his Lewis guns. Although Dewey reported in 1928 that Erwin and Easterbrook drove to the crash site the next morning to gain confirmation, the 82nd Division did not secure a line south of Sommerance until October 10. Erwin apparently visited the site later, however, because he found the wreck not badly smashed, with steel armor plates covering all its vital parts, this being the reason his bullets failed to take effect. It had to have been a Junkers J.I, the fuselage length and wingspan of which are both longer than that of a Rumpler C-IV. The Junkers J.I had a completely armored nose capsule of 5 mm chrome-nickel sheet steel that enclosed the engine and crew compartment. It ended in a solid bulkhead behind the observer's cockpit that gave protection from immediately astern, although the rear half of the fuselage, consisting of alloy tube frame, was fabric-covered.[25]

As a result of the American advances, the Germans started withdrawing from the Argonne on October 9, removing the menace of their presence in the forest to I Corps, from which 1st Aero Squadron was once again receiving their orders. They were ordered to locate the front lines at 9:30 a.m., 11:45 a.m., 2:10 p.m., and 4:00 p.m. A surveillance plane had to fly over the division sector from 8:30 a.m. until dark. Erwin was ordered to fly the early evening patrol near Saint-Juvin with Lieutenant Kibbs as his observer. Leaving at 4:15 p.m., they flew at between 25 and 600 meters in fair visibility, with another 1st Aero Squadron Salmson supplying protection. Although the air in the vicinity was still ferociously contested, their two aerial combats with enemy planes produced no results and they returned to Remicourt at 6:30 p.m.

The following day, Erwin took off at 9:15 a.m. with Easterbrook as his observer, flying within the Saint-Juvin, Sommerance, St. Georges triangular area at between 20 and 1,500 meters. The 1st Division took the Côte de Maldah, and about the same time they advanced through the nearest part of the large woods of the Bois de Romagne. Even finding front line positions was a difficult task, since the vicious ground combat resulted in many places changing hands that morning. Easterbrook reported: "Picked up our lines three times this flight, and the last time they had advanced a mile from where they were when I first picked them up. Fired 150 rounds at enemy troops in shell holes from fifty meters altitude." Erwin reported: "Four enemy planes attacked but after a brief combat they returned within their lines." That, however, could have been less than a mile north.

Using up all his available fuel on a successful mission, Erwin returned to Remicourt at 12:15 p.m. From October 11/12, 42nd Division relieved 1st Division, then occupying a position in a line running northeast from the Côte de Maldah just east of Sommerance through the Bois de Romagne. The 32nd Division was in line to their right, while 82nd Division reinforced the line to their left. During 12 days of battle, 1st Division had advanced more than 6.4 km through the difficult terrain of the Romagne Heights. Its casualties reached the heavy total of over 8,200 men, the greatest number of any division in the Meuse–Argonne offensive.[26]

Second Lieutenant Baucom returned from his duty as a 1st Division liaison officer during their recent battle, and the replacement 42nd Division jumped off all along its front during the general attack of the First Army. On October 14, 77th Division captured Saint-Juvin and 82nd Division took the ridge east of it. Upon returning, Baucom reported his experiences over the previous two weeks:

> I was with the Division all the time they were in the line and was at the Division Headquarters all the time.
>
> Each night, upon the instructions of the Chief of Staff or G-2, I would telephone, through the CAS 1st Army Corps, the kind, character and time of each mission of our Squadron for the following day. As we lost nine machines the first day, trying to find the front lines, I had the Division authorities bear in mind that we were operating with only about a third strength. The Division authorities appreciated the difficulties under which we were working and gave us good cooperation. I want to mention especially the splendid cooperation of Major Horsely, Divisional Signal Officer, and Lieut. Brown, Divisional Radio Officer, Lieut. Col. Creely, chief of staff, and also Major Sheppard, Capt. Beesely, and Lieut. Dean of the Artillery.
>
> During the whole time that the First Division was in the line, there was only one day during which the Air Service had an opportunity for efficient cooperation—that is, only one day fit for flying, and that golden opportunity was blighted because our [squadron] suffered 80% casualties by trying to work in impossible weather.[27]

Doing a good job while working with much higher-ranking officers earned Baucom a promotion 11 days later. It is unclear, however, how he derived "lost nine machines the first day." Squadron loss records show the greatest loss of Salmsons on any given date to be five, occurring on October 5, at least four of which were due to combat damage. Perhaps he was counting three 50th Aero Squadron DH-4s lost and six shot to pieces and no longer serviceable on October 6, while trying to find the "Lost Battalion" six companies of the 308th Infantry, parts of two companies of the 306th Machine Gun Battalion, and one company of the 307th Infantry, with an initial effective strength of more than 600 men from the 77th Division, isolated for six days by German troops after an American attack in the Argonne Forest. There are only seven 1st Aero Squadron known losses during this entire time.[28]

The 82nd Division captured Hill 182 north of Saint-Juvin on October 15, while 42nd Division launched its second assault on Côte de Châtillon, a stronghold in the Hindenburg Line. Gaining this ground was of exceptional importance because it opened the way for further advances. Lieutenants Erwin and Baucom left on a propaganda leaflet dropping mission to the German-held rear areas at 2:13 p.m., with four new 1st Aero Squadron Salmson crews protecting them while gaining experience. At the same time, Erwin and Baucom noted and reported enemy artillery battery positions back to the 77th and 82nd Divisions by wireless. This involved flying primarily over enemy-held territory, starting from Saint-Juvin, 8 km northeast over Chennery to Bayonville, then 5 km northwest to Buzancy, and finally 10.5 km south back to Saint-Juvin at an altitude of 350–1,600 meters in poor visibility. Erwin later detailed his sixth, and Baucom's second, confirmed victory:[29]

> We received a bunch of new pilots just a little after the beginning of the Argonne show. All of them seemed good material and anxious to have a run in with the Hun. So, on Oct. 15th Lt. Baucom and I took a formation of five out for a "party." We had some propaganda to drop and since parading around alone as much as we had, five machines looked like an Armada to us. Then I had to curb Baucom's desire to go and drop the propaganda on his majesty the Kaiser's personal residence in Berlin.
>
> We made quite an excursion into Germany to drop the propaganda and the Archies were unusually active. This extremely annoyed the new men, who began cutting so many antics to avoid them that I was really alarmed lest they should dive into a stray burst. We dropped our propaganda about ten kilometers in and started back. There was a dearth of Huns in the air, but the Archies continued when we almost reached our lines. Our own Archies, apparently not having had their daily target practice, started warming up on us. Not at all pleasant either, for some of our boys shoot remarkably well. Today it was a tossup, however the Boche gunners came nearly as near to us as our own, so we decided to go back into Germany and come into our own lines at a more favorable place.
>
> This time we went back almost to Buzancy (the lines were then south of Grandpré, Sommerance, etc.) [and] while cruising around back there, we sighted a bi-place enemy Rumpler who had evidently just got his altitude from his field near the little town of Bar [1.6 km northwest of Buzancy] about one kilometer from where we were. He did not see us, or if he did, thought that no one but Germans would be so far back and paid us no heed. As he came nearer and slightly over us, we noticed he had some red and white streamers on his upper wing. As he passed directly over, Lt. Baucom gave him a burst from both guns. He *viraged* to the left and started for home, then for some reason turned and faced us.

I headed into him, pouring lead into his engine and fuselage until he slid off on a wing and shot under our side.[30]

As he passed, Lt. Baucom gave him another burst, which I believe killed the observer, for his guns flew up and he hung limp over the side of the fuselage for the rest of the scrap. I put the machine into a *vrille* turn and by doing so got on his tail and started shooting at him. His machine began belching out heavy smoke and he started into a steep spiral, ending up in a slip as he was very near the ground and clearly out of control. I pulled off him to observe the crash. As I pulled away, Baucom who always wants to finish an argument with the last word, gave him a parting burst. He crashed about a mile from his field a complete wreck. We were fortunate to have had a formation along because we were able to obtain our confirmation on returning home. Seeing no others in the air and our gas beginning to run low, we returned to our field [at 4:15 p.m.], the "party" having been a complete success.[31]

On October 23, Headquarters, First Army Air Service confirmed their victory for the encounter, which occurred at 3:35 p.m., via General Orders Number 20.[32]

On October 18, an artillery surveillance plane was ordered to be on alert in the 78th Division's sector. Lieutenant Erwin left on such a surveillance mission at 3:10 p.m. with Lieutenant Baucom, flying between Sommerance and Grandpré at an altitude between 400 and 1,600 meters. Although Erwin remembered a slightly different version of events, five 94th Aero Squadron pilots wrote reconnaissance reports, one of them seeking confirmation for the German observation plane that Erwin mentioned seeing falling. He had happened upon a scene where a nine-Spad low patrol led by Capt. Hamilton Coolidge—also comprising Lieutenants Edward G. Garnsey, John N. Jeffers, Harvey Weir Cook, Raymond J. Saunders, Samuel Kaye, Jr., Alden B. Sherry, Charles I. Crocker, and Dudley M. Outcalt—were in the process of attacking a Halberstadt between Exermont and Fléville at 800 meters. One of the Spads, flown by Lieutenant Crocker, was approaching Erwin and heading south at 3:25 p.m. with motor trouble.

Ten Fokkers were perched above the Spads and Halberstadt, although none dove to chase Crocker, whom Erwin, Baucom, and the other protecting 1st Aero Squadron Salmson were ready to defend. Erwin thought that the 94th Aero Spads had been carrying light bombs that day. That was not the case—they were simply on a low patrol. What Erwin thought was a general melee was a swirling dogfight with the Halberstadt at 3:35 p.m., in which Lieutenant Cook fired 150 rounds at it, Kaye 50 rounds, Outcalt 100 rounds, Garnsey 100 rounds, and Sherry about the same. Lieutenant Outcalt followed the Halberstadt all the way to the ground, watching it crash on landing and turn over.

One of the 10 Fokkers meanwhile dropped down and attacked the Spads, firing about 50 rounds at Garnsey and shooting at Sherry too. Although both Erwin and the 94th Aero Squadron pilots agreed that there were 10 Fokkers sitting above, only Erwin thought there was more than one Fokker involved in the skirmish. This appears to be the same Fokker that Erwin attacked from an altitude of 1,400 meters, using his new chandelle technique, diving on the Fokker with his front gun, pulling up and then letting Baucom shoot with his twin Lewis guns. Baucom had trained his guns along the Fokker's perceived path of flight, the Fokker flew into it, there was a puff of smoke, and then flames burst from its gasoline tank. The Fokker suddenly nosed upward into a stall, but before it fell over into a sideslip, the pilot luckily took to his parachute. Erwin spiraled around him as he was coming down. When he landed, he crumpled up as though he was wounded but stood up at once. When Erwin flew low over him, he waved, and they waved back.[33]

Leutnant der Reserve Gustav Boehren of *Jasta* 10, who was indeed wounded and taken prisoner, had made a safe landing, his Fokker falling within the American lines near Sommerance at 3:50 p.m. This was Erwin's seventh confirmed victory, scored on his 23rd birthday. On November 2, General Orders Number 22 from Headquarters, First Army Air Service, confirmed what was also Baucom's third and final victory. Similarly, on October 27, General Orders Number 21 confirmed the 94th Aero Squadron's Halberstadt victory near Exermont at 3:35 p.m., credited to Lieutenants Cook (his fifth), Kaye, and Sherry.

Afterwards, Erwin invited *Ltn. d. R.* Boehren to be his guest at dinner. They dined together and he and the German, a scholar and graduate of Heidelberg University, became good friends. Boehren was firm in his belief that the Huns would still win the war, expressing himself in no uncertain terms. "We'll retire to the Rhine, put a ring of steel around Germany and you'll pay hell in getting through," was his confident assertion. Twenty-three days later, with the war over, Germany was a conquered nation.[34]

Meanwhile, Lieutenant Easterbrook flew two missions with 1st Lieutenant Coyle, the first one a photo mission between Landres-et-Saint-Georges and Grandpré at an altitude of 600 meters in poor visibility. This was a quick trip, leaving at 11:49 a.m., taking 15 oblique photos, 10 of which were good, and returning at 12:10 p.m. with their escort of two 1st Aero Squadron Salmsons. They left again at 3:40 p.m. on an infantry contact patrol between Landres-et-Saint-Georges and Champigneulle. Flying at altitudes ranging between 100 and 1,500 meters in poor visibility, they found German troop

Far right, *Leutnant der Reserve* Gustav Boehren, alongside other *Jasta* 10 pilots displaying "immediate readiness" circa September 1918, all seated on the ground in their parachute harnesses, with their Fokker D.VIIs behind them. From left to right: *Unteroffizier* Oskar Hennig, *Leutnant* Kurt Schibilsky, *Leutnant* Justus Grassmann, *Leutnant* Alois Heldmann (acting *Staffelführer*), *Offizierstellvertreter* Paul Aue, *Leutnant* Wilhelm Kohlbach, *Unteroffizier* Rudolf Klamt, and Boehren. (Via Greg VanWyngarden)

positions bunched closely in trenches of the *Kriemhilde Stellung*, part of the Hindenburg Line. They then similarly noted friendly 42nd and 82nd Division troop locations on the south side of the *Kriemhilde Stellung* before returning to base at 5:10 p.m.[35]

At 9:30 a.m. on October 19 on the aviation field at Belrain, Major General Mason T. Patrick, Chief of the Air Service, conferred DSCs to 1st Lieutenant Erwin, 2nd Lieutenant Baucom, and 1st Lieutenant Easterbrook in the name of the president for their heroic actions during the St. Mihiel offensive. Note that the Chicago address given below was actually Bill Erwin's apartment address while he attended the Chicago Musical College, rather than his father's address in Pawhuska, Oklahoma. This confusion later hampered the Army's ability to find Bill postwar. The citations read as follows:[36]

> The Commander in Chief, American Expeditionary Forces, has awarded the distinguished service cross to the following officers and soldiers for the acts of extraordinary heroism after their names:
>
> First Lieutenant William P. Erwin, Air Service, First Aero Squadron. "For extraordinary heroism in action in the Château-Thierry and Saint Mihiel salients, France. Lieutenant Erwin, with Second Lieutenant Byrne E. [*sic*] Baucom, observer, by a long period of faithful and heroic operations, set an inspiring example of courage and devotion to duty to his entire squadron. Throughout the Château-Thierry actions in June and July 1918, he flew under the worst weather conditions and successfully carried out his missions in the face of heavy odds. In the Saint Mihiel sector, September 12–15, 1918, he repeated his previous

courageous work. He flew as low as fifty feet from the ground behind the enemy's lines, harassing German troops with machine gun fire and subjected himself to attack from the ground batteries, machine guns and rifles. He twice drove off enemy planes which were attempting to destroy an American observation balloon. On September 12–13, 1918, he flew at extremely low altitudes and carried out infantry contact patrols successfully. Again, on September 12 he attacked a German battery, forced the crew to abandon it, shot off his horse a German officer who was trying to escape, drove the cannoneers to their dugouts, and kept them there until the infantry could come up and capture them." Home address: William A. Erwin, father, 814 Fine Arts Building, Chicago, Ill.[37]

Second Lieutenant Byrne V. Baucom, S.C., observer, First Aero Squadron. "For extraordinary heroism in action in the Château-Thierry and St Mihiel salients, France. Lieutenant Baucom, with First Lieutenant William P. Erwin, pilot, by a long period of faithful and heroic operations, set an inspiring example of courage and devotion to duty to his entire squadron. Throughout the Château-Thierry actions in June and July 1918, he flew under the worst weather conditions and successfully carried out his missions in the face of heavy odds. In the Saint Mihiel sector, September 12–16, 1918, he repeated his previous courageous work. He flew as low as fifty feet from the ground behind the enemy's lines, harassing German troops with machine guns. He twice drove off enemy planes which were attempting to destroy an American observation balloon. On September 12–13, 1918, he flew at extremely low altitudes and carried out infantry contact patrols successfully. Again, on September 12 he attacked a German battery, forced the crew to abandon it, shot off his horse a German officer who was trying to escape, drove the cannoneers to their dugouts, and kept them there until the infantry could come up and capture them." Home address: Mrs. Edith Elizabeth Baucom, mother, Milford, Texas.[38]

First Lieutenant A. E. Easterbrook, Air Service, observer, First Aero Squadron. "For extraordinary heroism in action near Saint Mihiel, France, September 12, 1918. Because of intense aerial activity on the opening day of the Saint Mihiel offensive, Lieutenant Easterbrook, observer, and Second Lieutenant R. E. DeCastro, pilot, volunteered to fly over the enemy's lines on a photographic mission without the usual protection of accompanying battle planes. Notwithstanding the low-hanging clouds, which necessitated operation at an altitude of only 400 meters, they penetrated 4 kilometers beyond the German lines. Attacked by four enemy machines, they fought off their foes, completed their photographic mission, and returned safely." Home address: Major E. P. Easterbrook, Father, Fort Flagler, Washington.[39]

On October 21, the 1st Aero Squadron was ordered to carry out an infantry control exercise previously arranged with the 1st Division. Erwin and Baucom were sent out on a photography mission at 11:55 a.m., but poor visibility between 400 and 1,600 meters prevented them from taking any photos. They flew to Saint-Juvin, east to Sommerance, northeast to St. Georges in the Hindenburg Line, and returned to Remicourt at 1:55 p.m.[40]

The following day, Erwin gained his eighth and final confirmed victory, with Easterbrook scoring his fourth victory as his observer. They left at 1:50 p.m. on a reconnaissance and propaganda-dropping mission within German lines in poor visibility. Soon after crossing the lines, an enemy machine-gun nest fired on them, with good effect, which they engaged from an altitude of 50

First Lieutenant Richard T. Pillings standing alongside Salmson 2A2 1161 "24" "Gertrude R," previously assigned to Lieutenant Arthur J. Coyle, who was promoted to captain and transferred to command the I Corps Observation Group on October 26. Note the German cross patches covering the bullet holes in the fuselage. (Pillings Album, National Museum USAF via Alan D. Toelle)

meters. They then went on to the town of Verpel, where they dropped 3,000 sheets of propaganda between it and Imécourt.

They attacked a German two-seater southwest of Imécourt at 2:55 p.m. During a combat starting at 850 meters, as the two ships strove to outmaneuver each other, they fought down to a bare 100 meters above the treetops, the enemy pilot fighting his way downward to seek protection from his own guns. Easterbrook then calmly trained his Lewis guns upon the enemy ship for one final burst, while watching it fall northwest of Rémonville. They were in turn shot up by ground machine-gun fire. Climbing out of this fire by dodging his way with banks and turns, they flew squarely into a formation of four Fokker D.VIIs. Erwin's Vickers gun jammed at this crucial moment, so Easterbrook kept them at bay. They evaded the Fokkers and regained their own lines, but with some 30 bullet holes in their Salmson.

Unsatisfied, they turned back into enemy territory, where they did more low-level strafing. Then at 3:20 p.m. they attacked another German two-seater over Beffu-et-le-Morthomme, "but without result, as he ran from us," Easterbrook noted in his logbook. Finally, low on fuel, they returned at 4:20 p.m. with their two 1st Aero Squadron Salmson escorting gunships. On November 7, 1918, Headquarters, First Army Air Service, issued General

By Lieutenant Erwin's personal count, he had a ninth German cross painted on his greyish brown/ brownish grey fuselage above the manufacturer's plate on Salmson 2A2 1286 "8" "Jo. 4." (Via Greg VanWyngarden)

Orders Number 24, confirming what was Erwin's eighth and Easterbrook's fourth victory at 2:55 p.m.[41]

Erwin and Easterbrook undertook two photography missions on October 23, the first at 9:15 a.m. in fair visibility, from west to east over Grandpré, Beffu and the sector in which the 78th Division operated, over Verpel and the sector in which the 77th Division operated, and Imécourt and the sector in which the 80th Division operated. Of the 36 photos taken at 2,500 meters, all were good. Grandpré, part of the outpost position of the Hindenburg Line, was situated against a steep bluff with a citadel of great strength, but which the 78th Division finally captured on this date. It was also one of the two main passes traversing the plateau upon which the Argonne Forest is located. One of the two escorting 1st Aero Squadron Salmsons had motor problems and was forced to land near Auzéville-en-Argonne, about 9.7 km northwest of Remicourt. The other Salmson, 1114 "19," flown by 1st Lt. Conrad G. Johnson and observer 2nd Lt. Chester E. Kennedy, was hit by an antiaircraft shell and exploded, just as Easterbrook turned to signal to them that his work was finished and they needed to return. "We went down to 100 meters," Easterbrook reported, "but the plane smashed into a thousand pieces."[42]

Erwin arrived back at Remicourt at 10:45 a.m., but then left again at 1:00 p.m. to take more photos from 2,000 meters over Imécourt, and the rest over St. Georges, a sector to the east in which the 2nd Division operated. Only one 1st Aero Squadron Salmson remained to protect them, and they dropped 1,000 sheets of propaganda in the enemy rear areas before their return to Remicourt at 2:20 p.m. All but two of their 36 photos taken were good. The most notable aspect of these photo missions was that they produced a different sort of record, as noted in Easterbrook's logbook: "Broke record for number of photos taken by one man in one day (72 exposures)."[43]

On October 24, per Operations Order No. 36, the First Army Air Corp Air Service assigned the 1st Aero Squadron to begin liaison with 80th Division. Their duties included visual reconnaissance; surveillance of enemy artillery activity and fugitive targets; infantry contact patrols; adjustment and control of division artillery; having alert planes available for special missions for the division and corps commander; and photographic missions required by the American I Corps. Field Orders No. 85 promoted Baucom to 1st lieutenant, outgoing 1st Aero Squadron CO Arthur J. Coyle's recommendation stating: "Since joining this Squadron, Lieut. Baucom has established for himself a truly remarkable record for bravery, perseverance and results. Easily one of the best observers in this organization, he is at the same time an Army officer of the highest order."[44]

The 1st Aero Squadron was ordered to reconnoiter the entire I Corps area as early as visibility allowed on October 28 and during the last hours of daylight. Erwin and newly promoted 1st Lieutenant Baucom left on a reconnaissance mission at 2:50 p.m. in poor visibility over Grandpré, flying at an altitude of between 400 and 2,200 meters, with partial success. They also tried to reconnoiter Landres-St. Georges but were driven back by a formation of 15 enemy planes and returned to Remicourt at 5:15 p.m.[45]

Erwin teamed up with Easterbrook the following day to photograph the woods of Argonne Forest north of Grandpré and south of Verpel, protected by four 1st Aero Squadron Salmsons. Leaving at 9:30 a.m. in fair visibility, they flew at 2,200 meters to take 36 photos, all of which were good, returning to Remicourt at 10:35 a.m. Easterbrook, like many observers with a burning desire to move to the front cockpit to become a pilot, also began informal training that day, with Erwin as his instructor. Two days later, Easterbrook managed a takeoff and landing.[46]

On October 30, Erwin and Baucom were ordered to photograph specific coordinates in the 78th Division sector around Landres-St. Georges, Saint-Juvin, and Grandpré from an altitude of 2,200 meters in fair visibility. After leaving at 9:15 a.m., they attacked one German two-seater at 1,800 meters over

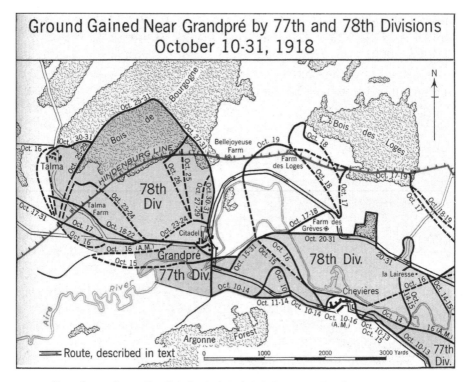

Ground gained near Grandpré by 77th and 78th Divisions, October 10–31, 1918.

St. Georges and drove it back over enemy lines. Baucom reported they shot and probably killed the observer of that plane. Four Fokker D.VIIs attacked them immediately afterwards at 10:30 a.m., but the four protecting 1st Aero Squadron Salmsons drove them off and the engagement was inconclusive. Thirty-two of the 36 photos taken were good, and they returned to Remicourt at 11:15 a.m.[47]

CHAPTER 5

The Final Assault

During October, the German Army had strongly held the Americans at the Hindenburg Line that stretched from Grandpré near the Aisne River all the way east beyond Brieulles on the Meuse River. The date fixed by the U.S. First Army for the general assault against the Hindenburg Line was November 1. The date of the attack had been postponed until then upon the request of the French, at which time the divisions of the First Army were stretched from the Meuse in the east to just north of the Argonne Forest in the west. The order of battle, from the Meuse to the west, was: III Corps with the 5th and 90th Divisions in line and the 32nd in reserve; V Corps with the 89th and 2nd Divisions in line, and the 1st and 42nd in reserve; and I Corps with the 80th, 77th, and 78th Divisions in line, and the 6th and 82nd in reserve. The 42nd Division was transferred to the reserve of I Corps soon after the beginning of the attack. The 3rd, 29th, and 36th Divisions in the rear areas composed the First Army reserve.

The First Army's general mission was to cut the Metz–Sedan–Mézières railroad. The detailed plan for the attack contemplated a deep penetration by V Corps in the center to secure the Barricourt Heights, followed by I Corps' drive to connect with the French near Boult-aux-Bois. The capture of the Barricourt Heights, a formidable natural obstacle, would compel a German retirement across the Meuse. Thus, III Corps, while aiding the main attack in the center, was directed to be prepared to force a crossing of the Meuse if the enemy withdrew. After having just faced extreme difficulties in advancing through the Argonne Forest, and with its 78th Division facing similar circumstances advancing through the Bois de Bourgogne on the left, I Corps planned to neutralize the Bois de Bourgogne with heavy artillery concentrations of persistent gas.

Meanwhile, the German Government, in a state of disarray, had further worsened the nation's military situation with unsuccessful calls for the Kaiser to abdicate. The German Navy was already in a state of mutiny and had refused orders to attack the British Navy. But the German Army generals had sworn an oath to the Kaiser and thus felt obliged to continue the war, despite talk of an armistice. Along the Western Front, the German Army resolved to make a stand at the Meuse, which would have a bearing on the terms of any armistice. The Americans held hopes of crossing the river, which would conversely weaken the German negotiating position. From November 1 on, the progress of the American First Army was exceptionally rapid as the German forces began a rapid withdrawal from the sector. The battle soon became a pursuit, the enemy merely fighting a delaying action. All American divisions pushed forward rapidly until they reached the Meuse, the pace primarily limited by the speed that the troops could walk. The Germans left nests of machine guns and artillery to impede the Americans, but these could be and were either bypassed or eliminated.[1]

A terrific two-hour artillery preparation on November 1 preceded the assault, which effectively bombarded the sensitive points of the enemy positions. When the infantry jumped off at 5:30 a.m., they concentrated all available artillery fire in a rolling barrage about 1,100 yards in depth, which progressively moved in front of the advancing lines. This intense and extremely effective fire and the severity of the infantry assault so overwhelmed the German defenders that the progress of the attack exceeded all expectations. Erwin and Baucom were ordered to fly an infantry contact mission to find the front lines of the 80th Division as soon as visibility allowed. Baucom later described their mission that morning:[2]

> On November 1st, the drive started again. For a third time Erwin and I played the role of "lead off" men. But we had hard luck that morning. There was a heavy ground mist, and visibility was impossible. Long before we reached the lines, it was impossible to see the ground. Above 800 meters the sky was clear, but you couldn't see anything below you. However, we thought we would go to where we believed the lines were and stick around for a while. Perhaps we would stumble into some lone Boche, which we could knock down. I had three of them to my credit, and I wanted two more so as to become an ace. Just as we reached the lines, judging by a balloon we could see sticking up through the clouds, we spotted a Boche bi-place machine. But just as we started to attack, our motor "pooped." Erwin juggled it along for a few seconds, then yelled back through the speaking tube, "Boy, get ready for a hell of a crash."
>
> That scared me a little; I had so much confidence in his ability to handle motors that I knew she must be in pretty bad shape if he gave it up. Since we couldn't see the ground even at twenty-five meters altitude, we knew what a forced landing in that rough country meant. I could hear the artillery down below us in the fog coughing away and had a picture

of ourselves and our wreckage piled up on top of some 155-mm long [cannon]. But shortly after we started down, Erwin got the motor to catch again, and we started home. About this time, they pulled the balloon down, as visibility was impossible, and that removed our only landmark. We then had to fly by instinct and with a sick motor. Erwin nursed it along until we got enough south that we could see the ground. Then we picked a place and landed. We were at Dommartin [-Dampierre], about eight kilometers west of St. Menehould and not more than fifteen kilometers north of our own field.[3]

The 80th Division, which Erwin and Baucom were supporting, formed the right half of the I Corps zone, north and east of Saint-Juvin, and attacked with brigades in column. They captured Imécourt at 11:00 a.m., 3.2 km north of their starting positions, but then had to repulse a severe counterattack. By nightfall it had reached the general line, a point about two kilometers northeast of Sivry-lès-Buzancy–Imécourt, to one kilometer south of Alliépont. That night, due to the deep advance of V Corps (on the right of I Corps), the German troops in front of I Corps retired, and from then on, its progress was exceptionally rapid.[4]

The 80th Division needed a recon plane over its sector throughout the hours of daylight on November 2, having still not yet met its goals on the previous day. Lieutenants Erwin and Baucom left at 6:40 a.m. in poor visibility to fly an infantry contact patrol over an area as far north as Authe, as far east as Sivry-lès-Buzancy and Imécourt, as far south as the Bois de Loges, south of Beffu-et-le-Morthomme, and as far west as Briquenay and Germont, at altitudes ranging from 20–400 meters. Baucom's 1st Army, Corps Observation Wing report ran as follows:

> Three Boche were going into Buzancy at 9:20 A.M. One Boche leaving Verpel going north at 9:00. American patrol of four men entered Verpel at 9:20. Three Americans were going into Sivry-lès-Buzancy at 9:20. We flew over this town at 50 meters altitude, and it looked deserted. The woods east of Verpel at 92.5–91.4 was occupied by two companies of our troops [77th Division] at 8:30 A.M. without any incident. Our troops (One Company) are in woods 400 meters southeast of Sivry-lès-Buzancy (8:30 A.M.). We flew over Buzancy several times at 50 meters altitude but could not see anyone, except the three lone Boche going back to the rear at 9:20 A.M. We also flew over Bar [-lès-Buzancy] at 50 meters but could not see anyone.
>
> At about 8:20 A.M. there were two companies in Harricourt but later they disappeared. At this same time there were five wagons at corner of road at 7.4–96.8. We strafed them with our machine guns and killed some horses. The lead wagon started in a gallop towards Bar [-lès-Buzancy].
>
> Our troops occupied Bois des Loges at 8:05 without resistance and at 9:15 one or two our companies were in the valley at 92.4–88.2 advancing north and we could see no Boche opposition.
>
> On road north of Authe at 93.4–00.4 was another convoy of about fifteen wagons going north at 9:00, and on the ground at 93.2–00.1 was this panel E.D. We were up at these

two towns at 300 meters altitude. The only place we were fired at by ground machine guns was just north of Thénorgues.

The following towns are apparently vacated. We flew over them at 50 and 100 meters and couldn't see any in them: Thénorgues, Beffu-et-le-Morthomme, Briquenay and perhaps Germont. There is a deserted Boche field piece (77mm) at 00.4–92.6. The railroad has two direct hits at the following points 94.7–89.7 and the bridge at 96.2–89.3.[5]

They dropped a message at Division HQ rather than I Corps headquarters, being short of gasoline after more than three hours of flying, and returned to Remicourt at 10:25 a.m. The 1st Aero Squadron closely followed this with a surveillance mission by Lieutenant Easterbrook, flying with pilot 2nd Lt. Ives Calhoun and protected by another 1st Aero Squadron Salmson. Departing at 10:55 a.m., they covered the same area, but Easterbrook noted different coordinates and engaged in ground-attack and aerial combat, as shown in his submitted 1st Army, Corps Observation Wing report:

> Friendly troops advancing in column A8-R5, time 12:00. Patrols at O7-R3 advancing in northeast direction 12:00. Patrols of two and three men were seen entering the southern part of Buzancy, time 12:00. Friendly troops in shell holes at O1-C6 in a line running northeast to A1-N7. About fifteen Boche seen at R1-A8, time 11:45. About two companies in trenches at O9-D1 to A8-D9, time 11:55. About three companies in good trenches at H7-D3 southeast to O2-X3, with machine gun nest front. Fired 150 rounds at same from 50 meters altitude. Small parties of Boche retreating at Y5-A5, time 11:40. Fired 50 at same.
>
> Enemy artillery of two guns going west at Y3-M6, time 11:35. Four guns going northeast at a dead run at Y5-S7, time 11:45. Fired at by Pilot and Observer. Total rounds 100. Six guns going southeast at Y5-X1 on a run and turned northeast at P9-U7, time 11:55. Three guns (150[mm]) going northeast out of Bar and also northeast at P9-U7. Fired 70 rounds (Pilot) 50 rounds Observer at same, from 25 meters, turning over one carriage. Two guns going in Germont, time 11:45. The whole retreat seems to be in a northeast direction as far as the artillery is concerned.
>
> The railroad tracks at Harricourt and Bar [-lès-Buzancy] were in good condition but no cars on tracks.
>
> Short combat south of Buzancy with enemy aircraft (Hannover) but with no result, time 11:30, altitude 50. Machine guns fired at us from A4-D8, time 11:35. At 11:30 friendly shots were falling at A3-R7.[6]

The 80th Division advanced northward from Imécourt that morning and captured Buzancy early in the afternoon after brisk fighting. They maintained a line north of Route Nationale No. 47 (National Road 47, currently D947). One of their support brigades acted as an assault brigade the following day to continue their advance northward. However, the Germans, knowing that the only road available for the 77th and 80th Divisions passed through Buzancy, responded by shelling and bombing the crossroads there for several days, making the movement of troops and supplies through this village a hazardous and difficult undertaking. This caused 80th Division Headquarters to move to Harricourt, 2 km west, but 2nd Division on their right made a march that night, temporarily creating a wide gap in the front lines.[7]

November 3: Easterbrook, Ace Observer's Fifth Victory

The 80th Division tried to fill the gap, and by nightfall its right elements had reached a line southwest of Ferme de Bellevue (Belval-Bois-des-Dames, Grand Est), in the zone of 2nd Division. At the end of the day, their zone of action extended from Saint Pierremont southeast to Ferme de Sartèles (Sartèles Farm).

In October, the I Corps Observation Group had decided to equip one Salmson with twin Marlin guns. An old 1st Aero Squadron Salmson 2A2, 3175 "13," received on July 1, 1918, was chosen to be retrofitted with these twin Marlin guns to fire through the propeller. After fitting, it was sent back to the squadron in early November. Captain Arthur J. Coyle, the former squadron commanding officer who had moved to command the I Corps Observation

Then 1st Lieutenant Arthur J. Coyle (left), 1st Aero Squadron commanding officer, and 1st Lieutenant Erwin stand along the left side of Coyle's Salmson 2A2 "24" "Mary A." (National Archives photo 11-SC-64294 via Greg VanWyngarden)

Group from October 26, wanted to test this new arrangement in combat to assess its effectiveness, but was not authorized to do so. He then selected an observer he could truly trust and rely upon—1st Lt. Arthur Easterbrook—to fly an infantry contact patrol for 80th Division, which was still on the front lines in its sector. The premise of the 11:00 a.m. patrol with Easterbrook in the Vaux–Buzancy–St. Pierremont area was to pinpoint advancing American troops and entrenched enemy forces, and engage various ground targets, while never flying above 100 meters. Easterbrook delivered a separate detailed observer's report to the American I Corps, G-2 intelligence staff, at 2:10 p.m., which was different in some key respects.

In this version they spent the first hour recording troop movements and firing at retreating troops in towns as far west as St. Pierremont, as far north as Sommauthe, and as far east as the castle at Château de Belval. They spotted and fired on what they believed to be four horse-drawn 150-mm guns. Easterbrook noted precisely where American troops were advancing and where they were entrenched in shell holes and foxholes. He also noted where German troops were entrenched. Then at noon, they attacked a German two-seater southeast of St. Pierremont. Coyle dove on it and chased it about 3 km north, losing altitude while firing about 100 rounds at it. The German observer fired back,

1st Aero Squadron Salmson 2A2 3175 "13," as it looked prior to the Marlin two-gun installation. It was shot down by Fokkers near the front lines south of Vaux-en-Dieulet on November 3, 1918, with pilot Captain Arthur J. Coyle and observer 1st Lieutenant Easterbrook. Discarded due to combat damage, it was more than likely a complete wreck. (Via Greg VanWyngarden)

striking the Salmson, and then Coyle's Marlin guns jammed. Ten minutes later, they were headed back south to Buzancy to drop a note to American troops, giving information about the German troops retreating from Sommauthe and Vaux-en-Dieulet. That was when they were attacked by four Fokkers and had to retreat at once.

In the official G-2 American I Corps report, Easterbrook did not even admit to being shot down, but said first that they shot the first Fokker down about 2 km southwest of Vaux-en-Dieulet, which was barely inside American lines on November 3. Then he said that the other three Fokkers chased them almost 5 km south-southwest at treetop level, inside American lines, as far south as Buzancy before turning back. Then they supposedly force-landed near Chevières due to bullets fired into their gas tank, 17.7 km south-southwest of Vaux. As shown below, this version brings up two questions: 1) how could they have flown that far south with gasoline flowing in streams from their gas tank; and 2) how could or why would three Fokkers fly at treetop level almost 5 km inside American lines with troops firing at them? That report was included in the squadron history, even though Easterbrook probably assumed that it would not be.[8]

Easterbrook later wrote a separate version for the squadron history that portrayed the outcome differently. In this version they were shot down and most likely crashed about 2.5 km south of Vaux and Hill 308 in a relatively flat area, pockmarked with shell holes and a few trees. When Arthur Coyle described this battle in a letter to his daughter a few years later, he said they landed between the first and second line of trenches, both of which fired upon the Fokkers. However, 80th Division's November 3 line of advance south of Vaux formed a "V" wedge pointing southward, such that trench lines extended on both their left and right as they emerged from their wrecked Salmson. This apparently left Coyle with the impression that there were two trench lines.[9] Easterbrook's second-version mission report describes his patrol that day:

It was on such a mission that Capt. Arthur Coyle and myself were sent. We picked up our troops, entrenched in shell holes with patrols advancing into the woods. Then going northeast, I saw about 30 Boche retreating into a town. I fired about 50 rounds at them, and they ran in all directions. As we flew over the town there was a company of Germans in the main street, and I fired about 80 rounds at them and they also ran for cover, but several never went further into Germany. We saw several convoys and also artillery retreating, which we shot up, killing men and horses, and turning over wagons and guns.

About this time four Fokkers, that were covering the German retreat, dropped down on us; we had our fun and now it was their turn. Four against one is nothing to be overjoyed about, especially when it is at 50 meters altitude and some 20 kilometers in Germany. I began firing at them, and the pilot headed towards home, at the same time gaining altitude;

but it was useless, as the Huns had position on us, and we were cut off in no time. The only thing left for Capt. Coyle was to maneuver his ship so as to make it hard for the Huns, and at the same time give me good shooting position.

On giving one of the Fokkers a burst of ten, my left gun jammed, and my right gun had but four shots left in it, as I had been using it quite freely on the retreating artillery. (I forgot to mention that Capt. Coyle's guns had jammed while diving on a retreating battery, just before the Fokkers jumped us.) So, there was nothing for us to do but to take what was coming to us and try and fix my guns, knowing that this was our only chance. The Fokker quartet noticed that I had stopped shooting, so they closed in, one coming so close that I expected every second for him to crash into us and both planes go down together. Tracer bullets were going by us like sparks from a dirty chimney, but I was busy fixing my guns. One bullet grazed my cheek, drawing blood, another shot off my ear tube about three inches from my head, another hit my wireless key, and goodness knows how many more were as close. But once the jam was cleared and new drums of ammunition were on, the guns were able to talk again. They spoke directly to one of the Fokkers just as he banked to keep from crashing into us, which pitched down and crashed in a condition scarcely fit to be turned over to the Allies.

For a few seconds I had an opportunity to breathe, and it's a good thing I did for I could smell gasoline very strongly. Looking at the gas tank I saw that it was badly hit and in spite of several G.O's [instrument readings?] to the contrary, it was coming in streams and giving precious essence away to the whole countryside. It had four sizeable bullet holes in it.

We were now quite low but near out lines. I kept firing at the remaining Fokkers, but without any apparent result, however, as they followed us to our lines, where we landed

The twin Marlin gun installation applied to Salmson 2A2 3175 "13" while still in the shop. (Ray Rimell via Alan D. Toelle)

in a field of shell holes. The German machines returned, satisfied, I suppose that they had another plane to their credit, but Capt. Coyle and his newly created observer ace, had nothing to worry about.[10]

Sommauthe and Vaux-en-Dieulet, towns that Easterbrook and Coyle had been shooting up, were then closer to 2 km north of the front lines, rather than 20 km. The squadron later tried to cover up specific details of this patrol, such as who the pilot and observer were when the plane was lost; where it actually landed; and whether it had one or two front guns for the pilot. First, in their "Report of Planes Lost From July 1st to November 20, 1918," they correctly listed Salmson 3175 as being "discarded owing to damage by enemy aircraft" on November 3. But then they listed the pilot as "Lt. Benson," a new pilot who had just joined the squadron on October 9; they left the observer's name blank and listed the location as "Argonne" without specifying location. Secondly, Easterbrook's squadron report given above was just the first copy made. It reflects Coyle firing two guns, but rather than crossing out the "s" in "guns," apparently since the first report had already been accepted, the clerk-typist then typed an almost duplicate second report on the following page. The only difference is that the second report says, "Capt. Coyle's gun had jammed," thereby sowing doubt to make the reader think the first version was wrong.

This apparently was the only time Marlin guns were ever used in combat on a Salmson 2A2 in World War I; unfortunately, not very successfully. Below is Coyle's letter, which seems to confirm the Marlin two-gun installation. One can probably assume that the records would have looked significantly different if Coyle and Easterbrook had instead returned from a successful mission that day. Their victory was later confirmed in General Order Number 5, 1919.[11]

I was so busy that I lost all sense of direction as I had to skim the ground so the Germans could not get under the tail of my plane. In a short time, both of my guns were destroyed six inches in front of my face by machine gun bullets. Our gasoline tank was riddled with bullets and there were holes in the tank as big as my hand. Gasoline was sloshing around in the cockpit. By all the rules of the game we should have been afire. I was running on an emergency tank in a wing that carried a 15-minute supply of gasoline.

One of the Easterbrook's guns was destroyed and the other empty. One German plane flew in within 50 feet of us, the pilot emptied his guns, then raised his goggles to look at us. He could not figure out why we were still there. About that time Easterbrook put a new drum of ammunition on his only machine gun. Another German plane flew right into us just as Easterbrook got his drum on. Easterbrook's first burst set him afire, and he hit the ground almost under us. Another plane was following him, and I knew we could not live in the air another minute.

It was my intention to run into some trees along the road and tear the wings off, hoping that we might survive the crash. We never made it to the trees. Easterbrook was cut across the face with a bullet and, of course, the wind blew the blood all over his face. I thought he was done for.

About that time an explosive bullet hit our gas tank and the jacket of the bullet hit me dead center in the spine. I thought that I had been completely shot away in the middle and I tried to turn the plane up on its wing so that I could run into the German plane and take him with me. My vision became blurred and my body so numb that I didn't have the strength to pull the stick back, which would have enabled us to hit the German plane. We were only 50 feet off the ground, and I had lost control of the plane. The wing hit the ground first, cushioning the fall.

The German planes shot into us when we were on the ground but fortunately, we went down between our first and second line of trenches and both infantry lines opened fire on the German planes, so they took off. I reached down to feel my stomach, expecting the worst, and you can imagine my surprise when I didn't find any damage. As a matter of fact, neither one of us were badly hurt. The war was over before I was able to fly again.[12]

Erwin and Baucom also flew an infantry contact patrol that day, leaving at noon. Pilot 1st Lt. John F. McCormick and observer 1st Lt. John H.

First Lieutenant Arthur E. Easterbrook, rear cockpit, and 1st Lieutenant Arthur J. Coyle, then 1st Aero Squadron CO, with Coyle's Salmson 2A2 1161 "24." Easterbrook was Coyle's primary observer, but since Easterbrook flew 10⅔ more hours than Coyle from August 26 to September 22, 1918, and 15¼ more hours than him between September 22 and November 3, 1918, he obviously flew many missions with other pilots, including Erwin. Note the German cross patches covering the bullet holes in the fuselage. "Gertrude A" stands for Gertrude Augustine, Easterbrook's fiancée whom he married after the war. (Via Greg VanWyngarden)

East in Salmson 2A2 1338 "15" flew along as their protecting gunship. Covering the area between Fontenoy, Verrières, Sommauthe, Oches, and Vaux-en-Dieulet at heights between 10 and 300 meters in fair visibility, Erwin and Baucom checked the new locations that marked the day's advance towards each of these towns. As they observed columns of German troops and artillery convoys retreating northward, they elected to dive and strafe the columns their entire length, with Erwin firing his Vickers gun and then Baucom his Lewis guns as Erwin nosed upward. First Erwin would charge and then McCormick would follow valiantly. Then just south of Oches, Erwin looked back to see that McCormick was no longer there. He swung back to find McCormick's Salmson laying on the ground a couple of hundred meters off the road.

A few days later, they learned from the Germans that McCormick had been shot in the middle of his body. Mortally wounded, he still brought his plane to the ground and saved Lieutenant East, who managed to lift him from the burning ship. McCormick died a few minutes later while first aid was being given, the last 1st Aero Squadron man to die during the war. East was made a POW but was liberated under the terms of the Armistice and rejoined the squadron on November 15. Erwin and Baucom returned to Remicourt at 3:35 p.m. Reporting coordinates from his map board, Baucom filed the following mission report:[13]

> At 3:00 P.M. our troops were advancing at 99.4–00.8, 99.7–00.8 and were going into St. Pierremont from the south. Twelve mounted cavalrymen were on the road between Fontenoy and St. Pierremont. Our troops were advancing at 94.7–02.4, 95.3–02.4, 96.0–02.5.
>
> There was about one or two platoons of Boche in Verrières, burning material that could not be gotten away. There were about twenty caissons on the side track there to be loaded on the train but no train ever came.[14]
>
> There were some new barracks being built in Verrières and a lot of new lumber there. At 1:15 P.M. there was a convoy of eight or twelve wagons and one or two companies of Boche leaving Oches going north. Boche convoys and troops were leaving Sommauthe and Vaux-en-Dieulet between 1:00 and 2:00 P.M. By 3:00 P.M. both towns were almost evacuated. We were pretty badly machine gunned at Sommauthe and Oches in the early afternoon. We were over Le Chesne at 200 meters and saw only a few Boche there and no traffic at all.
>
> A bi-place Rumpler tried for two hours to get across our lines and locate our positions and we drove him off each time.
>
> We dropped five or six messages to our advancing troops, giving them information of what was in front of them. We scattered these messages across the entire Corps sector and the infantry got them all. We each used 750 rounds of ammunition strafing troops and convoys. We flew most of the time at 50 meters back of the Boche lines and I lost my wireless antenna on the treetops. A few anti-shells northeast of Sommauthe.[15]

Note that Le Chesne is 8 km west-northwest of Verrières, completely out of I Corps' area, and controlled by the French Fourth Army. The 78th Division captured Verrières, 2.4 km south of Sy, about 5:00 p.m. on November 3 after a sharp fight.[16]

Lieutenants Erwin and Baucom observed the German Army's retreat during their three-hour infantry contact patrol in fair visibility, although rear guards with machine guns in shell holes, with German Fokkers overhead covering their retreat, could still slow down the pursuing American divisions. Departing at 11:40 a.m., the next day they flew over the area of Sommauthe and La Besace for 80th Division, and Sy for 78th Division, at altitudes varying between 20 and 2,200 meters. Reading coordinates from his map board, Baucom filed his mission report, as follows:

> At 1:30 P.M. our troops were at 91.0–05.4, about one company, and two or three hundred meters [away] were six or eight Boche machine gun nests in shell holes. About two of our companies were at point 98.5–04.1 and 98.9–03.9 and 300 meters in front of them were ten or fifteen shell holes with Boche machine guns in them, [at] 1:30 P.M. At 4:30 about two platoons of our troops were at 00.5–05.5 and 01.4–03.8. About two platoons of Boche were in shell holes at 00.7–03.9.
>
> At 1:30 P.M. a convoy of eight or ten wagons at crossroad 00.3–09.5, La Bagnolle and other traffic on road to La Besace. La Besace was burning. Could see nothing in big woods between Sommauthe and La Besace. The railroad going through these woods from Oches north [and] east seems destroyed.
>
> Every place we found Boche in shell holes, we dropped messages to our infantry and told them the position.
>
> We had a fight with six Fokkers and one with three Fokkers. Would have gotten a Boche biplane if our guns had not jammed.
>
> Used about 300 rounds of ammunition for strafing.[17]

Their return from this mission coincided with the German Third Army's issue of an order at 2:40 p.m., instructing the units facing 80th Division to withdraw by successive stages and cross the Meuse River at either Villemontry, 4 km east of Yoncq, or Létanne, 2 km east of Beaumont-en-Argonne, leaving rearguards who were to remain on the line until forced to retire by attacking troops. The U.S. First Army also issued orders that same afternoon, directing its divisions to continue pursuit of these rearguards the following day and capture or destroy their troops and transports before they could cross the Meuse.

First Army assigned I Corps the mission to continue pursuing the rearguards in the direction of Raucourt-et-Flaba, about 5 km north of La Besace, on November 5. The 80th Division continued the pursuit in its zone of action, moved out at 2:30 a.m., and reached Beaumont-en-Argonne by 4:30 a.m. At 11:25 a.m., its 159th Infantry Brigade ordered the attack to continue to the Beaumont–Yoncq road. This line was to be held while

A German antiaircraft machine-gun crew defending its position on a hillside, similar to that described by Lieutenant Baucom on the hillside southeast of Yoncq on November 5, 1918. (Courtesy of Blaine Pardoe)

patrols pushed to the Meuse. Its 317th Infantry Regiment requested artillery fire on the machine-gun positions in the small patches of woods about 1 km southeast of Yoncq. At 1:15 p.m., its 318th Infantry Regiment was reorganizing along the Beaumont–la Bagnolle road and awaiting the artillery concentration requested by 317th Infantry Regiment on its right. It was ordered to take advantage of this fire to open the road between Yoncq and Ferme la Harnoterie (Harnoterie farm), 1.8 km southeast of Yoncq, which it was supposed to consolidate and then patrol beyond. This fire was delivered, ceasing at 2:30 p.m., and at 3:30 p.m. the battalions of the 317th and 318th Infantry Regiments moved forward. After leaving Julvécourt, this was the scenario Erwin and Baucom later saw on the hill southeast of Yoncq, newly created shell holes.

The 1st Aero Squadron had moved from Remicourt to Julvécourt aerodrome that day, 27 km northeast (34 km by truck). The rapid advance of the American troops and the long distance between the front lines and the 1st Observation Group seriously hampered liaison at Remicourt, and telephonic communication became virtually impossible those last few days, making operations extremely difficult and prompting their move. Lieutenants Erwin and Baucom left Julvécourt on what turned out to be their last mission, a reconnaissance patrol in Salmson 2A2 1286 "8" "Jo. 4" at 2:40 p.m., flying at altitudes between 20 and 400 meters in fair visibility. There were two reports filed for November 5, the first one with coordinates from Baucom's map board probably written in the field at the 159th Infantry Brigade P.C. and then sent back that evening by mounted messenger, even though both the 1st Aero Squadron and 1st Observation Group had it dated November 6. The second part of the mission report, dated November 5, appears to be an overall summary of the events, perhaps written by Erwin rather than Baucom, after Erwin returned on a horse the following morning. This summary follows first below, followed by the November 6 report:[18]

> We found machine gunners on east and west side of Yoncq and strafed them with our guns. Then dropped a message to our troops, giving them the position and number of Boche. Then we went to Mouzon and Sedan. The Boche were leaving Mouzon and burning material in the railway yards west of the river at Mouzon. Convoys of forty or sixty wagons were going up the road east of the river towards Sedan. Material was burning at Villers, Mouzon and Remilly-sur-Meuse [now Remilly-Aillicourt].
>
> From Wadelincourt and Sedan heavily fired on by machine guns, firing a solid stream of incendiary bullets. We were flying at 400 meters altitude, and it was raining.
>
> We came back to Yoncq and began strafing the machine gun nests (six of them) on the hill west of Yoncq a few hundred meters. We were down to 80 meters, and they shot our controls away, causing us to land in no man's land. When I saw we were going to land, I concentrated my fire on them to take shelter in their holes until we glided over the hill out of sight. We walked back to our lines and there went to a Brigade P.C. There we made out a written report and sent it back by a mounted messenger.[19]
>
> Our troops north of Stonne and on ridge north of Besace, also at 01.0–09.0, and along road to Beaumont. Our troops are in Beaumont at 15:15. Enemy machine gun nests at 02.4–10.9 and 04.1–11.4 also in eastern side of Yoncq. Enemy troops leaving Mouzon, going towards Sedan.
>
> Material burning in railroad yards in Mouzon. Battery in woods at 05.9–11.2 at 15:30. Bridge at Villers-devant-Mouzon being burned at 15:35. Bridge at Remilly-sur-Meuse being burned at 15:40.
>
> Was shot down by enemy machine guns from the ground and landed just south of Yoncq in front of enemy machine guns nest at 16:00. Our lines were about one kilometer away but succeeded in reaching our lines in spite of heavy machine gun fire from enemy troops. Received much AA fire along Meuse valley.[20]

Both reports were then forwarded to the I Corps Observation Wing. They, however, only reported coordinates from the second report on their November 5 report. Two 1st Aero Squadron Salmsons were down and missing that day, but later a Command Reconnaissance plane found and reported both of them intact before dark. One Salmson was identified by its number "1" on the top wing and it "Looked to be in good condition. No one seen near the plane." The number of the other Salmson down could not be identified, but their reported coordinates of the Erwin–Baucom crash site were "03.7–10.3." Erwin's listed coordinates of machine-gun nests "02.4–10.9 and 04.1–11.4" matched positions on the south slope of Hill

Jo. 4 restored! Above the upper left corner of the flag on Salmson 2A2 "8," behind 1st Aero Squadron pilot 1st Lieutenant Richard T. Pillings, is a black spot that is a patched bullet hole. The original insignia and numeral were saved from this plane, now at the University of Texas at Dallas, with all details being in the same exact position and proportion. The other slightly smaller black dots on the fuselage, particularly five forward of the flagstaff, may also be bullet-hole patches. Snow first occurred in northern France on December 19, 1918, intimating this photograph may have been taken at Weißenthurm aerodrome, located about 8 miles northwest of Coblenz, Germany, where they were stationed from December 21, 1918. The camouflage paint seen here on "8," and the insignia fabric, is all considered to be original factory-applied with no painting over earlier numbers. It is also the same one retrieved from the battlefield southeast of Yoncq on November 6 and painted as "8" throughout its career as the only 1st Aero Squadron Salmson with distinctive white cowling panels aft of the exhaust collector rings. The factory-applied cellulose-acetate dope's pigmentation (except black) had 42 percent aluminum powder. This produced a somewhat neutral effect in photographs. In contrast, paint added in the field to alter numerals or insignia or make repairs did not hold any aluminum powder in the pigment, and therefore often stood out in sharp contrast with the factory-applied camouflage. The Americans never had access to the French factory dope in the field. (Byrne V. Baucom Collection, History of Aviation Collection, Special Collections and Archives Division, Eugene McDermott Library, the University of Texas at Dallas)

275 on the west side of Yoncq, and on the lower slope of the hill on the northeast side of Yoncq, respectively.[21]

The front lines of 77th Division's 305th Infantry Regiment were then located about 2 km west of Yoncq. An escape westward to reach them would have required Erwin and Baucom to descend back down the hill, cross the valley floor, and follow the road connecting Yoncq to La Besace, which was still controlled by German 10th Division rearguards. Those rearguards also then held the Yoncq–Beaumont line and controlled all territory east to the Beaumont–Mouzon highway, and south of Yoncq all the way to Ferme la Harnoterie. The 2nd Battalion of the 317th Infantry reached its objective, the Beaumont–Yoncq road, at 6:00 p.m., but then after its sister 1st Battalion, having advanced only 500 meters north of Ferme la Thibaudine, was checked by fire from Ferme la Harnoterie, both battalions retired generally along the Beaumont–la Thibaudine road. Lacking tank support, once the 318th Infantry's forward progress was stopped by machine-gun fire coming from the hill southeast of Yoncq that afternoon, the regiment started falling back to set up an outpost line at 6:00 p.m. This stretched generally along the La Bagnolle–la Thibaudine road, about 1.5 km south of where Erwin and Baucom landed. Patrols from Company H of the 318th Infantry also patrolled north that evening and were in liasion with 77th Division on their left. This raises the likelihood that the first American troops that Erwin and Baucom encountered were from the 318th Infantry. The German Third Army nevertheless ordered a continuation of its retirement across the Meuse that evening of November 5/6.[22] Baucom provided further details of their last battle:

> The last time Erwin and I went across the lines, on November 5th just shortly before the "*Guerre*" finished, we almost got it in the neck. We were driving on the last lap to the Meuse River. Our Corps sector was between Mouzon and Sedan. On our last few trips, we had been carrying all the ammunition we could possibly carry and using it for strafing Boche machine gun nests and convoys. On this trip we found ten or twelve nests around the little town of Yoncq, which was down in a narrow and deep valley. We strafed them considerably from an altitude of only fifty meters, then came back and dropped a message to our infantry, telling them what the Boche were doing up there. We got a lot of information and found he was still retreating. But we also got a hot reception. We were only flying four hundred meters, and it was raining pretty heavy … enough that our propeller was in danger of being splintered. Our presence back there on such an absurd day for flying took them by such surprise that as is characteristic of the thick headed Boche. We got our information before they realized we were there. By the time we reached Sedan, however, they had awakened from their temporary mental stupor and opened up on us with machine guns, firing a solid stream of bullets, and incendiary bullets. I've never in my life seen so many flaming objects in the air at once as there were then. How they ever missed us I don't know. They were going all around us. On account of the rain, I could not tell exactly where they were coming from, but I turned my guns in the general direction and blazed away as hard as

I could. Once in a while I was changing drums on my guns, I saw one of the flaming balls coming straight towards me. I held up the empty drum I had in my hand to ward it off, but it went slightly over me.

We came on back to Yoncq to pay another visit to friend Boche down there. This time we were down to twenty meters, dealing them all the hell that an airplane can deal and that is a whole lot. These were the only Boche we could find between our troops and the Meuse River, and we were determined to break them up. It was a battle royal between a Salmson airplane and ten or twelve machine gun nests. We were shooting the very life out of them. I know our damage to them must have been great, for I could see my tracer bullets going right into their midst. Those of them that were able to shoot were returning the fire with compound interest. Finally, as we were passing over a cluster of five or six of them, with our nose pointed towards our lines, they shot away our controls. I looked around at Erwin for an explanation. He yelled back thru the speaking tube that we were shot down. About that time, he set the wheels on the ground, not more than fifty or seventy-five meters in front of the Boche.[23]

We were in No-man's land and gliding up a slope towards the top of a flat hill. As Erwin put the tail on the ground, it gave me a good field of fire directly behind us. Without a second thought I took the last and only chance. I blazed away with both guns at the head of the Boche just back of us and made them duck down into their holes out of sight and stay there until we glided over the "military crest" of the hill just out of sight of them. Then we didn't have time to lose. If the Boche were wise they would soon have us surrounded, and we knew about how much mercy we could expect from them.

I tried to get my guns off the machine, but the rain had caused them to stick in their sockets, and I did not have time to fool with them. I realized too that I could not carry my guns and my map boards too, and it was imperative that I should take the latter as they held the codes and P.C. locations. By this time Erwin was out of the machine with his automatic ready for an emergency. I grabbed my maps and away we went. About that time the Boche started to shell the plane and there were lots of overs, which kept us dropping to the ground pretty frequently. After falling into all the shell holes in France and getting tangled in acres of barbed wire, we finally reached our lines.[24]

Erwin had also coincidentally landed near the road connecting Yoncq to Ferme la Harnoterie. The road's pathway has not significantly changed in the last 100 years, a somewhat depressed roadway traversing mostly straight up the hill. The Salmson's motor had not yet died, and the nearest German machine-gun nests were about 50 meters away. From the listed crash site coordinates, Erwin coasted upwards until they reached the military crest, high enough to put them in defilade. This allowed Baucom to keep those gunners pinned down, while Salmson 1286 "8" was barely out of sight after stopping. The I Corps Observation Wing published further details in their November 6 report that must have come from Erwin, since they present alternative facts to Baucom's above account:

They landed between two enemy machine gun nests and the observer Baucom turned his machine gun on the enemy nest while the pilot got out and as soon as the pilot had gotten into a shell-hole the observer left his machine gun and got out safely. Lieutenant Erwin

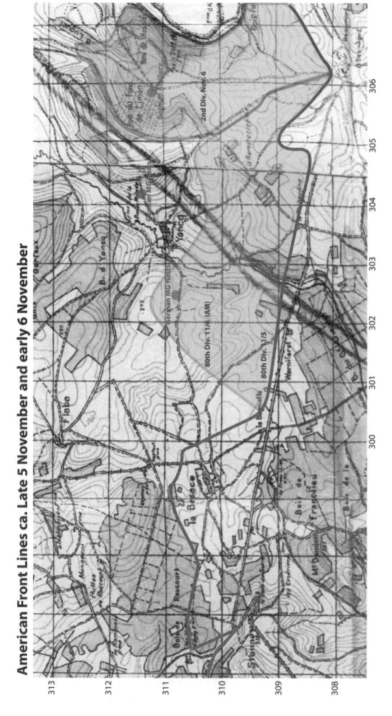

American front lines, late November 5–early November 6, 1918

traveled from there on foot until he was able to obtain a horse, when he returned to this field, this morning.[25]

The official American I Corps Headquarters version of the same report more closely matched Baucom's November 5 report. Baucom was also able to return to Julvécourt the next day, a trip of 76 km.

November 6 was also an important day in 1st Division history as it again entered the front line to relieve 80th Division. Ordered to attack in the direction of Mouzon, it occupied a 6 km front, extending from Beaumont-en-Argonne to La Besace, by 4:00 a.m. Marching up the Yoncq–Mouzon road at dawn, 1st Division advanced rapidly. Its 18th Infantry Regiment occupied Yoncq by 7:00 a.m. Major differences from the 80th Division plan of attack the previous day were that each battalion was accompanied by a machine-gun company, the 5th Field Artillery covered the division's front, and accompanying guns were designated for the assault battalions. The 6th and 7th Field Artillery and the 1st Battalion, 5th Field Artillery, which had followed closely behind the infantry, then went into position near Yoncq to support their follow-up assault on Mouzon.

All regiments overcame the resistance met and by noon they reached their goals along the Meuse, having covered more than 6 km. Here the 1st Division met elements of the 10th, 31st, 41st, 52nd, 115th, and 236th German Divisions. The 18th Infantry Regiment and patrols from the 26th Infantry occupied the part of Mouzon on the west bank of the Meuse after some sharp fighting. As the advance patrols were approaching the bridge there, it was blown up. Mines simultaneously exploded about the town on both sides of the river, and the buildings were soon in flames. German machine guns and artillery poured a violent fire into the town, causing several casualties among 1st Division troops. It was not until midnight on November 7 that the division arrived back at its bivouacs in the woods in the vicinity of Yoncq. Between then and 5:30 p.m. on November 5, its regiments had marched or fought without sleep or rest, each covering between 52 km and 71 km.[26]

The reconnaissance missions flown by Erwin, Baucom, Easterbrook, Calhoun, and Coyle, and the valuable information they provided during the first week of November 1918, set the stage for the First Army divisions' final assault to establish bridgeheads on the Meuse River, terminate the war, and complete the victory. Acknowledgment of their heroism came first to Baucom, General Pershing—commander of all American forces in France—awarding his second DSC, as announced on May 10, 1919, via General Orders Number 64, War Department. Erwin was awarded an Oak Leaf Cluster to his DSC

Standing here in the rear cockpit of Salmson 2A2 1286 "8" "Jo. 4" in Trier, Germany, postwar, 2nd Lieutenant F. W. De Haven first arrived at the 1st Aero Squadron on November 7, 1918. The hole behind the observer's cockpit has still not been repaired after the aircraft was retrieved from the battlefield on November 6, but the black spots on the fuselage forward of the flagstaff indicate bullet-hole patch repair, "Jo. 4" being hit about 30 times on the October 22 mission. The streak across the flag is a blemish in the original photo print. (Alan D. Toelle via F. W. De Haven)

on May 29, 1919, per General Orders Number 70, War Department. While there is some duplicative text, the overall descriptions vary somewhat:[27]

DISTINGUISHED SERVICE CROSS

The Distinguished Service Cross is presented to Byrne V. Baucom, Captain (Air Service), U.S. Army, for extraordinary heroism in action near Sedan, France, November 5, 1918. With atmospheric conditions such that flying was nearly impossible, Captain Baucom voluntarily undertook a flight as observer to locate the position of enemy troops and machine-gun nests which had been holding up our advance and causing severe casualties. Forced to fly at a very low altitude and subjected to almost constant antiaircraft, and rifle fire, he obtained the information that was vital to the success of our operations and dropped the message at division headquarters. He then penetrated far into the enemy lines, and opening fire upon enemy crews, routed them from a series of machine-gun nests. When his machine was finally shot down, he succeeded in operating the gun, and beat off an attack by the enemy in force. Armed only with revolvers and German grenades which they found in an enemy emplacement, he and his pilot then worked their way back to the American lines with valuable information, repeatedly subjected to enemy fire on their way.[28]

The Commander-in-Chief, in the name of the President, has awarded the Distinguished Service Cross to the following officer for the act of extraordinary heroism set forth after his name:

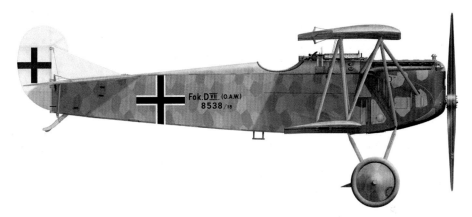

Fokker D VII (OAW) 8538/18 as flown by Capt. William P. Erwin over Jackson, Mississippi, on April 11, 1919. (Ronny Bar)

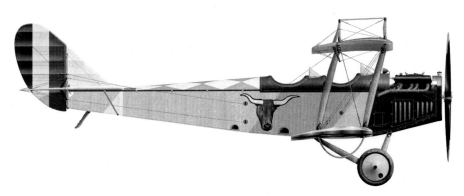

Curtiss JN-4H "Texas Longhorn" Jenny as flown by Capt. William P. Erwin over Wichita, Kansas, on May 1, 1919. Note that the blue and white diamond pattern was painted on the fuselage turtledeck and both sides of the lower wings. (Ronny Bar)

DH-4 32517 of 1st Lt. Floyd M. Pickrell, 50th Aero Squadron, who flew gunship protection for Lieutenants Erwin and Easterbrook's October 1, 1918, photo recon mission. Pickrell's DH-4 was slightly damaged by AA fire during the mission. (Juanita Franzi Aero Illustrations)

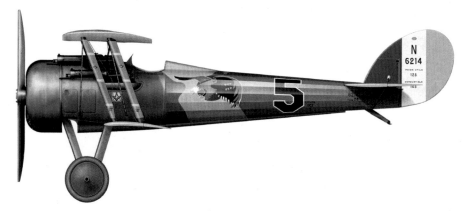

Nieuport 28 N6214 1st Lt. Clifford A. McElvain, 27th Aero Squadron, as it looked on August 1, 1918, when forced to land by *Ltn. d. R.* Fleischer, *Jasta* 17. Note the Masonic symbol below the Vickers gun mounting. (Juanita Franzi Aero Illustrations)

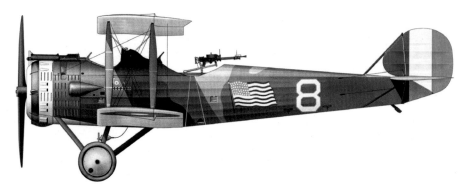

Salmson 2A2 1286 "Jo.4" of 1st Lt. William P. Erwin, received by the 1st Aero Squadron September 30, 1918, and forced to land by groundfire during his final mission, November 5, 1918. Six of his eight confirmed victories were scored in this ship. (Observers 1st Lt. Arthur Easterbrook shared four of these victories and 1st Lt. Byrne Baucom shared the other two.) (Juanita Franzi Aero Illustrations)

FIRST LIEUTENANT WILLIAM P. ERWIN, First Aero Squadron, (Pilot). For the following act of extraordinary heroism in action near Sedan, France, November 5, 1918. Lieutenant Erwin is awarded an Oak Leaf Cluster to be worn with the Distinguished Service Cross awarded him October 1, 1918. Against the advice of experienced officers Lieutenant Erwin undertook a reconnaissance flight in the face of atmospheric conditions that rendered flying most dangerous. In order that his observer might gain the necessary information, he was forced to fly at a perilously low altitude and was subject to continuous antiaircraft and rifle fire. When information gained on the flight had been dropped at division headquarters, he circled and returned over the enemy lines, although on the first reconnaissance mission his plane had been repeatedly hit by bullets. Penetrating far into enemy territory, he maneuvered most skillfully, and with shells bursting near him, flew low while his observer poured deadly fire upon machine-gun nests that had been holding up the advance of our troops. When his machine was crippled by enemy fire, he displayed exceptional skill in effecting a landing upon rocky land within the enemy lines. With his observer, he beat off repeated enemy attacks and fought his way back to the American lines, with information of vital importance to our troops.

Home address: W. A. Erwin, (Father), 814 Fine Arts Bldg., Chicago, Ill.[29]

After the signing of the Armistice on November 11, the only important event was the receipt of orders making the 1st Aero Squadron part of the Army of Occupation. During the Meuse–Argonne offensive, Lt. William P. Erwin flew 54 hours 35 minutes over the front lines between September 22 and

In coats and muddy boots, 1st Aero Squadron officers gather for an impromptu post-Armistice Signal Corps photo at Julvécourt aerodrome in the Meuse sector on November 12, 1918. W. P. Erwin and B. V. Baucom are missing. From the dog, left to right: Lieutenants Elliott J. Tucker, Alfred M. Pouse, Joseph H. Farnham, Richard T. Pillings, A. E. Easterbrook, Bruce M. Espy, Paul D. Meyers (CO), Capt. Arthur J. Coyle (1st Observation Group CO), Lieutenants Gordon M. Kibbs, Herbert K. Baisley, Edward J. Groteclose, James T. King, Charles A. Henry, Louis S. Burwash, Lee H. Rogers, Sanford L. Willits, John A. Benson, L. F. Pendleton, Veech T. Baird, W. D. Walsh, Francis V. Yates, Eckley B. Markle, Frederick J. Carr; Francis W. De Haven, Guy B. Bacon, Mahlon P. Bryan, and Knox W. Nicholson. Standing in the observer's cockpit of Salmson 2A2 "11" are Lieutenants Rudolph L. Gaalaas (left) and Raymond S. Coward. (National Archives #39361)

November 6, 1918. This time was double the number of hours flown by the next closest pilot, 1st Lieutenant Johnson (KIA, 27 hours). Easterbrook's 34¼ hours of flight time over the front lines during the Meuse–Argonne offensive, most by a 1st Aero Squadron observer, show his availability for duty on any given day, and particularly when Baucom was unavailable. Baucom still managed 32½ hours of flight time over the front lines during the Meuse–Argonne offensive, even with his 12-day assignment as 1st Division Liaison Officer, second highest of 27 1st Aero Squadron observers.[30]

Each of their shared victories had to be confirmed before official credit could be granted. That confirmation could be provided by any person who witnessed the combat from the air or the ground, or who saw the debris of the enemy airplane at the place specified by the claimant, except that a member of their pilot–observer team could not confirm a victory by the other crew member. This criterion nullified Erwin's first victory claim. The French and Americans awarded full credit to each person who contributed to a victory, giving credence to Erwin's eight victories, Baucom's three, and Easterbrook's five. However, the 1st Aero Squadron awarded its 13 confirmed victories to its pilot–observer teams, rather than individual pilots or observers. This is also the same concept that U.S. Air Force Historical Study No. 133 used to list victory credits as one credit for the destruction of one airplane, awarded to either the pilot or divided amongst however many crew members were involved in that airplane's destruction. According to that study, based on shared victories, Erwin's score is 3.75, Baucom's 1.5, and Easterbrook's 2.5. Moreover, as previously mentioned, because Easterbrook's five victory credits were lone combats scored entirely by him and his pilot, while most of the five aerial victories each credited to 91st Observation Squadron pilots Capt. Everett R. Cook (1.23) and Maj. Victor H. Strahm (2.0), and six and five aerial victories each credited to 91st Observation Squadron observers Capt. Leonard C. Hammond (1.48) and Lt. William T. Badham (1.57), were shared with other Salmson crews, Easterbrook should be considered as the highest-scoring American observer ace.[31]

CHAPTER 6

Postwar—Erwin's Early Return to Participate in America's Victory Loan Drive

Having been at Julvécourt aerodrome since November 5, 1918, the 1st Aero Squadron remained there after it was detached from the I Corps Observation Group on November 18. On November 21 it carried out 13 ferry flights from Julvécourt, 34 miles northeast to Mercy-le-Bas. One plane either had a forced landing or mistook the location 3 miles east at the aerodrome just north of Mercy-le-Haute, and then crashed on landing at Mercy-le-Bas the following day. The 1st Aero Squadron then flew what amounted to a replacement Salmson from Julvécourt to Mercy-le-Bas on November 22. The squadron was reassigned to the Third Army, Headquarters Third Army Air Corps Air Service, per General Orders Number 39, dated December 5, 1918, to serve as part of the occupation force of the Rhineland. They made their first advance into Germany on December 6 from Mercy-le-Bas to the Treves aerodrome, Rhineland-Palatinate. No ferry flights were attempted, since they were not permitted to fly over the neutral, landlocked country of Luxembourg to reach Treves. Finally, on December 21, they moved to the former Weißenthurm aerodrome, 5 km southeast of Andernach and 13 km northwest of Coblenz, Germany. One of its duties there was to fly over Cologne and other parts of the Rhineland occupied by the Third Army. The squadron was also able to perform test flights on surrendered German airplanes, including flights and evaluations of the Fokker D.VII, Pfalz D.XII, Roland D.VI, Halberstadts, and Rumpler planes.[1]

On November 29, 1918, Erwin was cited in General Order 12.028, French Armies in the East, with no medal awarded: "On 20 July 1918, he volunteered for an infantry liaison mission at night fall, executed this mission at 200 meters altitude. He brought back his observer, who was mortally wounded, and his plane was full of bullet holes."[2] This citation authorized him to wear the *Croix de Guerre* medal, and although one was not bestowed, they were common

Officers of 1st Aero Squadron at Julvécourt, France. Although labeled as November 12 on one copy, Lieutenants McKinney and Pitts did not rejoin the squadron until November 16, 1918. Missing are B. V. Baucom, who had already left on leave, and A. E. Easterbrook. From left to right, standing (middle row): Lieutenants R. T. Pillings, H. K. Baisley, Ross W. Bates, Lee H. Rogers, Fred E. D'Amour, Paul D. Meyers, W. P. Erwin, L. H. Wells, Roy U. Dabbs, E. J. Tucker, L. S. Burwash, C. A. Henry, Edward J. Groteclose, Arthur J. Butler, J. W. Gastreich, Philip T. Lyons, and S. L. Willits. Back row: Lieutenants Raymond S. Coward, Knox W. Nicholson, probably A. B. Pitts (labeled "Pitney" but no other officer had similar last name), John H. McKinney, Gordon M. Kibbs, and J. G. Bastow. Kneeling: Lieutenants F. W. De Haven, E. B. Markel, James T. King, L. F. Pendleton, Guy B. Bacon, Ives Calhoun, Bruce M. Espy, Herbert W. Crede, Joseph H. Farnham, Alfred M. Pouse, Francis V. Yates, W. D. Walsh, and R. L. Gaalaas. (Courtesy of San Diego Air and Space Museum)

enough at that time that one could buy one for five French francs. On March 22, 1919, the *Plane News* weekly Air Service newspaper published a list of all officers who had graduated from the 3rd AIC at Issoudun and since been awarded either a French *Croix de Guerre* medal or French citation. This list was further confirmed on March 29, 1919, when the Air Service published a list of awards recently bestowed on Air Service officers, showing that Erwin and 1st Lt. Easterbrook had both been awarded American citations (with no medals awarded), and Erwin had been awarded a French citation. On May 10, 1919, moreover, the Air Service announced that 1st Lt. Herman St. John

Boldt had been awarded the *Croix de Guerre* with Palm for their July 20, 1918, mission, but Erwin was still not similarly cited or awarded the same medal.[3]

A January 8, 1919, cable to the War Department, listing American aces, also showed Erwin with nine victories. Since he loaded aboard the SS *George Washington* to return home on January 11, 1919, and sailed from Brest, France, on January 12, he assumed that to be his final accepted score. However, those records were further compiled and finalized from First Army Air Service records on May 26, 1919, and this list showed his final victory total to be eight. His first victory claim of August 1, 1918, was never confirmed in a General Order. To add an ironic twist to his homeward voyage, one of his shipmates was a 27th Aero Squadron pilot who had protected him on the disastrous August 1 battle, A-Flight and former POW 1st Lt. Arthur L. Whiton. Erwin's former squadron commander, Capt. Arthur J. Coyle, after his memorable mission with Easterbrook on November 3, also returned on the same ship. Upon arrival, Erwin was transferred to Post Field, Oklahoma.[4]

On February 15, 1919, the War Department, Air Service, announced the promotion of 1st Lieutenant Erwin from Junior Military Aviator to Military Aviator status, effective September 12, 1918. The Military Aviator ratings award for flying duty carried with it a 75 percent increase in base pay, compared to his earlier JMA 50 percent increase in base pay.[5]

America Finances its Participation in World War I via Sales of War Bonds

There were four series of war bonds issued during World War I. Although the armistice of November 11, 1918 ended the actual fighting, it took six months of Allied negotiations at the Paris Peace Conference to conclude the peace treaty, culminating in the Treaty of Versailles on June 28, 1919. The one million men in the Army of Occupation in France and the Rhineland was costing the U.S. Department of the Treasury $1 million per day. Wanting to ride the surge of patriotism, they opted to finance the postwar as well, by once again selling war bonds to the general population. This led to the Victory Liberty Loan Act, which was signed into law on March 3, 1919. The resulting Victory Loan issue, consisting of $4.5 billion in tax-exempt bonds earning 4.75 percent interest, convertible into nontaxable American gold notes bearing interest at the rate of 3.75 percent, was the fifth and final war bond campaign relating to World War I. The Air Service played an especially important part in the Victory Loan Drive, it being the first time in American history that airplanes were used to support a national endeavor other than war.

The 12 Federal Reserve Districts each had bond quotas assigned to them by the Treasury Department. Each Federal Reserve District then assigned individual quotas to both the states within their district, as well as their larger cities. The individual states then assigned quotas to both their counties and smaller cities. Bonds were primarily sold either through banks or payroll deduction. Organizations such as the National Woman's Liberty Loan Committee (NWLLC) were instrumental in promoting and selling these bonds, having individual Victory Loan committees in every state, county, and larger city. They also oversaw publicity and staged strong educational programs throughout states and did much of the solicitation. More than one million women were members of the NWLLC during the Fourth Liberty Bond and Victory Loan campaigns, and they took credit for one-fourth of all Victory Loan sales, although this varied widely. In Kansas, for example, the NWLLC was credited with 9 percent of total bond sales in Topeka, 42 percent of bond sales in Kansas City, and one-third of all Victory Loan bond sales in Kansas.[6]

The Air Service planned to give air exhibitions in every large city during the drive, the success of which depended largely upon the enthusiasm brought out by the airplanes and their pilots. The best pilots, stateside flight instructors, and returning aces from France, were detailed by special order to participate in the exhibitions. The Director of Air Service notified the commanding officers of Rockwell Field (San Diego, CA), Ellington Field (Houston, TX), and Hazelhurst Field (Mineola, Long Island, NY) to each organize a flying circus at their respective field and stage rehearsals. He wanted assurance that every officer and man would do their part when they arrived at the various cities to perform aerial exhibitions, that they would be a great credit to the Air Service, and that they would not fail to be of great assistance in the Victory Loan Drive. Those executive officers determined whether or to what extent the returning aces would be permitted to fly in their respective region. The Far West Flight Executive Officer, Maj. Carl Spatz, did not permit his aces to fly. It is unknown how often the Eastern Flight executive officer permitted his seven aces to fly, but these included one Italian ace, one Italian Ansaldo S.V.A. reconnaissance biplane, and three Italian mechanics to service it, so it is likely that Eastern Flight aces flew to some extent. Mid-West Flight Executive Officer Maj. George E. Stratemeyer allowed his aces to fly at will, except that he apparently grounded them all for the last four air shows in Oklahoma and Arkansas, after Capt. Erwin crashed his Curtiss Jenny in Wichita, Kansas.[7]

The three Far West, Mid-West, and Eastern flying circus flights were ordered to travel by train over their respective sections of the United States, putting on air shows each day in three different locations for 30 days. The special trains consisted of nine Pullman wide end-door baggage cars, three sleeping cars, and one diner car.

First Lieutenant Erwin was assigned to the Mid-West Flight. Their airplanes included four Curtiss JN-4H Jennys, a Curtiss JN-6H photo ship, four SE-5s, four Spad VIIs, and five Fokker D.VIIs. The dismantled airplanes were stored in the baggage cars, with wings, wing assemblies, and fuselages stored separately. Although the Treasury Department's Victory Loan drive ran from April 21 to May 10, 1919, its Victory Loan Flying Circus (VLFC) tour started on April 10 in New Orleans.

On April 5, 1919, according to the Air Service weekly newsletter in announcing the officer and ace assignments for the Mid-West Flight, Erwin was still listed as a 1st lieutenant, and six-victory ace Edgar G. Tobin (from the since-disbanded 103rd Aero Squadron, later assigned to Kelly Field, San Antonio) was still listed as a captain. However, Special Orders No. 87 of March 28, 1919, per Colonel Fechet, Headquarters, Kelly Field, assigned Tobin to Flying Circus duties as a "major." Mid-West Flight executive officer, Maj. George E. Stratemeyer, acknowledging Tobin's temporary duty promotion, and with the two British aces soon to join their Flying Circus both being captains, decided to also grant Erwin a temporary duty promotion, nothing similar having occurred in either the Far West or Eastern flights. Erwin flew from Post Field to Ellington Field with two Post Field flight instructors, 2nd Lieutenants J. W. Maxey and P. T. Wagner, to take part in the VLFC tour.[8]

There were promotions in Headquarters, III Army Corps, but they were otherwise rare in the postwar U.S. Army as it sought to discharge as many officers as possible and downsize the Army Air Service. This should have directly affected Erwin's promotion, his ability to keep it, and his later discharge. Secretary of War Newton D. Baker's comments on how this affected the Army Air Service were published, with excerpts shown below:

> Appointments to any commissioned grade in the United States Army have been made, and can properly be made, only when vacancies exist. Immediately upon the conclusion of the armistice, November 11, 1918, the demobilization of the temporary army was begun and has been proceeding with great rapidity. From and after that date, therefore, instead of there being any vacancies in any grade, there has been a surplus of officers in every grade, which it has been necessary to reduce by discharge. To increase the surplus by further appointments would have been unjustifiable, and such appointments were therefore discontinued. As it is necessary to continue the discharge of officers at the rate of more than 1,000 a day, it is not contemplated to resume appointments.

… The matter may briefly be summed up as follows: The demobilization of the Army makes it impossible to employ any additional officers on active duty, but on the contrary necessitates the discharge of many already in the service … The War Department, therefore, discontinued the appointment of officers for active duty, but offers to every man who has been found qualified for it, a commission in the United States Army with inactive status.[9]

There was a notable difference between how executive officer Maj. George E. Stratemeyer operated the Mid-West Flight, also known as Flying Circus No. 2, and how Maj. Carl Spatz commanded the Far West Flight. Stratemeyer selected his senior officer, Major Tobin, as his Officer-in-Charge of Flying, and Tobin often allowed his fellow aces to fly at their discretion. This worked out quite well after RAF 54-victory ace Capt. Andrew Beauchamp-Proctor (84 Squadron, flying S.E.5as) and RAF eight-victory ace Capt. Thomas C. Traill (20 Squadron, a Bristol Fighter pilot) joined the VLFC tour on its third day, in Memphis, Tennessee. Captain Beauchamp-Proctor was an unparalleled aerobatic pilot, whose skills far surpassed those of any of the stateside flight instructors.

Including himself, however, Tobin had to schedule 17 pilots to fly, when no more than 11 airplanes flew on any given day, and sometimes as few as seven. Ten of the training/flight instructor pilots on the VLFC tour were experienced pilots from Kelly Field. By April 15, this had already become a valid concern, such that Major Stratemeyer sent a telegram to Major Baldinger in the Director of Air Service office regarding "surplus number pilots on board train," sent from Springfield, Illinois. This problem did not occur in the Far West Flight because Spatz did not allow any of his aces to fly in air shows. It similarly did not occur in the Eastern Flight, which carried the same number of officers onboard its train, but its aces also did not fly as often as those from the Mid-West Flight.[10]

The VLFC tour left Ellington Field on April 9, 1919, bound for New Orleans. As they traveled northward through the Mississippi River Valley, they performed aerial exhibitions in 23 cities in 13 Mid-West states in 30 days, starting at 1:30 p.m. each day. An advance man traveled one week ahead of the Mid-West Flight train and visited each of the cities in which they flew air shows. He had to pick out the fields where the airplanes could take off and land; decide where the proper railway sidings were situated for the unloading and loading of the train; arrange for proper police protection; make the necessary arrangements to assure that high-test gasoline was available in 100-gallon quantities for the airplanes; plan for the feeding of all officers and men in the flying circus; and arrange for their transportation to and from the field. This generally required coordination with each city's local Victory

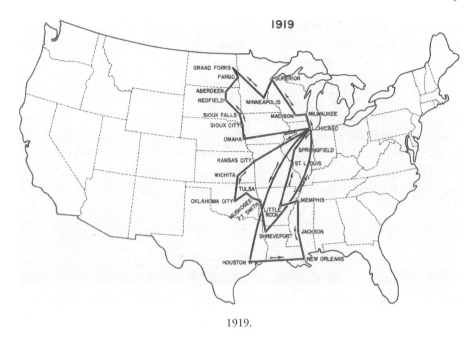

1919.

Loan committee, which also usually supplied entertainment afterwards. The local Victory Loan committees and recruiting officers generally set up booths to promote sales and distribute recruiting literature.[11]

Demobilization of the Air Service had continued until enlisted personnel were reduced to 15,000, and they planned on keeping only 21 aero squadrons at the time of the VLFC tour. (This comprised the 27th, 94th, 95th, and 147th Pursuit Squadrons; the 11th, 20th, 96th, and 166th Bombardment Squadrons; the 9th, 24th, and 91st Army Observation Squadrons; the 99th, 135th, and 258th Army Artillery Squadrons; the 1st, 12th, 50th, and 88th Corps Observation Squadrons; and the 8th, 90th, and 104th Surveillance Squadrons.) Upon their return to the United States from France in 1919, all Air Service men who were enlisted or drafted were discharged without delay if they so desired and were eligible for discharge. Without waiting for stabilization of the 15,000 enlisted personnel number, local recruiters worked with Mid-West Flight recruiting officer 1st Lt. P. E. MacGregor to recruit enlisted men for the Air Service at each air show.[12]

Regardless of the Mid-West Flight's efforts to help local Victory Loan committees sell Victory Loan bonds, air show crowds could not directly purchase those bonds that same day until the actual April 21 opening date of the Victory Loan sale itself. And that did not occur until they had reached Fort Snell, St. Paul, Minnesota. Up until that time, air shows in some cities were more highly regarded than in others; the flying fields chosen were not always the best and were sometimes dangerous, being somewhat affected by the quality of police protection provided; and their air shows were rained out in New Orleans on April 10, Chicago on April 16–17 and May 8, and Shreveport, Louisiana, on May 6. Some local Victory Loan committees were also already highly organized and did not necessarily need the VLFC Mid-West Flight to help them meet their assigned quotas of Victory Loan bonds to sell.

All the Kelly Field pilots were assigned to fly one of the designated airplane types during the VLFC tour: Fokker D.VII, SE-5, Spad VII, or Curtiss H. As one of the aces who joined after that order was issued, Erwin was not assigned

First Lieutenant William P. Erwin. Location unknown, but probably Coblenz, Germany, along the Rhine River, 13 kilometers southeast of Weißenthurm aerodrome, where 1st Aero Squadron was stationed postwar from December 21, 1918, to January 10, 1919. (George H. Williams via Greg VanWyngarden)

to fly any particular airplane type, but mostly flew one of the Fokker D.VIIs, a type he likely learned to fly at Weißenthurm aerodrome. His fellow Post Field flight instructors were assigned to fly Curtiss JN-4Hs. Although he may have flown one of the four Curtiss JN-4Hs used during air shows when pilots were taking "short hops," as they called it, there was only one documented case of him flying a Curtiss JN-4H during the VLFC tour. Below is a summary of events that happened during noteworthy Mid-West Flight air shows between April 11 and May 10, 1919.[13]

April 11, 1919, Jackson, Mississippi

At Sykes Field, approximately 5 miles north of Jackson, "There were two flying fields within a short distance, both of them were very rolly and cut up by

Captain Erwin sits in one of the two Fokkers flown at Sykes Field, about 5 miles north of Jackson, Mississippi, on April 11, 1919. The Fokker had motor problems during the 1:30 p.m. VLFC air show, causing Erwin to make a forced landing in which he broke his propeller. (Via Franklin O. Carroll)

ditches." They exhibited nine airplanes, but after one of the Curtiss Hs had motor problems, they only flew eight that afternoon. Starting at 1:30 p.m., this first air show only lasted for an hour, and included two Fokkers, one Spad, one SE-5, and four Curtiss Hs. "During the afternoon, Capt. Erwin, flying Fokker 8538, made a forced landing on account of motor trouble. He alighted in the only cleared field available, but due to ditch in center of field, broke propeller. This was the only damage to plane, Capt. Erwin being uninjured." This compromised the show's most spectacular routine—the dogfight between Fokkers, Spads, and SE-5s, something the crowd had not likely seen before. Although good luck seemed to follow him from France, spare parts were not as easy to replace.[14]

April 12, 1919, Memphis, Tennessee

The Mid-West Flight sent a telegram to McCook Field in Dayton, Ohio, about construction of new Fokker propellers. The two RAF aces finally arrived; Major Tobin allowed Captain Beauchamp-Proctor, affectionately nicknamed "Proccy," to pilot one of the Spads, and he was clearly the star of the air show at the North Memphis Driving Park. Of the two Fokkers, two SE-5s, two Spads, and five Curtiss Hs flown, Major Tobin flew one of the Fokkers, but was forced to leave the mimic air battle because of engine trouble and a broken wire brace. He misjudged the length of the landing field and almost ran into the surrounding fence. Mechanics averted an accident, however, when they swung onto the lower wings of the Fokker to slow it down. Although Erwin did not fly in Memphis, the *Commercial Appeal* newspaper extensively interviewed him about his exploits in France and his actions of November 5, 1918, that led to his being awarded an Oak Leaf Cluster to his DSC:

> I was fighting some German machine gunners behind the German line. They were keeping up a rear-guard action and had their guns in shell holes. Finally, a shell got my plane and it fell to the ground just a short distance behind these machine gunners. I turned my machine gun on this nest and in a few minutes had them subdued, and I only had a slight wound in my left leg. But then the gas came along, which sent me back to the hospital, where I was when the armistice was signed.[15]

April 13, 1919, North Little Rock, Arkansas

Captain Erwin also did not fly at Camp Pike but returned to where his military career started. Soon after he entered officer training camp at Fort Roots in April 1917, military officials realized that Fort Roots was insufficient to train the necessary troops to fight the war in Europe. As the Department of War looked to set up larger training facilities, on June 17, 1917, they selected

North Little Rock as the site for a post. The new facility, called Camp Pike, was easier to access and could accommodate a larger number of men. Camp Pike was ready to accept soldiers by September 1917, effectively replacing Fort Roots as the major military training facility.

During the afternoon air show, Mid-West Flight pilot 2nd Lt. Edward H. Hill successfully flew a Curtiss JN-4H Jenny under four successive bridges spanning the Arkansas River in Little Rock. A motion picture man with Pathé Weekly Motion Picture Company (a.k.a. Pathé-Cinéma) filmed the stunt and thousands of people saw it. Lieutenant Hill performed the stunt "As an additional attraction" to their air show over Camp Pike, although all the media attention focused on what happened over Little Rock. The one pedestrian and three railroad bridges that Hill flew under were (from west to east): the Baring Cross Bridge (aka Missouri Pacific Bridge, with a toll for pedestrian and wagon traffic); the Junction Bridge (found at the foot of Rock Street in what is now the River Market District); the Pulaski County Free Bridge (carrying pedestrian traffic, with no tolls); and the Rock Island Bridge. What the Mid-West Flight did not acknowledge was that "Lieut. C. E. Johnson from Eberts Field flew 12 times under the bridges," the *Arkansas Gazette* specifying both the Rock Island and Missouri Pacific railroad bridges. Their rationale was perhaps that it was a violation of direct orders from the

Camp Pike, North Little Rock, April 13, 1919. From left to right: Captain Howard H. Powell (formerly 85 Squadron RAF), Major George E. Stratemeyer, Lewis Lewyn, and Captain William P. Erwin stand in front of the Curtiss JN-4H "Dragon" Jenny. Lewyn represented the Pathé Weekly Motion Picture Company (aka Pathé-Cinéma) and joined Flying Circus No. 2 in Jackson, Mississippi, two days before, staying with them for the rest of the Mid-West Flight's tour. (Via Franklin O. Carroll)

Director of Air Service that their air shows should not include extra pilots who had not rehearsed the program with the Flying Circus pilots.[16]

April 14, 1919, St. Louis, Missouri

Forest Park, the flying field, was only 275 yards by 175 yards in size, with trees in the center. With an estimated 50,000 people in attendance, the police protection was inadequate and impossible to keep the crowd away from the point just beyond where the wheels of the airplanes left the ground. After five Curtiss Jennys dropped Victory Loan literature and finished their aerobatics in the air show, which began at 1:35 p.m., the program called for two German Fokkers to attack them, and then the Spad and two SE-5s to come to the Jennys' defense by attacking the Fokkers and forcing them to land. The Spad and SE-5s would then indulge in maneuvers and aerobatics for 15 or 20 minutes before landing. SE-5 C.8745 was unable to be flown from Forest Park after a flying wire broke during assembly. First Lieutenant Franklin O. Carroll took off in his Spad VII B.1374 at 1:55 p.m., followed at once by 1st Lt. George M. Belser in a Fokker, Captain Erwin in the other Fokker, and Captain Proccy in the other SE-5.[17]

If there was any doubt whether Captain Proccy would live up to his billing as the star of the air show, it was soon put to rest as his talent was quickly clear. The South African held his plane on the ground until he acquired a terrific speed, then rose steeply in a beautiful corkscrew turn that brought him back down the field before he had reached the other end of it. Almost simultaneously, the Curtiss Jennys piloted by Lieutenants Frank B. Estell and Alvin M. St. John came down, Estell rounding into the field with a bank in which his wings were virtually vertical.

A battle reenactment, representative of the air war on the Western Front, then occurred at a height of 1,500 feet. Lieutenant Belser's Fokker, previously "stalking" at a much higher altitude, attacked the Curtiss JN-6H Jenny piloted by 1st Lt. Paul A. Smith, waiting for just such prey. After squirming about desperately, but unavailingly, to evade the much faster pursuing Fokker, the slower Jenny went fluttering to earth in a "falling leaf" spin. But with the Fokker losing altitude during the duel, Belser had not seen Captain Proccy's SE-5 hurtling toward him from above at 150 mph. Then a real contest began, as every time Proccy dashed for a position on his opponent's tail, the wily Belser looped upward or side-slipped daringly out of range.

Soon, however, Proccy maneuvered as if to dive. As Belser looped, Proccy dashed straight at him, catching him in the middle of the loop with a "burst" in the back that would have riddled both pilot and machine. Carrying out his part of the sham, Belser let his Fokker reel drunkenly toward the ground in a hopeless spinning nosedive.

Meanwhile, Captain Erwin in his Fokker staged an aerial combat with 1st Lieutenant Carroll in his Spad at the eastern end of the field. Erwin's Fokker was faring differently; he spiraled to an altitude of 2,000 feet while diving on Carroll's Spad, which dodged about like a swallow but could not shake off his pursuer. In steady, concentric circles, Erwin's Fokker D.VII kept relentlessly on the tail of the Spad, never quite getting in range but never losing control of the situation. At a height of 500 feet, Carroll gave up, signifying that he was beaten, the analogy being that in real aerial combat his plane would have been forced to land, either in his own or enemy territory.

With the aerial duel ended, the two Fokkers, the Spad, and the SE-5 formed over Art Hill and raced northward across the field at a height not exceeding 200 feet. The Fokkers were definitely leading, as Proccy sped desperately to close the gap. As they rushed over the heads of the crowd, the rolled steel flying wires of his SE-5 were singing shrilly. He passed one Fokker near Lindell Boulevard but never caught the other. The Spad was last.

During both "combats," 1st Lt. H. C. Roberts in his "Dynamite" Jenny had been going through a series of beautiful maneuvers over the center of the field that challenged the combat planes for the crowd's attention. Once he saw the four scouts racing along Lindell Boulevard, Roberts knew it was time to land. He brought his Curtiss in and landed with little difficulty, except that he needed practically the whole length of the field. The crowd at the end of the field clearly did not understand the danger involved.

Next to land was Erwin in his Fokker. After having made a forced landing in a Fokker three days before and plunged into a ditch at the air show near Jackson, now he was trying to land with a crosswind. As he was about to land on the golf course at Forest Park, the wind blew the plane around so that it was at an angle to its flight path, which resulted in the wheels striking the ground sideways, breaking the landing gear and a wheel but causing no other damage. Yet even after landing with this much trouble, he still managed to stop the Fokker just short of the crowd. Again, the spectators were implored to move back, but such efforts were fruitless and they at once crowded back to their original positions.

Next it was Proccy's turn to descend. Fortunately, his SE-5 was structurally strong and stable, yet light on the controls, allowing the wily veteran to make a successful landing. Carroll closely followed Proccy's landing at 2:45 p.m.,

Left to right: Lieutenants Harry C. Roberts and George M. Belser, Captains W. P. Erwin and Thomas C. Traill (an eight-victory Bristol Fighter ace from 20 Squadron RAF), and Ewin T. Carroll (1st Lieutenant Frank Carroll's father and a prominent Evangelical Methodist preacher in Illinois) at Forest Park in St. Louis on April 14, 1919. (Via Franklin O. Carroll)

his Spad, with its 150hp Wright-Martin Model A motor being smaller and slower than those in the SE-5 and Fokkers, helping him make a successful landing at Forest Park.[18]

This left Lieutenant Belser as the only pilot still in the air. Without radio contact with the ground, he did not know that the 20-mph southwesterly wind he faced in taking off had suddenly changed to the north and northwest, requiring landings to be made crosswind and partially with the wind. Major Tobin, his officer-in-charge of flying, sensing the impending crisis, at once went to the far end of the field and implored the crowds to leave the area, but even police efforts were unsuccessful at moving them back.

On Belser's first landing attempt, he realized that he did not have room to land and applied full throttle just as he was about to touch the ground. With the Fokker's high angle of incidence, or stalling angle, this gave his ship the boost he needed to make another circle of the field. On the second attempt, he descended too slowly to maintain the Fokker's normal landing speed of about 80 mph. When the Fokker thus became nose-heavy in his glide, Belser had to apply some opposite rudder in the last 45 degrees and sideslip down with a touch of aft stick. In doing so, he barely cleared the treetops, but it appeared as though he would reach the field. It became clear, however, that he had misjudged and might overrun the field, endangering the crowd at the far end. Belser quickly cut his switch and tried to swing his ship around, but the crosswind prevented him from bringing his wings level while applying enough rudder to bring him exactly into the wind.

Mid-West Flight mechanics raced onto the field to help but were unable to grasp the wings, as was customary, because the Fokker was going too fast when it passed them. The crowd at the end of the landing field stood behind a heavy steel cable. With no brakes, the airplane coasted over the ground and into the cable against which spectators were packed. When the propeller hit the cable, the Fokker ground-looped, causing it to somersault onto its nose.

The result of the impact was catastrophic, the Fokker striking several people in the crowd. The seriously wounded were evacuated by ambulance to Barnes Children's Hospital and Barnes Hospital. One boy later died from a skull fracture and shock, while another suffered abdominal injuries in addition to an abrasion on his right hip. A third boy had abrasions on his right cheek and right thigh. A 62-year-old man suffered a fractured rib, a probable fractured right thigh, and abrasions on his left leg. Another boy was taken to St. Luke's Hospital with lacerations on his scalp. Belser was unhurt, except for slight lacerations on his hands. Another man, who worked at the Anheuser-Busch Brewery, reportedly went home after the accident to wash the blood from a cut on his face but was apparently not badly injured. No other injury-causing accidents occurred during the Mid-West Flight's 30-day tour.[19]

Examination of a photograph of Belser's Fokker shows that the plywood leading edge of the top wing was broken in at least two places, while the left wing interplane "N" strut was bent and the plywood leading edge immediately in front of the lower wing strut attachment was broken. It also had a broken axle fairing structure, exposing the aluminum axle box spar. The right side of the propeller was split just above the metal cladding on the bottom edge. Some of the wing fabric was torn and the tail was said to be damaged, although the engine and fuselage were unharmed.[20]

April 15, 1919, Springfield, Illinois

This was only the fifth air show and three Fokkers had already been damaged, two of them by Captain Erwin. The Mid-West Flight announced that two Fokkers and one Spad were undergoing repair. They opted to only fly the five Curtiss Jennys, two SE-5s, and one Spad from the fairgrounds in Springfield. Captain Proccy, who was photographed talking to Erwin prior to the event's late 2:30 p.m. start time, was once again the star attraction of the air show, flying an SE-5.[21]

Looking south with the Illinois State Fairgrounds, Barn M, and Feed and Storage Barn in the background, left and center, (from left to right) Captains T. C. Traill, A. F. W. Beauchamp-Proctor, and W. P. Erwin on the morning of April 15, 1919. Behind them, the red and white fuselage of the Curtiss JN-4H "Dragon" Jenny and other VLFC airplane fuselages. They were transported to the State Fairgrounds racetrack with their tailskid mounted on a flatbed truck that had to drag the airplane 200 yards from the fairgrounds siding to the center section of the racetrack. (Via Franklin O. Carroll)

This closeup view of a war-weary Captain William P. Erwin, taken in Milwaukee on April 18, 1919, portrays the stress effects of flying and combat fatigue on a young man only having just reached 23½ years of age. (Via Franklin O. Carroll)

April 19, 1919, Madison, Wisconsin

This show proved a great success for both pilots and spectators. "Madison has the best flying field of any place we have ever visited. The field is level and much better than the field we used in Milwaukee," said 1st Lt. J. M. Sullivan. Major Tobin allowed Erwin to fly the only available Fokker D.VII in that afternoon's air show. When the three Curtiss Jennys ranged over Madison, "bombing" the city with Victory Loan literature, that was Erwin's signal to attack them in his Fokker. The SE-5s and Spad came to the rescue, the battle raged, and thousands of sightseers, watching along the shore of Lake Monona and literally covering the tops of every tall building, were held spellbound as the machines dived at one another, sometimes flying for great distances upside down. Their first battle lasted only briefly. The SE-5 and Fokker routinely landed after short flights and then switched pilots. That gave everyone a chance to fly under such favorable conditions: Erwin had no problems in landing this time.[22]

April 22, 1919, Grand Forks, North Dakota

The Mid-West Flight flew two Fokkers, two Spads, two SE-5s, and five Curtiss Hs from the Lilac Hedge farm that afternoon, located about 5 miles north of Grand Forks. Starting at 1:30 p.m., Captain Erwin flew one of the Fokkers and Captain Traill the other. However, after it started raining at about 2:00 p.m., Major Tobin called an immediate halt to the air show, had everyone land and packed up all the airplanes so they would not get wet. The *Grand Forks Herald* interviewed Erwin and reported: "Capt. William P. Erwin ... has nine German machines to his credit and has an irrepressible tendency to talk all the time about what his fellow aviators did while on the front, but persistently refuses to say anything about his own heroic feats."[23]

April 26, 1919, Sioux Falls, South Dakota

The highlight of this air show was Captain Proccy flying in one of the SE-5s. First, he headed straight for the line of Pullman cars of the Victory Loan

"The Gang" assembles in Sioux Falls, South Dakota prior to their April 26, 1919, air show there. From left to right (sitting or kneeling): Captains Erwin, unknown, A. F. W. Beauchamp-Proctor, and Howard H. Powell (looking over Proctor's left shoulder), Lieutenants Whitney, Alvin M. St. John, Harris C. Roberts, Franklin O. Carroll (behind Roberts), and Frank B. Estell (flying goggles on head). (Standing): unknown, unknown, Major Stratemeyer (Executive Officer in Command), Lieutenants Hewitt, A. E. Selberg (Traffic Officer), and Edward H. Hill. (Via Franklin O. Carroll)

Special train on the siding near Lyon's Field, where he seemed to fairly crawl up the sides and over it. While the German Fokker and other scouts indulged in "crowd strafing" and a sham air battle that afternoon, Proccy would have none of that. Instead, while the other seven airplanes were returning in battle formation from over the city, Proccy was just approaching the downtown area, where he performed aerobatics for nearly an hour with daring dives and spins. Captain Erwin was photographed with the rest of "The Gang."[24]

April 28, 1919, Omaha, Nebraska

As reported in the *Omaha Daily Bee*, "Capt. W. P. Erwin, American ace with eleven German planes to his credit, was in one of the Fokkers."[25] Erwin was shadowing the formation of four Curtiss JN-4H Jennys that had just finished 15 minutes of various exhibition flying over downtown Omaha. Their "protection patrol" consisted of Captain Powell in an SE-5 and 2nd Lt. Joseph L. Whitney in a Spad VII. Once they released their leaflets over the city, that was the signal for Erwin and 2nd Lt. Charles M. Potter in the other Fokker to make a sham attack on the formation of four Jennys. While trying to maneuver out of harm's way and descend at the same time, the Jennys were eventually rescued by the Spad and SE-5. Powell and Whitney then chased the two Fokkers, soon driving both down and back to Ak-Sar-Ben Field. The Spad and SE-5 then indulged in maneuvers and aerobatics before returning to Ak-Sar-Ben Field. The star of the air show was Captain Proccy, who flew through downtown Omaha. He pulled up to barely clear the top of the 18-story Woodmen building, and then skimmed along the muddy waters of the Missouri River before diving cleanly through the center span of the Douglas Street Bridge.[26]

Just as was his victory total in the *Omaha Daily Bee*, however, some of the Omaha *World-Herald*'s published statements about Erwin were both misleading and false:

> Captain W. P. Erwin, pilot of an observation airplane and one of four observation pilots of the Air Service, with a record of nine German planes to his credit, this morning told of a thrilling flight and fight in which he figured at the Argonne on November 5 of last year, where Captain Erwin and his observer, Captain B. V. Baucom, won the Congressional Medal of Honor for heroism at that time.
>
> While strafing German machine gun nests, one of these nests shot away the control from Captain Erwin's machine and he was compelled to make a landing within twenty feet of the German lines, right in front of a nest. It was necessary to do some quick thinking and still quicker acting. They did.
>
> Captain Baucom, the observer, turned his swivel machine gun attached to the plane right into the German lines, wiped out two nests and killed seven men.

Then the two American flyers crawled into one of the nests for safety and remained there all night. At daybreak they crawled on their stomachs back to the American lines and safety—a distance of one and one-half miles. Captain Erwin was wounded in the leg and gassed in his memorable encounter and was compelled to spend six weeks in a hospital as a result.

Erwin's second DSC citation had not even been issued by that time, let alone a Medal of Honor. Neither Baucom's report, the DSC citations, or 1st Aero Squadron records list Erwin as having been wounded. Landing within 20 feet of the German lines, wiping out two machine-gun nests and killing seven men, staying in that shell hole all night until daybreak, and then crawling on their stomachs 1½ miles is all new information. The latter figure equates to almost 2.5 km, while Baucom reported being shot down just 1 km north of American lines on November 5, 1918. The American I Corps reported Erwin riding back to Julvécourt aerodrome on a horse the following morning. Even the

Captain Anthony Beauchamp-Proctor, 54 victories, VC, DFC, DSO, MC, and Bar, of 84 Squadron RAF, in SE-5 C.8747 at Ak-Sar-Ben Field, Omaha, Nebraska, on April 28, 1919. (BF4-242 from the Bostwick-Frohardt Collection, owned by KM3TV and on permanent loan to The Durham Museum, Omaha, Nebraska)

Looking northeast with Ak-Sar-Ben field running north to their left, Captain Anthony Beauchamp-Proctor (left) confers with three other officers, including the officer-in-charge of flying, Major Edgar G. Tobin (third from left), prior to the air show in Omaha on April 28, 1919. (Via Franklin O. Carroll)

statement that Erwin was one of four Air Service observation pilots with nine German planes to his credit was misleading, based on the War Department's then current list. The other three pilots—1st Lt. Thomas G. Cassady (28th Aero Squadron), 1st Lt. Chester E. Wright (93rd Aero Squadron), and Capt. Elliot W. Springs (148th Aero Squadron and 85 Squadron RAF)—were all pursuit pilots. He also had three more victories than the other two leading observation pilot aces, Capt. Everett Cook and Maj. Victor Strahm, both with five victories with 91st Observation Squadron.[27]

April 29, 1919, Chicago, Illinois

The Mid-West Flight cancelled the scheduled air show in Des Moines, Iowa, on this day and came back to Chicago instead to compensate for their earlier rained-out air shows there. While the Army Air Service listed Rev. W. A. Erwin as living in the 10-story Fine Arts Building, across the street from Grant Park, where the air show was staged, Bill had told the Omaha *World-Herald* that Chicago was his home at that time. It is more likely, however, that it was his residence while he was on a musical tour in 1917, and then he never returned after he joined the Army. With no preliminary advertisement, things went well in the air, but the Victory Loan tour had an overall disastrous day:

"Four Aces"—left to right: Major E. G. Tobin, Captains W. P. Erwin, T. C. Traill, and A. F. W. Beauchamp-Proctor alongside one of the Mid-West Flight's Fokkers in Chicago on April 29, 1919. They canceled their scheduled air show in Des Moines, Iowa, that day and flew in Chicago instead after their earlier air show there was rained out. Tobin wears the *Fourragère* of the *Croix de Guerre* cord because his 103rd Aero Squadron, formerly the Lafayette *Escadrille* N124, received two citations of the French Orders of the Army. (Via Franklin O. Carroll)

All ships on several occasions flew down Michigan Avenue at altitudes varying from ten feet to fifty feet. Ships were continually flying around the Blackstone Hotel at less than two hundred feet altitude. Several pilots flew down State and West Adams Streets between the buildings. The Curtiss and Scouts did aerobatics at very low altitudes, and the usual combat between the Scouts and Curtiss ships was given. This account is given with an idea of showing how the circus tried to assist Chicago with her loan drive, but it is believed that we met with the biggest failure the circus has thus far encountered. All pilots flew their ships with exceptional skill and have been told by unbiased civilians who were present at the exhibition, that Chicago saw, without doubt, the most daring and at the same time most skillful maneuvering ever before accomplished in this Country, as well as having the opportunity to see the very latest types and designs of war planes ... The War Department paid some three thousand dollars to give this exhibition but owing to absolutely no advertising of any kind, it is believed that our performance amounted to very little, notwithstanding that the exhibition in itself was a most excellent one.[28]

May 1, 1919, Wichita, Kansas

A serious accident was narrowly avoided in the morning, when Capt. William Erwin flew a Curtiss JN-4H, carrying *Wichita Beacon* reporter Keith J. Fanshier as his passenger. Fortunately, nobody was hurt in the incident. "Capt. Erwin, driving a Curtiss plane for the first time, misjudged a landing and smashed the nose of his machine into the ground, breaking the propeller," the *Wichita Eagle* reported, while providing other relevant information. "Low places on Jones field, caused by excessive rainfall the past few days, put ... [one] of the Flying Circus airplanes temporarily out of commission. One of these went into a rut during the morning exhibition."

After his landing accident, Erwin related the following: "I told the reporter who went up with me this morning that I have never driven a Curtiss before, and you should have seen the expression on his face. When I met that little mishap on making a landing, he raised his head and stammering asked if there was anything wrong with the motor."[29] The Mid-West Flight's *War Diary* Wichita show summary later stated: "Capt. W. P. Erwin in a Curtiss H plane used very poor judgment in landing during the morning, consequently the propeller and both lower wing panels were broken, also the undercarriage struts, braces and wheels were also badly damaged, the ship, however, was

 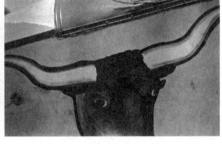

Captain William P. Erwin was flying this Curtiss JN-4H "Texas Longhorn" Jenny on the morning of May 1, 1919, at Jones aviation field in Wichita when he hit a rut or ditch, concealed by the cut alfalfa shown, which resulted in him breaking the propeller and both lower wing panels. The undercarriage struts, braces, and wheels were also badly damaged. Both Erwin and his passenger, Keith J. Fanshier, a *Wichita Beacon* reporter, were uninjured. (Via Joe Coomer)

A closer view of the "Texas Longhorn" on Erwin's Curtiss JN-4H Jenny's right fuselage. (Tim Culbert Collection via Alan D. Toelle)

Captain Erwin stands in front of one of the two Spad VIIs flown at Brookins Field in Tulsa on May 3, 1919. (Via Franklin O. Carroll)

immediately put back in flying condition without delay." Luckily, they had taken on a new shipment of Curtiss H lower wing panels in Redfield, South Dakota, on April 25 and carried the other Curtiss H spare parts with them in one of the baggage cars.[30]

May 5, 1919, Fort Smith, Arkansas

This was the 23rd air show on their tour. After Captain Erwin's disastrous flight in Wichita, it does not appear that Major Stratemeyer allowed him to fly any more Mid-West Flight airplanes during this or their previous air shows in Oklahoma City, Tulsa and Muskogee, Oklahoma. The *Southwest American* newspaper misreported Erwin's victory total as "11 German planes to his credit," but then underreported Captain Traill's eight confirmed victories, crediting him "with six German planes to his credit." No flights were made by any of the famous aces and Erwin apparently remained tightlipped: "When asked concerning his experiences, Capt. Erwin remarked, 'Oh, nothing exciting!'"[31]

May 8–10, 1919, Chicago, Illinois

The Mid-West Flight went first to Shreveport, Louisiana, from Fort Smith on May 6, but the air show there was rained off. They were originally supposed to stage air shows in Dallas, Waco, Austin, and perhaps even Houston, Texas, over the following four days. Instead, politics prevailed, and they were sent 865 miles northward again, back to Chicago for the third time. Captain Bill Erwin had been back in Chicago for the first time on April 16 and 17, when he stayed at the Congress Hotel, 520 South Michigan Avenue, on the night of the 16th. Cold weather, intermittent downpours of rain, and fog at 50 feet

"Sour Grapes"—Captain Erwin, Major Tobin, and Captain Beauchamp-Proctor sit forlorn, dejected, and simply worn out in Fort Smith, Arkansas, on May 5, 1919. After leaving Houston at 5:47 p.m. on April 9 and eating and sleeping for a month on a train traveling 4,908 miles up to that point, the daily stress of flying air shows was finally taking its toll. None of these men were allowed to fly in the Fort Smith air show that day, the tour's 23rd. Tobin was faring the worst and Flying Circus No. 2's surgeon sent him back to Kelly Field, San Antonio, Texas, after they reached their next stop in Shreveport, Louisiana, the following day. (Via Franklin O. Carroll)

had kept the VLFC from having any air show those two days. His hotel being only one block south from his old apartment at 410 South Michigan Avenue, and Chicago Musical College at 430 South Michigan Avenue, gave Bill an opportunity to look at opportunities in the musical field postwar. Although he was only back in Chicago for about eight-and-a-half hours on April 29, this third trip back on May 8 was for three full days. Heavy downpours of rain also made it impossible to exhibit or fly planes on May 8, giving Bill another free day to explore his postwar musical opportunities and realize it was not quite the same feeling as before the war. Somehow his sudden growth to maturity and acquiring skills as a military aviator had changed his outlook in life.

On May 9, the wind coming in off Lake Michigan was so strong that when one of the SE-5s, flown by 2nd Lt. Alvin M. St. John, was taxiing with the wind, and then turned to take off into the wind, the crosswind blew the SE-5 completely up and over onto its back. St. John was uninjured, but the SE-5 was temporarily out of commission.[32]

Sergeant 1st Class C. W. Peckham, a 103rd Aero Squadron crew chief, supplied the air show highlights this time by wing walking on the "Deuce of Spades" Jenny, flown by 2nd Lt. J. W. Maxey, from Post Field. The *Chicago Daily Tribune* described his antics:

> Far above the tip of the tallest flagpole of the Michigan Avenue skyline, a youth stepped from an airplane cockpit, walked to the edge of the lower port wing, and waved a nonchalant greeting to the landlubbers a mile below. The airplane zoomed into a loop the loop, and when it had regained the horizontal, the youth was seen to have changed his position to the top wing. There he remained while the airplane volplaned [performed a controlled dive] to within a few hundred feet of terra firma. Suddenly he jumped lightly to his feet, skipped to the rear, and best rode the chassis just in front of the rudder.
>
> … Throughout the maneuvers yesterday, Sergt. Peckham continued his aerobatics. He frisked about all over the airplane with the agility one of [zookeeper] Cy De Vry's pet primates.
>
> Once he climbed under the machine and sat on the axle of the two landing wheels. The machine volplaned to within ten feet of the ground and Sergt. Peckham doubled up his knees. Spectators feared his legs would be broken. But the machine flew up in a safer altitude.[33]

On May 10, the *Chicago Daily Tribune*'s front page showed Mid-West Flight photographer 2nd Lt. Grafton Wiggins's image of Peckham standing on a Jenny's lower starboard wing from 40 feet ahead and just below. They flew air show exhibitions from Grant Park both morning and afternoon on May 9 and 10. Captain Erwin is not known to have flown on these two days, after which their flight surgeon gave his assessment of the personnel:

> It was noticeable that at the completion of the final exhibition, both the officers and enlisted men were worn from the tension caused by nervous strain due to travelling in a moving train all night for so many successive nights, and assembling and disassembling planes

each day, and flying out of strange fields each day. The flight surgeon reported each pilot as suffering from neuro cardiac asthenia [clinical syndrome characterized by palpitations, shortness of breath, fatigue, or insomnia] due to continuous flying over a long period of time over strange fields and recommended a leave for all officers in order that they might secure a much-needed rest.[34]

May 11–12, 1919, Memphis, Tennessee, to Houston

After packing up and leaving at 1:00 a.m., it was another 1,196 miles back to Houston and Ellington Field, their average speed turning out to be 27½ mph. Although he still needed to report back to Post Field, the Victory Loan Special train dropped off Erwin in Memphis along the way. The Mid-West *War Diary* said: "Captain W. P. Erwin … was relieved enroute at Memphis, Tenn., and ordered to his proper station [on] account of urgent affairs needing his attention." Although his separation date from the Air Service cannot be found, there are some clues. He most likely saw a future in aviation, not in

The Curtiss JN-6H "Red Devil" Jenny from the 50th Photo Section at Grant Park, Chicago, on May 10, 1919. Center left is 2nd Lieutenant Grafton Wiggins, while center right is his pilot, 2nd Lieutenant C. M. Potter. Before the war, Erwin lived in the 10-story Fine Arts Building, which then housed the Chicago Little Theatre and Studebaker Theatre, across from Grant Park at 410 S. Michigan Avenue. (Via Franklin O. Carroll)

the Air Service, but still wanted to keep his "captain" title into civilian life. If he returned to Ellington Field, he would face pressure to return to Post Field with Lieutenants Maxey and Wagner. If he asked for an honorable discharge at Post Field, since his promotion was only "temporary" rather than "permanent," they would have discharged him as a 1st lieutenant rather than captain.

Major Tobin, when they were in Shreveport on May 6, upon the recommendation of the flight surgeon, was relieved from further duty and ordered back to Kelly Field. After returning to Kelly Field, Tobin, a San Antonio resident, was reverted to his former rank of captain. He was finally able to regain his rank of major by the spring of 1922, but by then he was an Air Service reserve officer, assigned to the Organized Reserves in the San Antonio area. The *Dallas Morning News* article series "Erwin: From the War Letters and Diary of an American Ace" completely overlooked Erwin's VLFC tour. "It was not until he was about to leave the service that word came from Washington that the higher rank had been established," said the newspaper's page six article on October 22, 1928. But then the article intimates that Erwin and Capt. Arthur J. Coyle were discharged together at Fort Sill, Oklahoma. That implies Erwin returned to Fort Sill to be discharged, but if so, he would have reverted to his permanent rank of 1st lieutenant, just as Tobin was reverted to his permanent rank upon return.[35]

The Victory Loan Special train carried a recruiting officer, whose job it was to coordinate with the local recruiting officer in each city in which they flew an air show. Those local recruiting officers were always at the air shows and met the aces, who also served as a recruiting tool. Their train's return route from Chicago was via the Illinois Central Lines to Memphis, then the Yazoo and Mississippi Valley Railroad Lines to Baton Rouge, Louisiana, and finally the Gulf Coast Lines to Houston.

Erwin had met the Memphis recruiting officer during the April 12 air show at the North Memphis Driving Park. He fulfilled his commitment to the VLFC tour and was present at one more air show than each of the other aces. He also flew in at least six of those air shows, even though he had landing accidents in three of them. The 17½ hours it likely took to travel the 483 miles between Chicago and Memphis gave him plenty of time to have Major Stratemeyer finish any paperwork authorizing his temporary field promotion to captain. Memphis would also be the only Flying Circus air show city they would stop in along their way back, and they should have arrived there about 6:30 p.m. on May 11. If he wanted to keep his title as "captain," he needed to find a friendly recruiting officer who would offer him an honorable discharge, which he was entitled to after almost two years and one month of service in

	Eastern	Mid-West	Far West
Total hours flown	202¼	202	234
Total civilian passengers carried	144	144	142
Total flights made	291	391	425

the U.S. Army. Of that time, he spent almost 15 months overseas. Thus, it is this author's belief that the "urgent affairs needing his attention" were his trip to the Memphis recruiting office on Monday, May 12, 1919, paperwork in hand, so that he could seek an honorable discharge from a sympathetic officer who knew him, forever after allowing him to retain his title "Capt. William P. Erwin." Not bad compensation after serving just one month on the VLFC tour in that capacity.

The *Air Service News Letter* typically published the names of officers receiving honorable discharges on a weekly basis in 1919. They never published Erwin's name, however, something quite unusual for an ace of his stature. A possible reason for this could be the issue regarding his rank. They may not have wanted to list his discharge rank as "captain," since he never served on active-duty status at that rank. His former squadron mates still in Germany would not have been aware of his field promotion during the VLFC tour. Even the May 26, 1919, General Order authorizing his second DSC still listed his permanent rank of 1st lieutenant.

By the time the train arrived back at Ellington Field at 8:25 p.m. on May 12, Flying Circus No. 2 had traveled 7,747 miles. Considering that the Far West Flight traveled 6,626 miles (although they added another 413 miles in one "side show"), one would not believe this disparity at first glance, but the Mid-West Flight's extra trips back to Chicago skewed this data. The Eastern Flight had traveled 4,338 miles. While more time on the rails should equate to less time in the air, statistics of the enterprise for all three flying circuses that covered 86 cities in 44 states during the April 10–May 10 tour are as follows:

The Mid-West Flight's only area where it excelled was the total number of civilian passengers carried. While they claimed 144 civilian passengers carried, their actual number was much higher. The Mid-West Flight tended to fly former soldiers who were aviators, and then not count them on their *War Diary* log sheets. Local newspapers, however, supplied those names otherwise left off the *War Diary* log sheets. The observations gained regarding the value of the fields used, the nature of the country, the altitude difficulties encountered in the Far West, and the resulting aerial photographs were all of aid to military, postal, commercial, and sporting aeronautics for years to come in the 1920s.[36]

CHAPTER 7

"Lone Star Bill" and the Dole Air Race

Bill Erwin thought civilian aviation had all the potential of reshaping people's transportation needs. With his parents then living in the Fort Worth/Dallas area and his father still preaching, Bill returned to Texas and leased some acreage on the north side of Azle Avenue in Fort Worth. The grazing land had been used as an airport, had acquired some flimsy wood hangars, and was known as Aviation Gardens. Bill then went to Dallas to buy a surplus trainer from a pilot formerly with the 11th Aero (Observation) Squadron, (then) 1st Lt. Frederick L. Koons, a Standard JR-1B with a 170hp Hispano-Suiza engine, for a few hundred dollars.[1]

He soon met Guy Warren, another pilot who was also in the oil land lease business, whose office was in downtown Fort Worth. Warren developed and promoted oilfields and offered Bill the opportunity of working with him. Warren agreed to share profits and back Erwin in buying some surplus military planes, to fly supplies and personnel into the new oilfield being drilled in East Texas. When Howard Woodall and Thomas F. Cook (former 2nd lieutenant pilot, 88th Aero Squadron) flew into Carrollton, Texas, from Muskogee, Oklahoma, with their surplus planes, Erwin met and welcomed them. He offered them his airport at Aviation Gardens as a home base, and they accepted his offer. Woodall also had a love affair with flying and a businessman's desire to be successful in his vocation. He had barnstormed continually, giving flying lessons and 15-minute passenger rides, also servicing airplanes.[2]

Business was also then improving for "Lone Star Bill" Erwin (his Texas nickname) and Guy Warren, requiring frequent trips to the East Texas Oil Field. Woodall would fly oilfield workers in Erwin's plane and bring the airplane back to Fort Worth, as there were no airports with proper airplane storage facilities nearby. By 1920, the financial and trade center of the East Texas Oil Field boom had entrenched itself in Dallas. After the Army Air

Service deactivated Love Field as an active-duty airfield and converted it into a storage facility for surplus DH-4 and JN-4 airplanes in December 1919, the city of Dallas leased space there. Erwin and Warren then moved to Dallas in April 1920 and based their planes at Love Field. Their new venture was chartered as the Aero Auto Club of Dallas on April 7, with former squadron mate Byrne Baucom as one of the partners. Here they met Tom Paine, another wheeler dealer in oil leases.[3]

Erwin, Warren, and Paine were on the rollercoaster. Their lucrative business and direct factory connections were also attractive to another buyer—Major Bill Long (formerly Lieutenant Hilton W. Long, 93rd Aero Squadron). They eventually sold their business venture to Long after Erwin and Warren became determined to diversify from the on-again/off-again oil business. Seeking an opportunity in commercial aviation, Warren and Erwin decided to open their own International Flying Service at Love Field. After first obtaining a contract to deliver Dallas newspapers to West Texas, they developed a plan to deliver mail and carry passengers from Love Field to Amarillo.

When Howard Woodall returned from working a stint at the Douglas Aircraft Company in Santa Monica, California, Erwin hired him as a flight instructor and charter pilot, and later became friends with Colonel William (Bill) E. Easterwood, Jr. In 1926, when the $25,000 purse was once again offered for the first transatlantic flight from New York to Paris, Easterwood tried to interest Bill Erwin into entering that venture. But by then Bill was dating Constance Ohl, an ex-student of the School of Industrial Arts in Philadelphia, who shared familiar musical talents and was well known in musical circles as a player of the cello and banjo. His engagement to Constance and efforts to make what was then called "International Airways" a profitable business prompted him to cease consideration as a contestant.[4]

On July 27, 1926, Capt. William P. Erwin married Constance Sarah Ohl, daughter of Mrs. John Wallis Ohl, at their 1030 Rosemount Avenue home in Dallas. Bill's father, Rev. W. A. Erwin of Pawhuska, Oklahoma, performed the ceremony. Their fathers also shared similar backgrounds, her late father having been the rector at Christ Episcopal Church in Oak Cliff, a Dallas neighborhood. Following their wedding trip by airplane, Bill and Constance set up their residence in Dallas. He was then general manager of International Airways. According to the 1927 Dallas City Directory, they were living in the Allen Apartments, "201," 3321 Oak Lawn Avenue, located between North Hall and Rawlins Streets.[5]

On August 21, 1927, the *Washington Sunday Star* reported: "Erwin was not awarded the Distinguished Service Cross in person until a year and a half ago.

The War Department had the coveted honor for him, but efforts to locate his address proved unavailing. Further search brought to light his whereabouts and the honors were bestowed upon him." While the Army assumed his father lived in Chicago's Fine Arts Building, it listed his father as living in Sabanno, Eastland County, Texas, even while Bill noted in his personal records that his father was living in Pawhuska, Oklahoma, in the spring of 1918.

This would mean Erwin not receiving the second DSC in person until early 1926. Erwin received his first DSC before the war ended and is shown wearing it in 1st Aero Squadron records. His second DSC (Oak Leaf Cluster) was publicly announced on May 29, 1919. Photographs do not show him wearing the Oak Leaf Cluster during his April–May 1919 VLFC tour. This evidence further shows that the Army Air Service discharged Erwin sometime between when the Victory Loan Special train dropped him off in Memphis on May 11, and May 29 when the second DSC award was announced. The *Dallas Morning News* reported that "he was mustered out of the army in June 1919," after his VLFC tour on behalf of the U.S. Treasury Department. If that statement was true, the Army could obviously have either presented him the Oak Leaf Cluster then or known where to send it to him after his discharge.[6]

In early June 1927, Captain Erwin addressed the Dallas Real Estate Board luncheon at the Baker Hotel in Dallas. He was the first flyer to enter the Dallas-to-Hong Kong flight for the $25,000 prize offered by Easterwood. "Texas has an ideal climate and an ideal topography for aviation development," Erwin told the luncheon, before continuing:

> An aviator can fly 100, 200 or 300 miles in any direction from the center of the State and find a place to land without difficulty, an important item in testing planes. The topography of other States will not permit this. Detroit is making every effort to become the aviation center of the United Sates, but it is working under a weather and topography handicap. Yet they are making progress. Here we can fly the year round, while in the North there are only five months of the year in which flying is practicable as a regular thing.[7]

Dallas held a contest in July 1927 to find a name for Lone Star Bill Erwin's new plane, which he planned to fly from Dallas to California, thence across the Pacific Ocean in the Dole Air Race. Thirteen people submitted the winning name *Dallas Spirit*, and honorable mention went to those who added "the," i.e., "The Dallas Spirit." The Swallow Airplane Company completed construction of *Dallas Spirit* in Wichita, Kansas, in 33 days. Bill, Constance, and *Dallas Morning News* journalist John Peyton Dewey drove there on August 3, 1927, and Captain Erwin took his first test flight in *Dallas Spirit*, a Swallow Monoplane, NX941, that evening. He made several more test flights there on August 4 to familiarize himself with the controls and Swallow made a few

Bill Erwin with his wife, Constance Ohl Erwin, on *Dallas Spirit* following the unveiling ceremonies at Love Field on August 6, 1927. Constance had planned on leaving with Bill on the flight to Hawaii but was ruled out at the last minute because she was under 20 years of age and was also pregnant at the time. (Courtesy of San Diego Air and Space Museum, Dole Air Race album)

minor adjustments. He returned to Love Field in Dallas the evening of August 5, greeted by a crowd of 5,000, even though his arrival was unannounced. Dewey drove Erwin's car back to Dallas.[8]

On August 6, before a crowd of 10,000 at Love Field, with Lieutenant Governor Barry Miller, G. B. Dealey, President of the *Dallas News*, Colonel W. E. Easterwood, Jr., Mayor Burt, and an even larger radio audience standing by throughout Texas, Governor Dan Moody unveiled *Dallas Spirit*, which had been wheeled over from its hangar to the platform. As Erwin spoke to the crowd, he made it clear that he intended to fly not only to Hawaii, but to continue to Hong Kong, Japan, and around the world before returning to Dallas. Below are highlights of Governor Moody's comments:

> I regard this as not only a great day for Dallas, but a great day for Texas. This flight will be an advertisement of Texas and the Texas spirit, that goes to make a great deal of what Texas is. The men who have financed this enterprise and made it possible have not only done a service to Dallas, but to the State.

> If Capt. Erwin's flight is a success, and all Texas joins with me in hoping that it is, it will add much to the progress of commercial aviation. The telegraph, the telephone and the radio already have eliminated time and distance. This thing you're doing in Dallas, sending an airship around world, to my mind is a forerunner of what is to come in aviation.[9]

Erwin made his first test flight in *Dallas Spirit* from Love Field on August 8, with federal inspectors Edison E. Mouton and Parker D. Cramer, before a gallery of 3,000–5,000 fans. Erwin made an early morning test flight on August 9, after which two more gasoline tanks—one of 20 gallons and the other 40 gallons—were installed, giving *Dallas Spirit* a total capacity of 515 gallons and a cruising range of 5,150 miles in one fueling. That afternoon he attended meetings downtown with sponsors of his flight, during which the National Aeronautical Association committee definitively ruled that his wife, Constance, could not fly with him because she was not 21 years of age. With more than 3,000 spectators on hand, Erwin left Love Field for Oakland that evening about 7:00 p.m. in *Dallas Spirit*, with 300 gallons of gasoline and 20 gallons of oil. His problems started when he thought the automatic pump in the motor was not pumping gasoline from the main and center section tanks, so he resorted to using his hand, or wobble pump, which only worked for a short time. Nearing Colorado City, Texas, 252 miles west, he decided to return to Love Field and not risk a forced landing. He reached Love Field at 11:45 p.m. and landed without any further problems.[10]

At the direction of federal inspector Cramer at Dallas, the entire system of gasoline leads from the various tanks to the motor, which had been installed at the factory, was removed and revised that same night and early morning of August 10. Erwin left Love Field for the second time that evening at 6:06 p.m. However, the revised system with its various cocks and pumps gave Erwin more trouble and made him make a forced landing in a wheatfield in Beaumont, California, with the same fuel line difficulties. He sent two telegrams describing his problems, the first of which read:

> Beaumont, Cal. 7 a.m.—Both engine and wobble pumps failed, forcing me down here, eighty miles from Los Angeles, between a couple of mountains at 5:30 a.m. Will fill gravity tanks and be in San Francisco by noon.

When Col. W. E. Easterwood learned that Erwin had alighted before reaching San Francisco, he said he was willing to waive the forced landing and still award the prize to Erwin if he went ahead and completed the flight. He also reiterated that he would present the Dallas aviator with the added $5,000 offered for reaching Hong Kong. However, Captain W. A. Southworth, acting head of the starting committee of the National Aeronautical Association for the Easterwood flight, said that Erwin's landing at Beaumont had disqualified him, unless he returned to Dallas to make what would have been his third start. The rules called for a nonstop flight from Dallas to San Francisco, Capt. Southworth said, and this rule could not be waived. Nevertheless, Dallas sponsor C. R. Miller, who was there in Oakland representing Erwin, declared that Erwin was flying under the rules of the Easterwood prize for the $25,000 award offered for the first airman to hop from Dallas to Hong Kong.

The second telegram, also from Beaumont, said:

> Engine pump never worked. Wobble pump passed out over mountains during storm at 2 a.m. Frisco by noon.[11]

Erwin left Beaumont at 7:50 a.m. on August 11 and landed at Oakland's airport at 1:38 p.m. (3:38 p.m. Dallas time). He was stiff and exhausted after his long flight, much of it flying with his left hand while pumping gas with his right hand. He landed wearing a light gray suit and a straw hat with a blue band. His right thumb was a solid water blister because of using the wobble pump, and he was badly splashed with black oil. Other than that, he looked like an ordinary citizen out in the park for a stroll. Aside from what he perceived as mechanical failures, he was delighted with *Dallas Spirit*, declaring confidently to Dallas friends that it was the fastest ship in the Dole Air Race lineup and that he was going to win the race. Chief mechanic Eddie Blom then took charge of *Dallas Spirit*, and with his assistants their first priority was to tear out and rebuild the gasoline system once again. Since Erwin had agreed to team up with the competent navigator Alvin Eichwaldt, of Hayward, California, this necessitated the cutting of trapdoors for observation in *Dallas Spirit*'s roof and bottom of the fuselage, which he could open when required and drop smoke bombs to determine drift.

Erwin could not have returned to Dallas a second time anyway, since the original race starting time had been scheduled for August 12 at 12:01 p.m. It was not until that date that the Dole aviators signed a unanimous agreement to postpone the race until August 16, which was ultimately approved. Although Erwin was originally scheduled to start fifth in the race, he was not one of the first four contestants to pass the federal inspection tests on August 12, and the new starting order was to be made in the order of their completing these tests. Federal inspector Cramer had released a statement on August 11 that summarized all of Erwin's mechanical problems—namely pilot failure to familiarize himself with his operating systems, problems traced back to Swallow Aircraft Company—and that unfairly tarnished its image:

Bill Erwin and his navigator for the Dole Air Race flight, Alvin H. Eichwaldt of Hayward, California. (Courtesy of San Diego Air and Space Museum, Dole Air Race album)

From my knowledge of the working of a gasoline system as installed in the *Dallas Spirit* when it made its first departure from Love Field en route to San Francisco, [I] will say that I have tested the particular hook-up as then installed and was satisfied that it was possible to flow the gasoline from the main tanks to any one of the wing tanks by a use of the wobble or hand pump.

Of course, it required a working knowledge of the system in order that the operator could open and close the correct valves. Upon the plane's return to Dallas, the report came out that the gasoline pumps failed to function. And as I felt it was reasonable to assume a lack of familiarity with the workings of the system as a more likely cause for the failure, I immediately went to Love Field, and upon questioning the mechanics and the pilot, and also checking the actual operation of the pilot, I was thoroughly convinced that there had been no mechanical failure.

It was thought advisable to simplify the system as long as there was time available by installing a bypass, which would allow the gasoline to flow around the wobble pump directly to the motor pump from the fuselage tanks, and to add [an] individual return line from the wobble pump to the center wing tank. After this installation had been made, it was checked by actually trying the flow of gasoline from each of the wing tanks to the carburetor, and by pumping with the wobble or hand pump, gasoline from the left-hand main fuselage tank to the center wing tank and allowing it to equalize itself into the right and left-wing tanks, thereby checking the feasibility of using practically all of the gasoline in the fuselage tank by flowing them through the gravity tank to the carburetor. This system necessitated thorough understanding of the hook-ups of all the gas lines and shut-off valves, as well as the method of functioning of both the motor and the wobble pump. It would be quite possible and highly probable that unfamiliarity with the system would cause a failure because the right shut-off valves were not operated properly and [this] seems more likely to have happened than an actual mechanical failure.

The operation of the motor pump in taking gasoline from the main tanks when checked before the flight was doubtful, but it was not deemed that a change was necessary, as we knew that with the proper handling of the gas valves, it was entirely possible to use the main gas supply by putting it through the center section as before described. Unless the wobble pump actually broke and would no longer pump gasoline, or unless there was an actual breakage or leak in the gas lines, it would seem to me to be an injustice to the aviation industry as a whole, and to the reliability of this particular machine, or of the mechanics who made the installation to give publicity to the fact that the return landing or the forced landing was caused by failure of any part of the gasoline system. It would seem that a fair statement to all concerned and one that would be more nearly correct would be that lack of familiarity with the system was the cause of its failure to function.[12]

From what Cramer reported, Erwin could replace his fuel system after every long flight and the results would probably be the same. There were too many gas tanks and pumps with separate lines and control valves, and Erwin never had time to learn how to effectively operate an intricate new system that was different from that originally installed by the Swallow Airplane Company.[13]

Captain Erwin spent August 12 consulting with his navigator, Alvin Eichwaldt, while his mechanics were working over *Dallas Spirit*. They installed a new earth inductor compass from one of the airplanes that was originally entered in the race, *Miss Hollydale*, but which withdrew at the last moment. In a Dallas meeting, sponsors J. Perry Burrus and Clarence R. Miller, who were already at the Oakland airport, were given full authority to act on behalf of the sponsors of Erwin's trans-Pacific flight. Burrus, however, was called away to Los Angeles on business, while Miller had to leave to visit his family in Yellowstone National Park, both missing the actual start of the race on the 16th.[14]

By August 13, Lone Star Bill Erwin had lost his fifth place in the starting lineup in the Dole race when John (Auggy) Pedlar's *Miss Doran* passed the Department of Commerce tests and was certified by the starting committee. "After all," said Eichwaldt, "a few minutes' difference in the hop-off, or even the difference of a few hours, will make no real difference. The race is partly one of speed, of course, but a great factor also is keeping straight on the course. In fact, this is the greatest factor."[15]

The mechanics had also installed a small window on the fuselage right side, just under the rear side of the right wing, a small window in the bottom from which the navigator could drop smoke bombs to determine wind drift, and a chart table in the fuselage behind the pilot's seat. Another former 1st Aero Squadron observer, 1st Lt. Charles Arthur Henry, arrived to help. Henry went to the Army post at the Presidio in San Francisco and borrowed two Very pistols and a couple of dozen rounds of ammunition for Erwin. Someone had stolen his original Very pistols from the cockpit of *Dallas Spirit* when it was in Dallas. Erwin and Eichwaldt could theoretically use these if forced down in the Pacific at night and they wanted to fire a flare to mark their location.

On August 14, two more entrants in the Dole race were qualified for the race, seven of the nine having already qualified, leaving only *Dallas Spirit* and *City of Peoria* to qualify on August 15. But then the *City of Peoria* was disqualified by the starting committee after the Department of Commerce reported that it did not have sufficient gasoline capacity to complete the trip. Eddie Blom changed the fuel system gas lines in *Dallas Spirit* one more time. W. M. Stearman, an engineer from the Swallow Aircraft Company in Wichita, said that the fuel lines were originally installed exactly as Charles Lindbergh had in his *Spirit of St. Louis* for his first solo nonstop transatlantic flight three months previously, and that they should not have been changed in Dallas. Even Captain W. C. Parkins, government inspector of aircraft and engines at the Department of Commerce, told Erwin on August 15 that he did not understand how he had flown from Dallas to Oakland with the fuel lines installed as they were when *Dallas Spirit* first landed there. He agreed with Inspector Cramer, but even though Lone Star Bill qualified that morning, leaving Erwin in last place, his knowledge of how to operate the complex system had not improved.[16]

At 12:38 p.m. on August 16, Erwin made a successful takeoff in *Dallas Spirit*, with 410 gallons of gas but no radio, the eighth and last aircraft in the contest to leave, 38 minutes behind *Oklahoma*. However, *Dallas Spirit* returned to the airport with fabric ripped from the fuselage at 1:10 p.m. The window cut in the bottom of *Dallas Spirit* had either broken or swung open while they were out over San Francisco Bay. This allowed a whirlwind of air to come inside the fuselage, resulting in the fabric from the tail nearly halfway up to the cockpit being torn off. Erwin had to turn around and successfully land *Dallas Spirit* with 325 gallons of gasoline still onboard, the heaviest load ever brought down safely in a single-motored airplane.[17]

This was the fuselage fabric tear after wind tore open the trap door on *Dallas Spirit*, creating a wind tunnel and aborting their Dole Air Race opportunity. (Courtesy of San Diego Air and Space Museum, Dole Air Race)

While the repairs were being made, *Woolaroc*, piloted by Art Goebel, reached Wheeler Field, 25 miles outside Honolulu in Hawaii, on August 17 at 12:23 p.m., after a flying time of 26 hours, 17 minutes. *Aloha*, piloted by Martin Jensen, arrived there at 2:22 p.m., after a flying time of 28 hours, 16 minutes, for second place. Two others—*Miss Doran* and *Golden Eagle*—had apparently disappeared. On August 18, National Airways, whose entry *City of Peoria* had been disqualified from the Dole race, filed a protest with the Department of Commerce in Washington. Their grievance was that under the rule of a 15 percent safety margin, *Golden Eagle* should have carried 397 gallons of gasoline but left with only 350 gallons on August 16. Applying the same Department of Commerce criteria of 13 gallons gasoline consumption per hour, and a cruising speed of 90 mph, they had disqualified *City of Peoria* due to its limited 368-gallon fuel capacity. Did the organizers unintentionally not check *Golden Eagle* as it was being fueled, and it later ran out of gas? While the fabric was being repaired on *Dallas Spirit*, Erwin purchased the radio set with which the monoplane *Oklahoma* had been equipped, to be installed in his aircraft. Colonel Easterwood sent the following telegram to Erwin:[18]

> For the sake of Dallas am willing to waive Beaumont stop, first Oakland hop from San Francisco, in attempted Dole flight, and for third and last time offer you $25,000 for hop to Hongkong [*sic*] China, with stops at Honolulu and Tokyo, and will require only 250 hours' time. Other original terms of contract hold good.

W. E. Easterwood.
The original offer for $25,000 for a Dallas to Hongkong flight still stands.

Even though the National Aeronautical Association had already disqualified Erwin for this prize, Easterwood said that the fund would not be handled by the National Aeronautical Association and would just be a private agreement between himself and Lone Star Bill. "If Erwin makes the trip from San Francisco and anybody wants to enter the original contest starting from Dallas, there will still be $25,000 for him if he can meet the terms. The new offer to Captain Erwin is just a little side show of my own," said Easterwood.[19]

Lone Star Bill had originally planned to leave mid-afternoon on August 18, but the Navy Department postponed his rescue flight until mid-afternoon the following day. Colonel Easterwood, however, sent another telegram to him on the evening of August 18, saying: "Dallas wants hop to Hongkong [sic]. My personal offer expires Friday 6 p.m., Dallas time, if you have not hopped." Easterwood further explained that this offer did not conflict with his original

August 17–18, 1927, mechanics have finished repairing the fabric on the starboard fuselage side. The fabric roll appears to be waiting to be cut underneath the fuselage at the trap door, while mechanics work on the engine. Dallas investors C. R. Miller and J. Perry Burrus meanwhile anxiously look on, since two of the six planes that had taken off successfully on August 16 were already down in the Pacific. Erwin and Eichwaldt were determined to join the search for the missing crews and were just waiting for *Dallas Spirit* to be repaired. (Courtesy of San Diego Air and Space Museum, Dole Air Race Album, "C. W. Hobson Extends Greetings to Erwin," *Dallas Morning News*, August 8, 1927, 7)

offer of $25,000 for a flight from Dallas to Hong Kong within 300 hours, with stops at San Francisco, Honolulu, and Tokyo, which was being handled by the National Aeronautical Association. Further inducement to make the flight was the $10,000 reward offered by James D. Dole for discovery of the occupants of either of the lost airplanes, or $20,000 for discovery of both crews. William F. Malloska of Flint, Michigan, backer of the airplane *Miss Doran*, also offered a reward of $10,000 for the recovery of the occupants of that plane, dead or alive.[20]

Captain Erwin replied with a telegram from Alameda that Friday before he left: "If my comrades have been found by the time I reach Honolulu I will make the attempt. Otherwise I will continue in the search for them." He thanked the colonel for his kind and generous offer and sent best regards. Easterwood wired in reply, commending Erwin for his desire to help his fallen comrades, expressed his heartiest support of this undertaking, and advising him to "show the people of Dallas, the city of your sponsors, that you can make it." If Erwin and Eichwaldt did not locate the missing flyers, and the huge armada of naval and merchant vessels also did not sight them by the time they reached Honolulu, they planned to have *Dallas Spirit* refueled, its engine examined, and then return to the mainland along a different route from that taken on the westward trip, starting within a few hours of their arrival.[21]

Lone Star Bill and Al Eichwaldt left on their final flight, their errand of mercy, from Oakland at 2:15 p.m. Pacific time on August 19. *Dallas Spirit* carried 480 gallons of gasoline and a gross load of 5,600 lb. on takeoff, the heaviest load any single-motored airplane up to that time had ever pulled into the air. The 15,000–20,000 spectators, gathered to witness the takeoff, cheered as *Dallas Spirit* slowly gained enough speed at the 5,000-foot mark for daylight to appear under its wheels. Soon thereafter, Eichwaldt started sending radio flashes; he could send messages but not receive them.

After leaving Oakland Field, Erwin rose to an altitude of 1,700 feet. If he kept flying at that altitude, he would have had the stars and the horizon to guide him in steering the plane, even if his instrument lights failed, as they did fail. But as soon as he reached the area overcast by low-hanging clouds, Erwin dropped down and flew under the clouds so he could see the surface of the water. He was on a mission of mercy, and his duty, as he saw it, was to seek the missing aviators, believed to be adrift in the Pacific.

Their radio reports said that by 2:50 p.m., *Dallas Spirit* was flying at 300 feet under the cloud strata. At 3:49 p.m., they were at 500 feet, with the clouds just above them at 700 feet. The last message giving their altitude was at 7:10 p.m., when they were flying at 900 feet, where it was partly cloudy

On August 19, 1927, Lone Star Bill Erwin, wearing the same oil-stained light gray suit that he was wearing when he landed at Oakland on August 11, folds up a tarp that was covering his engine or windshield as a gasoline truck behind and to the right tops off his tanks. Note the device at his feet that he had become so dependent upon—his wobble pump. (Courtesy of San Diego Air and Space Museum, Dole Air Race album)

with a smooth sea and visibility about 30 miles. Erwin knew he was in serious danger flying at that altitude but disregarded the risk, for he felt his duty was to scan the surface of the ocean. At 8:00 p.m., he radioed that it was getting dark and that they would not be able to see much until morning. Hence, for the next hour he could not see what he was flying into. Their last message said: "9:02 p.m. we went into a tailspin—SOS—belay that—we came out it but were sure scared. It was a close call. We thought it was all off, but we came out of it. The lights on the instrument board went out and it was so dark that Bill couldn't see the—we are in a spin—SOS."[22]

The missing word may well have been "horizon." Pilots learn from early training that if they are unable to see the horizon or other reference points around them—as can occur over water at night and in situations where visibility is limited—they must trust only their instruments and not their senses. This is because the senses easily become confused and convey to the pilot false information, leaving the pilot having to completely focus on his instruments as his only available mechanism for survival. Lone Star Bill apparently lost his sense of spatial awareness in the dark below the clouds, not being able to see anything on which to focus, the instant he was deprived of his instrument lights. At that point he literally lost the ability to distinguish the difference between up and down. Due to his state of spatial confusion, although Eichwaldt knew this to be a spin, Erwin may have unknowingly fallen into the spin, the sound of *Dallas Spirit*'s engine racing during the rapid descent possibly his only indication that things were not right.[23]

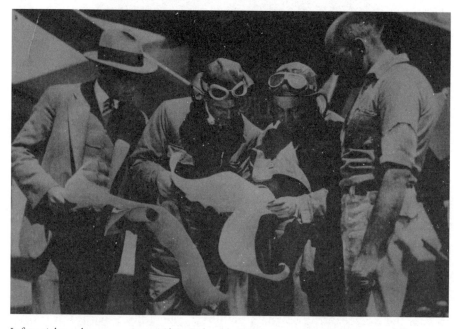

Left to right: unknown, navigator Alvin Eichwaldt, Bill Erwin, and Ralph Heintz check their maps one last time before taking off prior to either the August 16, 1927, Dole Air Race or the rescue mission that followed three days later. (Courtesy of San Diego Air and Space Museum, Dole Air Race)

Although the last of the message said "SOS," radio experts pointed out that there was a possibility that *Dallas Spirit* might still be in the air if it snapped out of the tailspin from an altitude of 900 feet within a short distance of the water. In recovering from his first spin, he was still without horizon or instrument direction, this blindness precipitating the second tailspin. That one probably started at an altitude so low as to prevent straightening the plane out before it struck the water. It is likely that the second SOS call was ended as the tail of the radio antenna struck the water. Their antenna was 250 feet long, so that was the probable distance of the fall. No pilot, however skillful, could have recovered from the second spin in so short a distance, and particularly with such a load as *Dallas Spirit* was carrying. The result was most likely a nosedive into the Pacific and the probable instantaneous death of both the pilot and his navigator.

Captain Andy Southworth of Dallas later said that if Erwin had flown at a higher altitude, he would not have been in danger of a tailspin. He added that it was also too dark after 8:00 p.m. for Erwin and Eichwaldt to scan the ocean for possible traces of the missing *Miss Doran* and the *Golden Eagle*. Flying that low was not worth the risk involved, and they should have risen above the cloud layer at that point. Erwin thus took his chances purposely and knowing its hazards when he left that afternoon.[24]

The radio suddenly was silenced, and nothing more was ever seen or heard of Erwin, Eichwaldt, or *Dallas Spirit*, raising the Dole Air Race death toll to 12. The 31-year-old Erwin left behind his wife of one year, Constance Ohl Erwin, who was also pregnant at the time. He also left behind a parting message for his sponsors, which the *Dallas Morning News* published on August 21, 1927:[25]

> Tomorrow brings the great adventure. Flying personifies the spirit of man. Our bodies are bound to the earth; our spirits are bound by God alone, and it is my firm belief that God will guide the course of *Dallas Spirit* over the shortest route from the Golden Gate to the Isle of Oahu. I want to thank each and every sponsor for the opportunity of doing this thing. If we succeed, it will be glorious.
>
> Should we fail, it will not be in vain, for a worthy attempt could never result in a mean failure.
>
> I believe with my whole heart that we will make it. I believed in it when I first conceived it, and I believe it more strongly now. We will win because *Dallas Spirit* always wins.
>
> But if it be His will that we should not make it, and from the exploration of the Pacific we should suddenly be called upon to chart our course over the Great Ocean of Eternity, then be of good cheer. I hold life dear, but I do not fear death. It is the last and most wonderful adventure of life. If something should happen to me, I know I don't have to ask you to look after Mrs. Erwin. It broke her heart that she could not accompany me. She is my life, gentlemen, and the sweetest, finest, truest girl the Almighty ever created.

Captain Bill Erwin lifts *Dallas Spirit* off from Oakland for his final journey, along with navigator Alvin Eichwaldt and 480 gallons of gasoline, at 2:15 p.m. Pacific time on August 19, 1927. (Courtesy of San Diego Air and Space Museum, Dole Air Race Album)

> Knowing that she is safe gives me confidence and vigor for the trial. We will make it because we must, but whatever comes, I am the master of my fate and, God willing, the captain of my soul.
> William P. Erwin[26]

Constance Erwin gave birth to a son on October 12, 1927, and named him Bill (William Portwood Erwin, Jr.).

Erwin had finally tempted fate once too often and ultimately lost his life due to several contributing factors. Although he hired the best help, such as Eddie Blom, he put too much trust in their work without checking the details himself, such as the "trap door placed in the bottom of the navigator's cabin [that] had been attached insecurely, permitting the wind to rush through and rip the cloth off the bottom of the fuselage," soon after leaving Oakland Municipal Airport on August 16. *Dallas Spirit's* fuel system had been extensively modified in the two weeks since he acquired it from the Swallow Airplane Company, and the amount of flight time he had in the airplane was minimal, especially at night, certainly not enough to learn how to successfully operate this hybrid fuel system, as cited by federal inspector Cramer. Erwin used poor judgment in not rising above the cloud layer at 8:00 p.m. when he could no longer see the ocean surface, had no visual horizon nor previous flying experience over the Pacific, and knew that he risked instrument panel failure in that situation.

He was under enormous pressure from William E. Easterwood, Jr. and his Dallas sponsors to attempt the Dallas to Hong Kong flight, which masked his desire to aid in the rescue of any possible survivors of the Dole Air Race. The farthest that Erwin had previously flown *Dallas Spirit* without a serious mishap was approximately 1,300 miles between Love Field in Dallas and Beaumont, California, but then he faced a 2,400-mile trip between Oakland airport and Honolulu. Having seen so much death in France during World War I, he did not grasp the gravity and enormity of the loss and potential death of so many other Dole Air Race participants, perhaps with the mindset that this was just another hazardous mission for the "unkillable."

Finally, he placed too much emphasis on searching for Dole Air Race survivors; even though he may have been the most experienced pilot in the race, he did not have experience in flying such a heavily loaded airplane, extensively modified from the manufacturer's specifications, over an ocean at low altitude in the dark. Experts nevertheless told Erwin that *Dallas Spirit* was a superior airplane to that of the *Spirit of St. Louis*, and that it was the best-designed and best-equipped plane in the Dole race. But that assumption was made without considering the unknown effect of *Dallas Spirit*'s extensive modifications and the pilot's ability to adapt to them. Charles Lindbergh flew the *Spirit of St. Louis* some 3,600 miles from Roosevelt Field, Garden City, New York, to Paris on May 20–21, 1927, with 450 gallons of fuel in 33½ hours. However, he did not add extra fuel tanks to the *Spirit of St. Louis* as Erwin did to *Dallas Spirit*. When Erwin left on his final flight in *Dallas Spirit* on August 19, carrying 480 gallons of fuel to fly approximately 2,400 miles, he was already exceeding Swallow's design fuel specifications by 25 gallons in addition to carrying a navigator, which further hampered its flight characteristics.[27]

CHAPTER 8

Byrne V. Baucom, the Epitome of a Career Officer Serving His Country

"The Bravest Man in the American Army"

This is what Bill Erwin called Byrne V. Baucom, the former newspaper reporter who generally supplied exact written accounts of their exploits in squadron records, while Erwin became a storyteller of the same events. Baucom's career was that of a soldier with a stellar resume of postwar duty assignments, as shown below. He was highly regarded in the Army Air Service, and later Air Corps Headquarters, and was well known in the Washington, D.C. area. If

First Lieutenant Byrne V. Baucom beside Salmson 2A2 "17," probably at Weißenthurm aerodrome, where the first major snowstorm of their stay occurred on December 19, 1918. The fabric from the left fuselage has been preserved by the National Air and Space Museum in Washington, D.C. (George H. Williams via Greg VanWyngarden)

he had survived and served into World War II, as several of his cohort did, he most certainly would have been promoted to a senior officer position. His loss in 1928 was a huge blow for the Army and everyone who knew him, his funeral being accorded honors due a celebrity.

Baucom served with his 1st Aero Squadron in 1919 as part of the Third Army occupation force of the Rhineland at the former Weißenthurm aerodrome. A cable received at the War Department, Washington, D.C., on January 8 that

Captain Byrne V. Baucom with his captain bars looking barely attached to his epaulet and hat, predicating this studio portrait was probably taken in Paris soon after being promoted to captain. Also note his new pilot's wings, DSC with palm, awarded the second week of May 1919, Victory Medal bar with five battle stars, three service stripes on his left sleeve, and dark blue and white Army III Corps patch on his left shoulder. This would be consistent with his new assignment and transfer to Camp Travis, San Antonio, Texas. (Byrne V. Baucom Collection, History of Aviation Collection, Special Collections and Archives Division, Eugene McDermott Library, the University of Texas at Dallas)

year included "1st Lieut. Byrne V. Baucom" among its list of 63 American officer aces credited with five victories. On January 11, both the *Temple (TX) Daily Telegram* and *Houston Post* published this cable in an Associated Press article listing Baucom with five victories, while giving Erwin nine victories and a home address of Chicago. However, their final compilation of confirmed victories in the AEF First Army Air Service, as of May 26, credited Baucom with three victories. The announced date of Baucom's second DSC was May 10. On May 12, the squadron moved to Colombey-les-Belles aerodrome in France. The date that he received his pilot's wings is unknown, although a studio portrait shows him wearing Air Service pilot's wings, captain's bars, DSC with palm, Victory medal bar with five battle stars, and Third Army shoulder patch. Previous photographs had shown him still wearing his observer's badge, Lieutenant's bar, and Air Service shoulder patch, so it is likely that the studio portrait was taken to celebrate his promotion to captain, which may have gone hand-in-hand with earning his pilot's wings. This would then date the studio portrait to the second week of May 1919 while still in Germany, prior to his return to America in August, when he was stationed back in San Antonio at Camp Travis. At the end of the war, flying officers who wanted to remain in the Air Service to make it a career were allowed to do so. However, career commissions in the Regular Army required written examinations, which did not begin until July 7, 1920. On November 8, Captain Baucom was discharged from the Army. There was a banquet held in his honor at the Gunter Hotel in San Antonio on the previous Thursday night. Five aces were among the 15 guest officers who attended his farewell party: Maj. Reed Chambers (seven victories), Capt. Clayton Bissell (six victories), Capt. Arthur "Ray" Brooks (six victories), Capt. Harvey Weir Cook (seven victories), and squadron mate 1st Lt. Arthur Easterbrook.[1]

On April 7, 1920, Baucom partnered with his old squadron mate Bill Erwin and W. R. Holcomb to charter the Aero Auto Club of Dallas corporation in Austin. After the primary election held on July 24, the Texas Election Bureau certified that Baucom was nominated, with no opposition, for Place 1 (of two) in the Texas House of Representatives for District 55 from Waxahachie. In the general election on November 2, he was elected to the Texas Legislature as one of the two Waxahachie Representatives from Ellis County for Legislative District 55. Baucom, however, resigned a month after the election. The *San Antonio Express* reported that he resigned to accept a commission in the Army Air Service. On December 6, the acting governor authorized a special election to be held in Ellis County on January 8, 1921, for the purpose of filling the vacancy.[2]

Baucom married Corinne Connor of Lexington, Lee County, Texas, in January 1921. He then re-entered the Army Air Service, assigned to Kelly Field, and attended the 1st Pursuit Group's January 31–February 4 scheduled flight training. Practicing group echelon, cross-country, and balloon attack formation flying, and flying patrols over a delineated battle sector, helped train him to assume command of the 94th Aero Squadron at Kelly Field on March 19 as a permanent captain. This Regular Army promotion showed that he had not lost seniority even after leaving the Air Service for over a year. On March 26, Kelly Field announced that Captain Baucom would soon teach a one-hour lecture on liaison with other arms of the Air Service. During the week of April 9, he took a five-day leave of absence. On May 16, Baucom was part of a contingent of five captains, 40 first lieutenants, 43 cadets, and 290 enlisted men of the 49th (Pursuit) and 96th (Bombardment) Squadrons, commanded by Maj. Henry J. F. Miller, that was sent to Langley Field, Virginia, by train to take part in naval ordnance tests between the Air Service and the Navy in the vicinity of Langley Field from June 20 to July 21. On November 9, Baucom led a formation of seven SE-5s at Ellington Field to demonstrate the method of pursuit bombing, using dummy bombs, developed at Langley Field during their June–July maneuvers. He and 10 first lieutenants who had recently returned from temporary duty at Langley Field were cited for their participation in the bombing maneuvers at Chesapeake Bay. While there, the 1 Brigade sank the hulk of the battleship *San Marcos* (6-22-21), the captured German submarine U-117, the destroyer G-102 (7-13-21), the armored light cruiser *Frankfort* (7-18-21), and the German battleship *Ostfriesland* (7-21-21). Their practice bombing of decommissioned Navy ships extended into September, when they took part in the sinking of the old battleship USS *Alabama* from the 23rd to the 25th.[3]

On January 21, 1922, the 94th Squadron was made a training squadron, where student pilots received their pursuit training at Ellington Field, and Captain Baucom was still the commanding officer. On February 4, he led a formation of three pursuit formations of five SE-5s apiece, composed of student pilots, during a review at Ellington Field. On March 14, Baucom was the acting group commander at Ellington Field and flight commander of Flight 1, as he led nine flights during an exhibition of dummy bomb dropping and machine-gunning on ground targets, for an aerial review in honor of Major General Mason M. Patrick, Chief of the Army Air Service. In mid-July, Baucom was commanding officer of the newly formed 39th (School) Squadron, which then consisted of three officers and 98 enlisted men, all of whom were formerly of the 1st Group (Pursuit). His first order of business was scheduling a series of three lectures on pursuit aviation to the reserve officers at Kelly Field, where Baucom had been transferred back to. In September he became director of pursuit training at the Advanced Flying School, Kelly Field. By October 7, he had been transferred to the 43rd (School) Squadron and took a weekend cross-country flight to Brenham, Texas. His students were also taking cross-country flights that same weekend, but they were going to fly to Austin instead, 76 flight miles west, and then attend a University of Texas football game.[4]

On April 24, 1923, Baucom took over as commanding officer of the 41st (School) Squadron at Kelly Field.[5]

In 1925, on May 24, Captain Baucom dropped poppies from a plane near the Francis Scott Key Bridge in Washington, D.C., in memory of airmen who died in World War I, during Memorial Day services conducted in conjunction with the National Woman's Relief Corps. On October 31, the American

As announced on May 10, 1919, 1st Lieutenant Baucom, wearing a Third Army shoulder patch, is presented with his Oak Leaf Cluster while standing alongside 1st Aero Squadron Salmson 2A2 1279 "7." (Richard T. Pillings album, National Air and Space Museum via Alan D. Toelle)

Society for Promotion of Aviation included "B. V. Baucom" in its list of 52 American aces from "official records." However, this list did not correspond with either the War Department's first January 8, 1919, list of 63 aces or the AEF First Army Air Service final compilation of May 26, 1919. Working in the Office of the Chief of the Air Service, he was one of the first of 73 witnesses scheduled to testify at the Emory Building on November 2 and the following week, when the general court-martial of Colonel (his permanent rank) William L. (Billy) Mitchell reopened. Mitchell was ultimately convicted of insubordination and resigned from the Air Service.[6] Illinois Representative Frank R. Reid, chief civilian defense counsel, examined Baucom in court on the afternoon of November 7.

On May 31, 1926, Baucom again dropped poppies from an Army plane in the Francis Scott Key Bridge program, as part of Memorial Day services to honor fallen wartime airmen. Having served two years with Training and Operations in the Office of the Chief of the Air Corps, he reported at Bolling Field in Anacostia, Washington, D.C., on November 1 and was assigned to the command of the 18th Headquarters Squadron. By the following month, he was also appointed to an Air Board to examine candidates for appointment as second lieutenant in the Army Air Corps.[7]

In 1927, Captain Baucom was ordered to proceed to Brooks Field, Texas, not later than June 30 for the purpose of pursuing a special course of instruction for instructors. He was detailed for duty at March Field, Riverside, California, on September 25, as commanding officer of the 47th (School) Squadron.[8]

On May 30, 1928, Byrne Baucom was killed in an airplane crash after leading Lieutenants Byron T. Burt and passenger W. C. White in one plane, and Lt. Clinton W. Davies and passenger Capt. C. L. Mullins in a de Havilland observation plane, in a formation of three from San Antonio, Texas, to his post at March Field. After something went wrong with his motor near Douglas, Arizona, Baucom signaled his intentions to his comrades and swooped down on the field selected for the forced landing. However, he struck power lines head-on, smashing to the ground. Lieutenant Harry Leubberman, his passenger, was thrown clear as the aircraft turned over and burst into flames, but Baucom was unable to extricate himself. He was flying one of the venerable DH-4 variants, most likely either a DH-4M-1 or DH-4M-2, known to have been in active service at Kelly Field in May 1928. First flown during World War I, the Air Corps finally condemned this type three years later. By October 1931, some Air Corps flying fields were using surviving DH-4s for gunnery target practice.[9]

On June 4, 1928, 3,000 people gathered in Milford—which at the time had a population of only 1,200—to honor Capt. Byrne Virchow Baucom and pay him a final tribute. After his body arrived by train from Douglas, Arizona, at 3:30 p.m., an overhead escorting plane dropped flowers as the casket was removed from the train. Four other planes from the 366th Observation Squadron, Love Field, flew overhead, one place left blank in the five-plane formation as a final tribute to Baucom. The procession then went to the Milford Presbyterian Church for the funeral service. Members of the Freemasons, whose lodge officers were all ex-servicemen, conducted the burial service at the hillside Milford Cemetery. Although he did not have any children, Baucom left behind an extended family throughout Texas and California.[10]

The previous year, the *Evening Star* in Washington, D.C., had noted that Baucom and Bill Erwin were roommates, "inseparable companions" who:

> lived together, slept together and flew and fought together … Their duty was to harass ground troops, break up batteries and destroy lines of communications while flying at the perilously low altitude of 50 feet, with the entire German Army shooting antiaircraft, machine gun and rifle bullets at them … Their tactics were to dive down on their target, at a terrific speed, while Erwin opened fire with … his fixed gun, which fired through the propeller. Then as he pulled up in a zoom, Baucom, standing up in the back seat, poured steel-jacketed bullets into the enemy. Invariably this had the desired effect—dead, wounded and fleeing troops.[11]

CHAPTER 9

Easterbrook, Observer Ace, Army Infantry Officer to Air Force General

"He Never Wasted a Shot"

This was the tribute Bill Erwin paid to 1st Lt. Arthur Easterbrook: "I would sometimes watch him lounging in his cockpit while some enemy would be coming up. All of a sudden, he would crouch at his guns. When he did this, I knew something was going to happen to somebody. When I heard his guns begin to talk, I began to look for falling Hun planes."[1]

On March 1, 1919, the War Department, Air Service, announced that Easterbrook had been awarded a Bar for his extraordinary acts of heroism on October 8, 1918, to be worn with the DSC previously awarded on October 3, 1918:

CITED FOR DISTINGUISHED SERVICE

First Lieut. Arthur E. Easterbrook, Infantry (observer). For the following acts of extraordinary heroism in action near Exermont and Varennes, France, October 8, 1918, a bar, to be worn with the Distinguished Service Cross awarded him on October 3, 1918, is awarded. On October 8 Lieut. Easterbrook, with Lieut. Erwin, pilot, successfully carried out a mission of locating our Infantry, despite five encounters with enemy planes. During these encounters he broke up a formation of three planes, sending one down out of control; killed or wounded an observer in an encounter with another formation; and sent a biplane crashing to the ground, besides driving away a formation of two planes and several single machines. Home address, Maj. E. P. Easterbrook, father, Fort Flagler, Wash.[2]

Easterbrook soloed in April 1919 from the Weißenthurm aerodrome, significant because he did not receive preliminary flight training in France or Germany prior to this first solo flight, served with the 1st Aero Squadron until June, and Brigadier General (temporary) Billy Mitchell apparently presented his new wings. On May 16, his 1st lieutenant rank was made permanent. Easterbrook returned from France in time to be the guest of honor at a luncheon given by Sigma Chi Fraternity at the Seattle Hotel on July 1. He then spent the

German *Feldwebel* Christian Donhauser, a *Jasta* 17 19-victory ace, and 1st Lieutenant Arthur Easterbrook pose on rail car 23872, carrying Fokker 8540 (OAW), at Coblenz, Germany, in late December 1918. This was part of a train that carried 27 surrendered German airplanes to the American depot at Romorantin in France. The airplanes were all inspected at Coblenz. Two Fokkers and one Roland D.VI were assembled and test flown by Donhauser on January 1, 1919. At least 14 of the Fokker airplanes were shipped to America, five of which were present at Rockwell Field, California, on April 1, 1919, and were used by the Victory Loan Flying Circus's Far West Flight. (Richard T. Pillings album; National Air and Space Museum via Alan D. Toelle)

following week in Tacoma, Washington. From October to December, he served with the 12th Aero Squadron, assigned to Border Operations, Surveillance Group, with Headquarters at Kelly Field.[3] On November 7, 1919, the award of an Oak Leaf Cluster for his extraordinary heroism during the St. Mihiel offensive the previous year was announced. The text is almost a recitation of his previous DSC award of October 3, 1918, combined with that of his Bar award announced on March 1, 1919:

DISTINGUISHED SERVICE CROSS

ARTHUR E. EASTERBROOK, first lieutenant, infantry, observer, 1st Aero Squadron, Air Service. For extraordinary heroism in action near St. Mihiel, France, September 12, 1918. Because of intense aerial activity on the opening day of the St. Mihiel offensive, Lieut. EASTERBROOK, observer, and Second Lieut. RALPH E. de CASTRO, pilot, volunteered to fly over the enemy's lines on a photographic mission without the usual protection of accompanying battle planes. Notwithstanding the low-hanging clouds, which necessitated operation at an altitude of only 400 meters, they penetrated 4 kilometers beyond the German lines. Attacked by four enemy machines, they fought off their foes, completed their photographic mission, and returned safely.

Lieut. EASTERBROOK is also awarded an oak-leaf cluster for the following acts of extraordinary heroism in action near Exermont and Varennes, France, October 8, 1918: Lieut. EASTERBROOK, with Lieut. ERWIN, pilot, successfully carried out a mission of locating our Infantry, despite five encounters with enemy planes. During these encounters he broke up a formation of three planes, sending one down out of control, killed or wounded an observer in an encounter with another formation, and sent a biplane crashing to the ground, besides driving away a formation of two planes and several single machines. Home address, Maj. E. P. Easterbrook, father, Fort Flagler, Wash.[4]

From December 30, Easterbrook spent the next 10 days visiting his mother at Fort Worden in Port Townsend, Jefferson County, Washington.[5]

Upon his return to international border operations duty, he transferred from the 12th Aero Squadron, Surveillance Group, to the 166th Aero Squadron, Bombardment Group, also at Kelly Field. By mid-January 1920, he was on their Kelly Field polo team. Other notable polo teammates included: Maj. George Stratemeyer, who gave Erwin his field promotion to captain in April 1919; six-victory ace Capt. Clayton Bissell, 148th Aero Squadron; five-victory ace Capt. Harold Buckley, 95th Aero Squadron; five-victory ace Capt. Everett Cook, 91st Aero Squadron; and Maj. William Schauffler, Kelly Field Wing Operations Officer, but former 90th Aero Squadron CO and III Corps Observation Group. By late January, the 1st Surveillance Group Headquarters had transferred from Kelly Field to El Paso, Texas. Their attached squadrons then transferred to border stations, and their group became part of the 1st Wing. Easterbrook, along with a dozen other 166th Aero Squadron officers, conducted an artillery shoot at Fort Crockett, Texas, the group being complimented for their excellent work. However, when the Headquarters moved to El Paso, he moved with them, attached to the 104th Aero Squadron as Group Operations Officer. That move turned out to be very temporary, because by the first week of March, he decided to transfer from the Air Service back to the infantry. This move most likely transferred him

In a photograph taken in Germany in 1919, 1st Lieutenant Arthur Easterbrook and his father, Lieutenant Colonel (Associate Senior Chaplain of the Third Army) Edmund P. Easterbrook, reminisce alongside Salmson 2A2 "13," the replacement ship for the Salmson 2A2 3175 "13" Arthur flew in to gain his fifth victory on November 3, 1918. (Via Greg VanWyngarden)

from the downsizing National Army and into the Regular Army infantry. His new position was Assistant Operations Officer of the VIII Corps area, based at Fort Sam Houston, Texas, still as a 1st lieutenant.[6]

On May 5, 1920, Easterbrook married Gertrude Augustine in Denver, Colorado, his longtime girlfriend whose name was painted beneath the right-side observer's cockpit of 1st Aero Squadron Salmson 2A2 "24." On May 11, the married couple returned to Fort Sam Houston. On July 1, he transferred back to the Air Service and was promoted to captain, serving as assistant operations officer at Fort Sam Houston until November 5. During the second week of November, he oversaw a detachment of eight officers, one cadet and 10 enlisted men, working with the Coast Artillery at Fort Crockett, Galveston, Texas. He accompanied a flight of four DH-4Bs of the 1st Day Bombardment Group, complete with radios, dual generators, and armament, which took off in formation en route to Ellington Field in Houston to establish a liaison with the Coast Artillery during their 15-day artillery shoot at Fort

Crockett. The shoot ended the week of November 23, the flight having its base at Ellington Field and flying each morning to Fort Crockett, landing on the parade ground.[7]

Easterbrook was afterwards transferred to Langley Field, Hampton, Virginia, where he was commanding officer of the 50th (Observation) Squadron. He also attended the Field Officers' School during his time at Langley Field, then located at that field. On October 6, 1921, he and his wife sailed from New York for two-and-a-half months' leave in Europe, most of their time spent in Coblenz.[8]

On February 1, 1922, Captain Easterbrook left for New York on business, pertaining to assemblage of the LWF Model H Owl, an American twin-boom tri-motor biplane, which was evaluated as a bomber by the U.S. Army Air Service later that year at Langley Field.[9]

On November 12, 1924, Easterbrook was transferred, and was on duty starting December 26 as an instructor with the 116th Observation Squadron with the Organized Reserves at Spokane, Washington. It was noted that he had been an efficient commanding officer of the 50th (Observation) Squadron at Langley Field for the previous three years.[10]

Easterbrook's duty at Spokane ended on March 21, 1927, after which the Air Corps transferred him to the Advanced Flying School, Kelly Field, Texas,

Lieutenant Arthur Easterbrook prepares Benedict Crowell, Assistant Secretary of War, 1917–20, for a flight alongside Salmson 2A2 "0" at Weißenthurm aerodrome, Germany, on June 10, 1919. (Courtesy of San Diego Air and Space Museum)

where he commanded the 40th School Squadron and performed various other duties.[11]

Between May and October 1929, Easterbrook was on duty at the Training Center Headquarters as adjutant and completed all his assignments on October 28. He then left Kelly Field on a 30-day leave of absence before reporting for a tour of duty in the Philippine Islands that started on December 28. He spent most of his leave at his home in Tacoma, Washington.[12]

In mid-September 1931, he was ordered to report to the Air Corps Training Center, Duncan Field, Texas.[13] He was stationed with the 4th Composite Group at Nichols Field, Philippines, in 1932 and commanded the 2nd Observation Squadron until March 3. He then transferred to Randolph Field, Texas, serving there until 1936 and commanding the 67th Service Squadron during this time.[14]

On March 16, 1935, Easterbrook, as executive officer, was advanced to lieutenant colonel (temporary) at the Air Corps Training Center, Randolph Field. On August 1, he was promoted to major (permanent).[15]

Effective February 15, 1936, Lieutenant Colonel (Major) Easterbrook was relieved from duty and temporary rank as executive officer, Air Corps Training Center, Randolph Field, and assigned to duty in the Office of the Chief of the Air Corps, Washington, D.C., By March 1, Major Easterbrook was transferred to the War Plans and Training Division. By that time, he was one of the very few officers remaining in the Air Corps who held the official title of "ace." He transferred to Wright Field, Ohio, in May as a member of a board to study and make recommendations on military characteristics of airplanes. But then on June 8, Easterbrook left the office on an extended navigation flight, with an inspection trip to the Air Corps Tactical School at Maxwell Field, the Air Corps Training Center at Randolph Field, and the Air Corps Technical School at Chanute Field. He returned on June 19. On August 28, he left for duty as umpire and was the senior Air Corps officer at the Third Army maneuvers. He returned to his office on October 2.[16]

In 1937, Easterbrook still occasionally left the Office of the Chief of the Air Corps to get back out in the field. On April 28, along with Maj. A. W. Marriner and Maj. James A. Mollison, he inspected Kelly Field airplanes and equipment. On October 12, Easterbrook was one of four majors promoted to a temporary rank of lieutenant colonel. The temporary promotions in grade were granted to those four majors, as well as 42 other Army Air Corps officers, under provisions of a June 16, 1937, act of Congress. On December 6, Lieutenant Colonel Easterbrook attended a monument dedication ceremony

USAF studio portrait of 1st Lieutenant Arthur Easterbrook taken in 1920. (Via Greg Van Wyngarden)

at the Washington, D.C., Cathedral in memory of Lt. Norman Prince, pursuit pilot and organizer of the famous Lafayette *Escadrille*. Easterbrook was among approximately 1,000 attending statesmen, diplomats, government officials, Army and Navy officers, veterans, relatives, and friends. General John J. Pershing, representing the armies of the United States, praised Lieutenant Prince as a chivalrous hero who gave up wealth and ease for martyrdom in the name of righteousness.[17]

On May 1, 1939, Lieutenant Colonel Easterbrook was reported as one of three Air Corps officers from the Office of the Chief of the Air Corps ordered for duty as students in the 1939–40 course at the Army Industrial College in Washington, D.C. But then on September 30, 1939, he retired on account of disability, which prevented him from continuing to serve on active duty.[18]

Although the 1934 *Air Corps News Letters* have not been republished, which would provide specific details, it is known that this image shows Captain Arthur Easterbrook at the 1934 presentation ceremony of his Purple Heart award. (Via Greg VanWyngarden)

However, he was recalled to active duty on April 16, 1940, and assigned to recruiting duty in Phoenix, Arizona. He transferred to the West Coast Air Corps Training Center at Moffett Field, California, in September 1940, for duty as Chief of Staff until January 1944, when he became Commanding General, Basic Training Center No. 12, Amarillo Army Air Field, Texas. His next World War II assignment was to Denver, Colorado, where he became Chief of Staff, Western Technical Training Command, four months later. In February 1945, he was announced as commanding the Santa Ana Army Air Base, California. He was awarded the Legion of Merit in July 1945 with the following citation:

> Brig. Gen. Arthur Easterbrook, as Assistant Chief of Staff (A-1), Army Air Forces Western Flying Training Command, from November 1941 to January 1944, displayed executive ability of the highest order, which was particularly outstanding during the early growth and

vast expansion of the Air Forces Training Program. His foresight and powerful planning resulted in the smooth and efficient transition from moderate peacetime training to the greatly accelerated war-time production of flying crews. With great skill, General Easterbrook organized and coordinated training activities and tirelessly applied himself to personnel problems, effecting the ultimate use of available manpower and rendering exceptionally meritorious services in the war effort.[19]

In April 1946, he was assigned to a separation center to revert to retired status on June 30 that year. Arthur E. Easterbrook, observer ace and longtime U.S. Air Force pilot, died of a heart attack at the Veterans Administration Hospital in Long Beach, California, on July 24, 1952. He had been a paraplegic patient since January 20, 1950, following a fall from a tree while he was picking avocados at the home of friends in Santa Ana, California, where he lived. He was buried in Arlington National Cemetery on July 30.[20]

CHAPTER 10

Byrne Baucom Gets the Last Word

"There never was another fellow on earth like Bill Erwin."

So said Byrne Baucom, whose service together with Erwin and the 1st Aero Squadron during World War I encompassed so many adventures and wreaked so much havoc upon the German Army. Fame and fortune awaited Lone Star Bill, something that "Bauc" had always eschewed.

Erwin's death was nevertheless a fitting climax to a spectacular career as an aviator, as well as ending the famous team of Erwin and Baucom. Although in 1927–28 they were bestowed the sobriquet "terror of the Western Front," that phrase may bring to mind many other Allied pilots. Yet Erwin and Baucom, as well as Erwin and Easterbrook, were feared by German ground troops and were certainly the most notable two-seater crews the *Luftstreitkräfte* anticipated facing in the American sectors. Ever since the start of the St. Mihiel offensive, Erwin's Salmson "8" was the only two-seater always marked with distinctive white cowling panels aft of the exhaust collector rings. Flouting their distinctive markings, Erwin—whether with Baucom or Easterbrook—rained death and destruction upon the enemy. It remains a mystery how Erwin could on some days bring his Salmson safely home, shredded with bullets and shrapnel, and perhaps a dead or wounded observer, and then crash land other airplanes in good, clear weather on other days.

The lives of Byrne V. Baucom and Arthur E. Easterbrook, career soldiers of the highest regard, were never controversial. But Bill Erwin was an enigma: musically gifted and talented, deeply religious, full of energy, driven to succeed, and yet simultaneously having another need—acclamation for his efforts. His motivations seemed at first to be nothing more than that of a young patriotic soldier headed for war. In a January 2, 1918, letter to his father from Châteauroux, France, then Cadet Erwin wrote: "I am every day more convinced of the righteousness of our war ... The men of this war are dying that others may know the blessings of liberty and equal rights of mankind, whether weak or strong. So where is anyone who would be bold to say that the spirit of sacrifice is dead"?[1]

Then there was the other side of Bill, the side rooted in his childhood, as evidenced in another paragraph of a later letter written home during his flight training in France:

> But I was really the happiest, I think, when Mamma used to go off with me perhaps for a walk or maybe just to a separate room, and there we'd talk about things we were both interested in, and she'd tell me things and I'd tell her. I'd think then I had to amount to something, or she'd be the most terribly disappointed person in the world.[2]

His mother was at Love Field with him when he left Dallas in *Dallas Spirit* on August 10, 1927, at 6:05 p.m.[3]

Lone Star Bill Erwin was ultimately a successful businessman who perhaps allowed his past flying experience to cloud his future business judgment; a businessman who could focus on important matters of primary interest to him and leave details for others to finish. It had been that way since France in World War I, where his mechanics prepared his Salmson for battle, his squadron commander gave him the mission map to follow, and either Baucom or Easterbrook mapped the coordinates at their objectives, took photographs, dropped messages, and kept enemy planes at bay with their twin Lewis guns. That freed him to decide when to attack enemy planes he spotted, troop columns, or gun emplacements.

Many people remembered his adventures as the larger-than-life, somewhat fictionalized character from the May 1934 pulp aviation *Flying Aces* magazine depiction, literally putting into pictures the 1919 Omaha *World Herald*'s account of Erwin's last few days before the Armistice. Regardless of prior journalism accounts, it is beyond doubt that 1st Lt. William P. Erwin's volunteering for every possible mission, bringing back dead and wounded observers, with airplanes full of bullet and shrapnel holes, wrecking three Salmsons in forced landings, escaping from behind enemy lines, and having eight confirmed victories with his front gun, was simply an astounding achievement.

Endnotes

Dedication

1   Colonel William B. Mitchell, US Air Service, Americus Times-Recorder (Americus, GA), November 5, 1925, 9.

Introduction

1   History of the AEF Air Service, National Archives Microfilm Publications, series E, vol. 1, 1st Aero Squadron, 29–30, 75, 80, hereafter Gorrell's History, E–1, or the applicable series letter and volume number, and then followed by the page number, also available at fold3. com/title/80/gorrells-history-aef-air-service.
2   John Peyton Dewey, "Erwin: From the War Letters and Diaries of an American Ace," *Dallas Morning News*, part X, October 9, 1928, 11, and part XIII, October 12, 1928, 12; Gorrell's History, E–1 52, 69, 78–80.
3   "Report of Enemy Planes and Balloons Brought Down, Confirmed and Unconfirmed, July 4th to Nov. 11th," Gorrell's History, E–1, 78; "U.S. Air Service Victory Credits, World War I," *USAF Historical Study No. 133*, Historical Research Division, Aerospace Studies Institute, Air University, Maxwell AFB, AL, June 1969, iii–iv, 1–2, 8–9, 16, 19–20, 26, 52–53.

Chapter 1: William P. Erwin, Byrne V. Baucom, and Château-Thierry Offensive Operations, July 1918

1   https://en.wikipedia.org/wiki/Ryan,_Oklahoma (History); John Peyton Dewey, "Erwin: From the War Letters and Diaries of an American Ace," part I, *Dallas Morning News*, September 30, 1928, 27; Joseph A. Weisberg Papers, manuscript notes, UTD, box 10/folder 7; Sanborn Fire Insurance Map from Ryan, Jefferson County, Oklahoma, April 1904, Image 3, Library of Congress; https://www.myheritage.com/research/record-1-365433081-2-8136/lula-portwood.
2   "Local News Items," *Twice-a-Week Herald*, Amarillo, Texas, December 26, 1905, 5; "Local News," *Twice-a-Week Herald*, Amarillo, Texas, July 24, 1906, 4; Advertisement, *Twice-a-Week Herald*, Amarillo, Texas, August 17, 1906, 1; Advertisement, *Twice-a-Week Herald*, Amarillo, Texas, September 28, 1906, 1; "To Take Postgraduate Course," *Weekly Herald*, Amarillo, TX, April 11, 1907, 3; Sanborn Fire Insurance Maps from Amarillo, Potter County, Texas, July 1908, Images 14 and 17, Library of Congress.

3 "Personal Mention," *Weekly Herald*, Amarillo, TX, April 11, 1907, 3; Sanborn Fire Insurance Maps from Amarillo, Potter County, Texas, November 1904, Image 3, July 1908, Image 7, March 1913, Images 16 and 21, Library of Congress; https://www.firstpres.com/history.

4 https://en.wikipedia.org/wiki/Pawhuska, Oklahoma; "Society, Presbyterian Church Men to Entertain," *Amarillo (TX) Daily News*, January 3, 1912, 5; "Society, Chapel Program," *Amarillo Daily News*, February 18, 1912, 10; "Local News," *Twice-a-Week Herald*, Amarillo, Texas, August 24, 1906, 4; Sanborn Fire Insurance Map from Amarillo, Potter County, Texas, July 1908, Image 9, Library of Congress; Dewey, "Erwin: From the War Letters and Diaries of an American Ace," part I, *Dallas Morning News*, September 30, 1928, 27; "Presbyterian Church," *Osage Journal* (Pawhuska, OK), May 2, 1912, 5; "Union Meeting," *Osage Journal*, May 9, 1912, 6; "Union Meeting," *Osage Journal*, May 16, 1912, 5; "The Methodist Church," *Osage Journal*, May 23, 1912, 5.

5 https://en.wikipedia.org/wiki/Chicago_College_of_Performing_Arts; Joseph A. Weisberg Papers, UTD, manuscript notes, box 10/folder 7.

6 "Erwin Won Fame For Valor in War," *Evening Star* (Washington, D.C.) August 20, 1927, 3; Norman Archibald, *Heaven High—Hell Deep* (New York: Albert & Charles Boni, Inc., 1935), 9–11; https://www.arlingtoncemetery.net/ehbarksdale.htm; https://www.wwiarkansas.com/sites-and-memorials/north-little-rock-history-commission; Donald M. Kingston, "The Plattsburg Movement and its Legacy," *Relevance* 6, no. 4 (Autumn 1997), also available at https://www.worldwar1.com/tgws/rel011.htm.

7 Archibald, *Heaven High—Hell Deep*, 11–19; War Dept. Memo, from General Superintendent, Army Transport Service, New York City, to Commanding General, Port of Embarkation, Hoboken, NJ, regarding SS *Megantic*, and Passenger List of Casuals, October 10, 1917, 2.

8 Gorrell's History, J–9 (Third Aviation Instruction Center, Issoudun, France), 16, 40; Dewey, "Erwin: From the War Letters and Diaries of an American Ace," part III, *Dallas Morning News*, October 2, 1928, 15.

9 Gorrell's History, J–10 (French School of Aviation, Châteauroux, France), 348, 350, 352, 354; Dewey, "Erwin: From the War Letters and Diaries of an American Ace," part IV, *Dallas Morning News*, October 3, 1928, 10.

10 Dewey, "Erwin: From the War Letters and Diaries of an American Ace," part VI, *Dallas Morning News*, October 5, 1928, 13; Gorrell's History, J–9, 24; Original National Archives, 3rd AIC. Issoudun records were copied by Alan D. Toelle.

11 Gorrell's History, J–9, 26; Dewey, "Erwin: From the War Letters and Diaries of an American Ace," part VI, *Dallas Morning News*, October 5, 1928, 13.

12 Gorrell's History, E–1 (1st Aero Squadron), 73, 79; J–9, 20, 23; M–12 (Files of Air Service Publications), Erwin specifically cited being at Field 8 and number of class graduates confirmed in "Intensive Combat Work at Field 8 Cram Full of Exciting Incidents," *Plane News* II, no. 12, February 8, 1919, 3; graduation date from 3rd AIC specifically stated in "Issoudun Products Constitute Major Portion of Flyer Aces," *Plane News* II, no. 13, February 15, 1919, 1.

13 Gorrell's History, Series I, Vol. 21 (History of American Aviation Acceptance Park No. 1 at Orly), 1, 98, 361; Dewey, "Erwin: From the War Letters and Diaries of an American Ace," *Dallas Morning News*, part VI, October 5, 1928, 13, and part VII, October 6, 1928, 21.

14 Gorrell's History, E–1, 70, 72–73; Dewey, "Erwin: From the War Letters and Diaries of an American Ace," part VI, *Dallas Morning News*, October 5, 1928, 13; Alan D. Toelle's study conducted since September 5, 2013, and 1st Aero Squadron List of Salmson Airplanes database, revised October 10, 2020 (hereafter 1st Aero Squadron Salmson data, rev. October 10, 2020).

15 Gorrell's History, E–1, 45, 77.

16 Dr. Sam H. Frank, "Air Service Combat Operations, Part 7, Operations on the Marne Salient—Château-Thierry," *Cross & Cockade* Journal 7, no. 4 (Winter 1966): 370.

17 Gorrell's History, E–1, 7, 38; 1st Aero Squadron Salmson data, rev. October 10, 2020; American Battle Monuments Commission, *American Armies and Battlefields in Europe* (Washington, D.C.: United States Government Printing Office, 1938), 36, American Operations in the Aisne-Marne Region, May 31–October 12, 1918, map, January 1, 1937; Thomas G. Miller, Jr., "Air Service Combat Organization," *Cross & Cockade* Journal 3, no. 1 (Spring 1962): 2; https://en.wikipedia.org/wiki/Francheville_Aerodrome.

18 *American Armies and Battlefields in Europe*, 36–37; The Society of the First Division, *History of the First Division During the World War, 1917–1919* (Philadelphia, PA: John C. Winston Company, 1922), 112–21.

19 *American Armies and Battlefields in Europe*, 39, 85–87, 499; *History of the First Division During the World War, 1917–1919*, 129, 136.

20 Although Gorrell's History, E–1, 7 states, "During the month of June the Squadron was equipped with Salmson airplanes," 1st Aero Squadron Salmson data, rev. October 10, 2020, indicates only one Salmson was received by the squadron prior to July 1, whereas the squadron received 17 Salmson 2A2s on July 1 and one on July 2, 1918.

21 Gorrell's History, E–1, 7–8, 12, 72, 90.

22 *American Armies and Battlefields in Europe*, 39, 87; *History of the First Division During the World War, 1917–1919*, 138.

23 https://www.utdallas.edu/library/specialcollections/hac/worldwar1/Baucom.

24 *Ibid.*; Jon Guttman, "Salmson 2A2," *Windsock Datafile* 109 (Hertfordshire, Great Britain: Albatros Productions, 2005), 5, 25; Colin A. Owers, Jon S. Guttman and James J. Davilla, *Salmson Aircraft of World War I* (Boulder, Colorado: Flying Machine Press, 2001), 22; "Reserve Officers on Furlough Will Return August 29," *San Antonio (TX) Express*, August 16, 1917, 8; "Standing of Class in Equitation is Given," *San Antonio Express*, November 22, 1917, 4.

25 Gorrell's History, E–1, 11.

26 *Ibid.* The discrepancy between Baucom's claimed arrival date of July 14 and the Squadron's official July 16 posted date is unknown.

27 Gorrell's History, E–1, 12.

28 *Ibid.*, 13.

29 Gorrell's History, N–6 (95th Aero Squadron), 10; Archibald, *Heaven High—Hell Deep*, 127–30; Dewey, "Erwin: From the War Letters and Diaries of an American Ace," part VIII, *Dallas Morning News*, October 7, 1928, 54.

30 Gorrell's History, E–1, 38.

31 Erwin logbook, Dewey, "Erwin: From the War Letters and Diaries of an American Ace," part VI, *Dallas Morning News*, October 5, 1928, 13; Notes on Weather, Northern France, June–December 1918, compiled from diaries and documents by Alan D. Toelle, September 19, 2012.

32 Erwin logbook, Dewey, "Erwin: From the War Letters and Diaries of an American Ace," part VI, *Dallas Morning News*, October 5, 1928, 13; Gorrell's History, E–1, 70, 77; Notes on Weather, Northern France, June–December 1918, compiled from diaries and documents by Alan D. Toelle, September 19, 2012.

Chapter 2: Black Thursday—1st Aero Squadron and 1st Pursuit Group's Worst Day

1   Gorrell's History, C–4 (1st Army Air Service report, September 20, 1918), 489.

2   Peter M. Bowers, "The Nieuport N.28C-I," *Profile Publications* (London & Watford, England: Hills & Lacey Ltd, 1966), 12; C. F. Andrews, "The Spad XIII C.1," *Aircraft in Profile* 1, part 2 (Garden City, NY: Doubleday & Company, Inc., 1965), 60; Guttman, "Salmson 2A2," *Windsock Datafile* 109, 36.

3   Frank, "Air Service Combat Operations, Part 7, Operations on the Marne Salient—Château-Thierry," 373–74.

4   Gorrell's History, E–1, 9, 11, 13, 77; E–6 (27th Aero Squadron), 170; *American Armies and Battlefields in Europe*, 99, American Operations in the Aisne-Marne Region, May 31–October 12, 1918, map; Dewey, "Erwin: From the War Letters and Diaries of an American Ace," part X, *Dallas Morning News*, October 9, 1928, 11.

5   Gorrell's History, E–1, 10, 75, 77.

6   Gorrell's History, E–1, 9, 13; E–6, 170, 253–54.

7   Gorrell's History, E–1, 9, 13; E–6, 253.

8   Gorrell's History, E–1, 13; E–6, 39.

9   Gorrell's History, E–6, 170; Richard Duiven and Jeffrey Sands, "The Original Flying Circus: The Combat Log of Royal Prussian *Jagdstaffel* 11," *Over the Front* 2, no. 1 (Spring 1987): 38; Bowman A. Brown, Jr., "*Jasta* 11 Revisited," *Over the Front* 2, no. 3 (Autumn 1987): 270, 273; the table holds 27th Aero Squadron Spad XIII and Nieuport 28 data by Alan D. Toelle, compiled February 19, 2017; Stephen Lucas and Alan D. Toelle, "Ten Days—Lt. Charles B. Sands, 27th Aero Squadron," *Over the Front* 19, no. 2 (Summer 2004): 106.

10 Gorrell's History, E–1, 9, 13; E–6, 252–53; William R. Puglisi, "The 27th Squadron's Black Day," *Cross & Cockade* Journal 3, no. 3 (Autumn 1962): 230–32; Greg VanWyngarden, "Richthofen's Circus" *Jagdgeschwader Nr 1* (New York, NY: Osprey Publishing, 2004), 103.

11 Gorrell's History, E–6, 252–253; VanWyngarden, *Jagdgeschwader Nr 1*, 125–26.

12 Gorrell's History, M–10 (Narratives of Experiences of Air Service Officers Who Were Prisoners of War in Germany), 192.

13 Marvin L. Skelton, "*Jagdgeschwader* Nr. 1 Pilots," *Cross & Cockade* Journal 18, no. 4 (Winter 1977): 326.

14 Gorrell's History, M–10, 314.

15 *Ibid.*; Skelton, "*Jagdgeschwader* Nr. 1 Pilots," 326; VanWyngarden, *Jagdgeschwader Nr 1*, 103; American *Armies and Battlefields in Europe*, American Operations in the Aisne-Marne Region, May 31–October 12, 1918, map; Gorrell's History, E–6, 38–39.

16 Gorrell's History, M–12 (Files of Air Service Publications), "McElvain Was 'Out of Luck' For His 'Twenty-Three Carrot' Soup," *Out of Control* 1, no. 3, December 13, 1918, 10.

17 This quotation and all information relating to this episode also found in Jon Guttman, *USAS 1st Pursuit Group* (Oxford: Osprey Publishing, 2008), 67–69.

18 *Ibid.*, 68.

19 *Ibid.*, 68–69.

20 Gorrell's History, E–6, 32, 40, 253; Skelton, "*Jagdgeschwader* Nr. 1 Pilots," 329.

21 Gorrell's History, E–1, 92; E–6, 170.

22 Gorrell's History E–1, 92; E–6, 253; *American Armies and Battlefields in Europe*, American Operations in the Aisne-Marne Region, May 31–October 12, 1918, map; https://earth.google.com/web/@49.23581085,3.52381127.

23 Gorrell's History, E–6, 253; Guttman, *USAS 1st Pursuit Group*, 67, 126; Lucas and Toelle, "Ten Days—Lt. Charles B. Sands, 27th Aero Squadron," 106; Beauchamp was later credited to *Ltn.* Lothar von Richthofen, *Jasta* 11, per Duiven & Sands, "The Original Flying Circus: The Combat Log of Royal Prussian *Jagdstaffel* 11," 38.

24 Gorrell's History, E–6, 252; Lucas and Toelle, "Ten Days—Lt. Charles B. Sands, 27th Aero Squadron," 106.

25 "Cited for Distinguished Service," *D.M.A. Weekly News Letter* I, OS 1311 (Washington, D.C.: War Dept. Air Service, February 8, 1919), 9.

26 Gorrell's History, E–6, 252; Lucas and Toelle, "Ten Days—Lt. Charles B. Sands, 27th Aero Squadron," 110.

27 Skelton, "*Jagdgeschwader* Nr. 1 Pilots," 340.

28 Gorrell's History, E–6, 252–53.

29 Gorrell's History, E–6, 40, 254.

30 Gorrell's History, E–1, 13.

31 *Ibid.*, 9.

32 *Ibid.*, 13.

33 *Ibid.*, 9.

34 *Ibid.*, 13–14.

35 *Ibid.*, 9–10; Guttman, *USAS 1st Pursuit Group*, 67.

36 Gorrell's History, E–1, 14; note that Baucom, as well as Erwin, were witnessing the descent of 1st Lieutenant Beauchamp—see table; Guttman, *USAS 1st Pursuit Group*, 67.

37 Gorrell's History, E–1, 10, 14; note that Erwin is being facetious here, as Vasconcells did not claim shooting a Fokker down in flames in his combat report; Baucom also did not say this attacking Fokker was shot down and only reported that an intervening Nieuport "drove him away."

38 Archibald, *Heaven High—Hell Deep*, 150–55; 95th Aero Squadron Spad data via Alan D. Toelle, rev. January 24, 2018; Dewey, "Erwin: From the War Letters and Diaries of an American Ace," part X, *Dallas Morning News*, October 9, 1928, 11.

39 Archibald, *Heaven High—Hell Deep*, 150–51.

40 Gorrell's History, E–1, 10.

41 *Ibid.*, 10–11.

42 *Ibid.*, 11.

43 Archibald, *Heaven High—Hell Deep*, 154–55; Dewey, "Erwin: From the War Letters and Diaries of an American Ace," part X, *Dallas Morning News*, October 9, 1928, 11.

44 *Ibid.*, 75, 90–91.

45 Gorrell's History, E–1, 70, 75; E–6, 32.

46 Gorrell's History, E–1, 78; E–6, 30, 252–54; 1st Aero Squadron Salmson data, rev. October 10, 2020; Guttman, *USAS 1st Pursuit Group*, 66–70; Norman L. R. Franks and Frank W. Bailey, *Over The Front* (London: Grub Street, 1992), 45, 77; note that Lieutenant Vasconcells' August 1 victory confirmation for a "Rumpler C" was an error and should have read "Fokker D.VII," as shown on page 45, and shared with Lieutenants Hudson and Nevius on August 1, 1918; VanWyngarden, *Jagdgeschwader Nr 1*, 103.

47 Gorrell's History, E–1, 77; Frank, "Air Service Combat Operations, Part 7, Operations on the Marne Salient—Château-Thierry," 368.

48 *American Armies and Battlefields in Europe*, 39, 73.

49 Dewey, "Erwin: From the War Letters and Diaries of an American Ace," part XI, *Dallas Morning News*, October 10, 1928, 11; Toelle, 1st Aero Squadron Salmson data, rev. October 10, 2020.

50 Dewey, "Erwin: From the War Letters and Diaries of an American Ace," part XI, *Dallas Morning News*, October 10, 1928, 11; Toelle, 1st Aero Squadron Salmson data, rev. October 10, 2020.

51 Dewey, "Erwin: From the War Letters and Diaries of an American Ace," part XI, *Dallas Morning News*, October 10, 1928, 11.

52 *Ibid.*

53 Gorrell's History, E–1, 14, 38; E–3 (12th Aero Squadron), 96; C–7 (Historical Account of the 1st Observation Group), 304; Puglisi, "The 27th Squadron's Black Day," 232–33.

54 Dewey, "Erwin: From the War Letters and Diaries of an American Ace," part XI, *Dallas Morning News*, October 10, 1928, 11; Toelle, 1st Aero Squadron Salmson data, rev. October 10, 2020.

55 Gorrell's History, N–5 (History of the 94th Aero Squadron), 451.

56 Dewey, "Erwin: From the War Letters and Diaries of an American Ace," part XI, *Dallas Morning News*, October 10, 1928, 11.

57 Gorrell's History, E–1, 38.

Chapter 3: St. Mihiel Operations and Easterbrook's Arrival

1 Gorrell's History, E–1, 39, 58; James J. Sloan, Jr., *Wings of Honor, American Airmen in World War I* (Atglen, PA: Schiffer Publishing, 1994), 310; *The Texas Spirit of '17, Ellis County, U.S.A.* (Dallas, TX: Army and Navy History Company, 1919), 34, also available at https://texashistory.unt.edu/ark:/67531/metapth20203/.

2 Olmsted, "Lieut. Arthur Easterbrook and the 1st Aero Squadron," 8–9; Franks and Bailey, *Over The Front*, 36; https://www.washington.edu/150/timeline/.

3 Olmsted, "Lieut. Arthur Easterbrook and the 1st Aero Squadron," 9; https://www.4thinfantry.org/content/division-history; https://www.army.mil/article/209676/a_look_back_at_fort_sills_early_aviation_days.

4 Olmsted, "Lieut. Arthur Easterbrook and the 1st Aero Squadron," 11.

5 *Ibid.*; "Summary of Combat Service of American Divisions in the Aisne-Marne Region," *American Armies and Battlefields in Europe*, 103.

6 Gorrell's History, E–1, 39.

7 *Ibid.*, 41.

8 *Ibid.*, 42; Dewey, "Erwin: From the War Letters and Diaries of an American Ace," part XII, *Dallas Morning News*, October 11, 1928, 15.

9 Gorrell's History, E–1, 42.

10 "A. E. Easterbrook Tells of His Work," *Seattle (WA) Daily Times*, October 25, 1918, clipping via the Arthur E. Easterbrook Collection/The Museum of Flight, page number unknown; Gorrell's History, E–3 (13th Aero Squadron), 212, 216.

11 Gorrell's History, E–3 (13th Aero Squadron), 375.

12 Dewey, "Erwin: From the War Letters and Diaries of an American Ace," part XIII, *Dallas Morning News*, October 12, 1928, 12.

13 Gorrell's History, N–23 (1st Army, St. Mihiel Offensive Summary), 4.

14 Gorrell's History, E–1, 15.

15 *Ibid.*, 16; note that Remenauville has since been renamed Limey-Remenauville, and all such villages can be viewed aerially via https://earth.google.com. Regniéville-en-Haye has since been renamed Thiaucourt-Regniéville.

16 Gorrell's History, E–1, 40; Lt. B. V. Baucom to Mrs. E. E. Baucom, Milford, TX, September 7, 1918, Byrne V. Baucom Collection, Box 1, Folder 8, UTD.

17 Gorrell's History, E–1, 40; "A History of the Activities and Operations of the 360th United States Infantry Regiment in the World War, 1914–1918," Zeltigen, Germany, April 15, 1919, www.90thdivisionassoc.org; https://earth.google.com/web/search/Villers-sous-Prény,+France.

18 Gorrell's History, E–1, 40; E–3 (12th Aero Squadron), 114; E–3 (13th Aero Squadron) 221, 382; E–8 (50th Aero Squadron), 82; "The 360 Infantry," Part II, The St. Mihiel Offensive; "A. E. Easterbrook Tells of His Work," *Seattle Daily Times*, October 25, 1918.

19 Gorrell's History, E–1, 40.

20 Gorrell's History, E–1, 43; E–5 (22nd Aero Squadron), 22, 149.

21 Gorrell's History, C–3 (Operations of Air Service, First Army—General Orders, Chief Air Service, 1st Army), (General Orders No. 7, Sept. 20, 1918) 55; E–3 (13th Aero Squadron), 394.

22 Gorrell's History, C–3 (General Orders No. 14, October 8, 1918), 64; also found in N–1 (History of Operations of 1st Army from Aug. 10–Nov. 11, 1918), 57; E–1, 43–44; N–3 (History of Balloon Operations with the 1st Army), 257, 283, 783–84; Dewey, "Erwin: From the War Letters and Diaries of an American Ace," part XV, *Dallas Morning News*, October 14, 1928, 9.

23 Gorrell's History, E–1, 43; *American Armies and Battlefields in Europe*, 143, 163.

24 Gorrell's History, N–23 (Historical Account of the Organization and Functioning of the Office of the Chief of Air Service Army Corps), Operations Order No. 1, September 14, 1918, Operations Order No. 2, September 15, 1918, 39–40; *American Armies and Battlefields in Europe*, 499, American Operations in the St. Mihiel Region, September 12–November 11, 1918, map, January 1, 1937.

25 Gorrell's History, E–1, 44; "A. E. Easterbrook Tells of His Work," *Seattle Daily Times*, October 25, 1918.

26 Gorrell's History, E–1, 44, 178.

27 *Ibid.*; Sloan, Jr., *Wings of Honor*, 319.

28 Gorrell's History, C-12 (History of the 1st Observation Group, I Corps, First Army), 305.

29 Gorrell's History, E–1, 38, 44, 59, 80; N–17, 12th Aero Squadron, 115; E–8, 90–91.

Chapter 4: Meuse–Argonne Offensive Operations

1 Gorrell's History, C–12, 9, 43.

2 *Ibid.*, 46, 49.

3 *Ibid.*, 45, 59; *American Armies and Battlefields in Europe*, 173.

4 Gorrell's History, C–10 (2nd Pursuit Group, Operations Order No. 73), 242–43; N–4 (1st Pursuit Group Operations Orders), 129–31.

5 Gorrell's History, E–3 (11th Aero Squadron), 55, 67; E–4 (20th Aero Squadron) 184, 219; C–8 (1st Day Bombardment Group), 103; C–11 (3rd Pursuit Group, Operations Orders No. 68–69), 19, 109, 111; M–38 (General Orders No. 17), 103.

6 Gorrell's History, E–1, 45; E–8, 60, 91.

7 Steve Ruffin, "'The Luckiest Man in the Army,' Milton K. Lockwood, Aerial Observer, 50th Aero Squadron," *Over the Front* 25, no. 2 (Summer 2010): 172–73.

8   Gorrell's History, E–1, 45; *American Armies and Battlefields in Europe*, Meuse–Argonne Offensive of the American First Army, September 26–November 11, 1918, map, January 1, 1937.

9   Gorrell's History, C–7 (Observation Wing of the Air Service), 117–18.

10 *Ibid.*; *American Armies and Battlefields in Europe*, 529–30.

11 Gorrell's History, C–3 (General Orders), 80; also found at N–1, 73; C–12, 9; E–1, 47, 59; N–23, First Army Corps, Chief of Air Service, September 29, 1918, Operations Order No. 12, para. 14, 59; Summary of Operations No. 20, V. Miscellaneous, 178; *American Armies and Battlefields in Europe*, Meuse–Argonne Offensive of the American First Army, September 26–November 11, 1918, map; Toelle, 1st Aero Squadron Salmson data, rev. October 10, 2020.

12 Gorrell's History, E–1, 47.

13 Gorrell's History, E–3 (11th Aero Squadron), 71; E–4 (20th Aero Squadron) 219; E–14 (96th Aero Squadron), 122; N–8 (2nd Pursuit Group, Report of Operations), 103; N–7 (1st Pursuit Wing), 158.

14 Gorrell's History, E–1, 48, 59; Toelle, 1st Aero Squadron Salmson data, rev. October 10, 2020; *American Armies and Battlefields in Europe*, Meuse–Argonne Offensive of the American First Army, September 26–November 11, 1918, map; *History of the First Division During the World War, 1917–1919*, 181; Dewey, "Erwin: From the War Letters and Diaries of an American Ace," part XVII, *Dallas Morning News*, October 16, 1928, 18.

15 Steve Ruffin, "Flying in France with the Fiftieth, 1/Lt. Floyd M. Pickrell, USAS," *Over the Front* 25, no. 2 (Summer 2010): 164.

16 Gorrell's History, E–1, 49, 66, 68, 77, 79; C–12, 9; Toelle, 1st Aero Squadron Salmson data, rev. October 10, 2020; Greg VanWyngarden, *Geschwader 'Berthold', Jagdgeschwader Nr II* (Oxford: Osprey Publishing, 2005), 108; Dewey, "Erwin: From the War Letters and Diaries of an American Ace," part XVII, *Dallas Morning News*, October 16, 1928, 18.

17 Gorrell's History, E–1, 49, 56, 59, 66; C–12, 9; N–23, Summary of Operations No. 24, I. Reconnaissance, 188.

18 Gorrell's History, E–1, 50, 70, 72–73; Dewey, "Erwin: From the War Letters and Diaries of an American Ace," part XVII, *Dallas Morning News*, October 16, 1928, 18; Toelle, 1st Aero Squadron Salmson data, rev. October 10, 2020.

19 Gorrell's History, E–1, 38, 50, 59; N–23, Summary of Operations No. 26, V. Miscellaneous, 194; Dewey, "Erwin: From the War Letters and Diaries of an American Ace," part XVII, *Dallas Morning News*, October 16, 1928, 18.

20 *History of the First Division During the World War, 1917–1919*, 201.

21 Gorrell's History, C–3 (General Orders), 83; also, N–1, 76; E–1, 50, 73, 78; Olmsted, "Lieut. Arthur Easterbrook and the 1st Aero Squadron," 16; Dewey, "Erwin: From the War Letters and Diaries of an American Ace," part XVIII, *Dallas Morning News*, October 17, 1928, 17.

22 Gorrell's History, E–1, 50, 59; *American Armies and Battlefields in Europe*, 226, 230; *History of the First Division During the World War, 1917–1919*, 204.

23 Gorrell's History, C–7 (Observation Wing of the Air Service), 103, 110; E–1, 29–30.

24 Gorrell's History, C–3 (General Orders), 66.

25 *Ibid.*, C–3 (General Orders), 80; also found in N–1, 73; Peter Gray and Owen Thetford, *German Aircraft of the First World War* (Garden City, NY: Doubleday & Company, Inc., 1970), 154–57; Dewey, "Erwin: From the War Letters and Diaries of an American Ace," part XVIII, *Dallas Morning News*, October 17, 1928, 17.

26 Gorrell's History, E–1, 51, 59; *American Armies and Battlefields in Europe*, 241–42; https://www.georgiaguardhistory.com/2018/10/september-25-october-16-1918-meuse.html; Dewey, "Erwin: From the War Letters and Diaries of an American Ace," part XIX, *Dallas Morning News*, October 18, 1928, 20.

27 Gorrell's History, E–1, 68.

28 Steve Ruffin, "'Dutch Girl' Over the Argonne, The 50th Aero Squadron in WWI," *Over the Front* 25, no. 2 (Summer 2010): 122; Toelle, 1st Aero Squadron Salmson data, rev. October 10, 2020; *American Armies and Battlefields in Europe*, 362–5.

29 Gorrell's History, E–1, 52, 78; *American Armies and Battlefields in Europe*, 181, Meuse–Argonne Offensive of the American First Army, September 26–November 11, 1918, map.

30 Gorrell's History, E–1, 19.

31 *Ibid.*, 20.

32 Gorrell's History, C–3 (General Orders), 77; also found in N–1, 70.

33 Gorrell's History, E–12 (94th Aero Squadron), 159–60, 253; Dewey, "Erwin: From the War Letters and Diaries of an American Ace," part XIX, *Dallas Morning News*, October 18, 1928, 20.

34 Gorrell's History, C–3 (General Orders), 81, 83; also found in N–1, 77; E–1, 52, 60, 78; "Captain Erwin, 'Ace', Saw Fierce Fighting," *World Herald* (Omaha, NE), April 29, 1919, 3; Greg VanWyngarden, personal communication, March 20, 2020.

35 Gorrell's History, E–1, 52; https://www.georgiaguardhistory.com/2018/10/september-25-october-16-1918-meuse.html.

36 Gorrell's History, N–23, Operations Order No. 20, 75–76; Operations Order No. 22, 80–81; Summary of Operations No. 40, V. Miscellaneous, 223–24; Dewey, "Erwin: From the War Letters and Diaries of an American Ace," part VI, *Dallas Morning News*, October 5, 1928, 13.

37 "For Immediate Release," *Air Service Weekly News Letter*, Aeronautical Information Branch, O.S. 863, October 26, 1918, 5.

38 *Ibid.*, 7.

39 *Ibid.*, 5; "A. E. Easterbrook Tells of His Work," *Seattle Daily Times*, October 25, 1918.

40 Gorrell's History, E–1, 52.

41 Gorrell's History, C–3 (General Orders), 91; also found in N–1, 84; E–1, 52–53, 60, 78; Olmsted, "Lieut. Arthur Easterbrook and the 1st Aero Squadron," 17; Dewey, "Erwin: From the War Letters and Diaries of an American Ace," part XX, *Dallas Morning News*, October 19, 1928, 15.

42 Gorrell's History, E–1, 53, 77; *American Armies and Battlefields in Europe*, 237, 239, Meuse–Argonne Offensive of the American First Army, September 26–November 11, 1918, map; Dewey, "Erwin: From the War Letters and Diaries of an American Ace," part XX, *Dallas Morning News*, October 19, 1928, 15.

43 Gorrell's History, E–1, 53; N–23, Summary of Operations No. 44, V. Miscellaneous (note that this was one of three missions dispatched for the purpose of dropping propaganda, during which a total of 3,000 sheets were dropped), 231; Olmsted, "Lieut. Arthur Easterbrook and the 1st Aero Squadron," 17.

44 Gorrell's History, C–12 (1st Army Corp Air Service), 106, (Annex No. 2 to Field Orders No. 85), 37; "Captain Baucom Dies in Airplane Crash," *Air Corps News* XII, no. 8 (Washington, D.C.: Information Division, June 5, 1928), 200.

45 Gorrell's History, E–1, 54, 60–61, 73.

46 *Ibid.*; Olmsted, "Lieut. Arthur Easterbrook and the 1st Aero Squadron," 17.

47 Gorrell's History, E–1, 55, 61.

Chapter 5: The Final Assault

1   *American Armies and Battlefields in Europe*, 186–87, 277–78; Toelle, personal communication, June 23, 2020.

2   Gorrell's History, E–1, 61; *American Armies and Battlefields in Europe*, 187.

3   Gorrell's History, E–1, 22.

4   *American Armies and Battlefields in Europe*, 276–77, 285, Meuse–Argonne Offensive of the American First Army, September 26–November 11, 1918, map; American Battle Monuments Commission, *80th Division Summary of Operations in the World War* (Washington, D.C.: U.S. Government Printing Office, 1944), 16.

5   Gorrell's History, C–7 (1st Observation Wing, Reports of Observers), 108.

6   *Ibid.*, 112; E–1, 56.

7   *American Armies and Battlefields in Europe*, 285, 287–88; *80th Division Summary of Operations in the World War*, 16.

8   Gorrell's History, E–1, 30–31.

9   *Ibid.*, Meuse–Argonne Offensive of the American First Army, September 26–November 11, 1918, map.

10   Gorrell's History, E–1, 23.

11   Gorrell's History, E–1, 24, 73, 77; M–38 (Victories and Casualties), 4.

12   Olmsted, "Lieut. Arthur Easterbrook and the 1st Aero Squadron," 18–20.

13   Gorrell's History, E–1, 61, 69, 72, 75, 77, 96; Dewey, "Erwin: From the War Letters and Diaries of an American Ace," part XXI, *Dallas Morning News*, October 20, 1928, 10.

14   Gorrell's History, E–1, 27; note that the spelling of "Fontenoy" comes from the Meuse–Argonne Offensive of the American First Army, September 26–November 11, 1918, map, as well as Baucom's report. Today, however, it is correctly spelled "Fontenois."

15   Gorrell's History, E–1, 28; C–7, 107.

16   *American Armies and Battlefields in Europe*, 289, Meuse–Argonne Offensive of the American First Army, September 26–November 11, 1918, map.

17   Gorrell's History, C–7 (1st Observation Wing, Reports of Observers), 106.

18   Gorrell's History, C–12 (Historical Account of the 1st Observation Group), 305.

19   Gorrell's History, C–7 (1st Observation Wing, Reports of Observers), 105.

20   *Ibid.*, 104.

21   Gorrell's History, C–3 (Report From 1st Corps Observation Wing, 5th November 15:30), 265; C–12 (1st Army Corps Air Service, Summary of Operations, 6 Nov.), 271, map on 308.

22   Gorrell's History, C–3, 265; *80th Division Summary of Operations in the World War*, 53–54; *History of the First Division During the World War, 1917–1919*, German divisions identified on the V Corps Front since September 26, 1918, with dates of withdrawal and sector occupied, 450.

23   Gorrell's History, E–1, 25.

24   *Ibid.*, 26.

25   Gorrell's History, C–3 (1st Army, Report from Corps Observation Wing), 268–69; Dewey, "Erwin: From the War Letters and Diaries of an American Ace," part XXII, *Dallas Morning News*, October 21, 1928, 8; https://earth.google.com/web/search/Yoncq,+France/.

26   Gorrell's History, C–12 (1st Army Corps Air Service, Summary of Operations), 271; N–17 (1st Army final reports on 1st Aero Squadron), 63; *80th Division Summary of Operations in the World War*, 53; *History of the First Division During the World War, 1917–1919*, 227–28.

27   "Milford, Texas, Soldier Awarded D.S. Cross," *Houston (TX) Post*, May 11, 1919, 3.

28   https://www.findagrave.com/memorial/26101629/byrne-virchow-baucom.

29 "Distinguished Service Cross," *Air Service News Letter* II, V–418, May 29, 1919, 4.

30 Gorrell's History, E–1, 35, 80.

31 "U.S. Air Service Victory Credits, World War I," Historical Research Division, Aerospace Studies Institute, Air University, Maxwell AFB, AL, June 1969, iii–iv, 1–2, 8–9, 16, 19–20, 26, 52–53.

Chapter 6: Postwar—Erwin's Early Return to Participate in America's Victory Loan Drive

1 https://en.wikipedia.org/wiki/1st_Reconnaissance_Squadron; "3rd Army Air Service Events" research spreadsheet, Alan D. Toelle, 2013, derived from Gorrell's History, P–2 (History of Air Service units attached to the 3rd Army).

2 Franks and Bailey, *Over The Front*, 37.

3 Gorrell's History, M–12 (Files of Air Service Publications), "Costly Honors," *Cent Soixante Six*, March 1, 1919, 3; "Aviators Receive Goodly Number *Croix de Guerre* and French Citations," *Plane News* II, no. 18, March 22, 1919, 1; "French Citations," *D.M.A. Weekly News Letter* I, V–37, March 29, 1919, 13–14; "Awards of French *Croix de Guerre*, With Palm," *Air Service News Letter* II, V-277, May 10, 1919, 6.

4 Landing Return form for SS *George Washington*, sailed from Brest January 12, 1919, List of Officers, Sheet 2; Gorrell's History, M–38 (Victories and Casualties), 4, 63.

5 "Advanced Ratings for Overseas Flying Officers for Distinguished Service," 1, "Honor Roll of the Air Service," 6, *D.M.A. Weekly News Letter* I, OS 1345, February 15, 1919; https://en.wikipedia.org/wiki/Organization_of_the_Air_Service_of_the_American_ Expeditionary_Force.

6 U.S. Treasury Department, "Report of National Woman's Liberty Loan Committee for the Victory Loan Campaign," April 21 to May 10, 1919, 34–35; "Wichita Kept Record Clear in Bond Drive," *Wichita Eagle*, May 11, 1919, 5.

7 "'Aces' to Fly for Loan," *D.M.A. Weekly News Letter* I, V–16, March 22, 1919, 7; "Air Battles Over All Big Cities in the Interest of Victory Liberty Loan Drive," *AIR SCOUT* I, no. 21 (Garden City, NY: U.S. Aviation Fields), April 15, 1919: 405.

8 "Army Aviators to Fly for Loan, Central or No. 2 Flight Personnel," *Air Service News Letter* II, V–100, April 5, 1919, 6; "War Diary, Victory Loan Mid-West Flight," p.1, April 9, 1919, boxes 1 and 2, compartment 14, row 39, stack 190, record group 18, Army Air Forces Entry NM53-135 Air Service Training and Operations Group, Training Division, Victory Loan Flight Correspondence, 1919–1920, National Archives and Records Administration, Washington, D.C. (hereafter cited as "War Diary," followed by the applicable sheet number and date).

9 "Promotions," *Air Service News Letter* 1, no. 11, December 22, 1919, 11–12.

10 Alan D. Toelle, "Wings Over America, Victory Loan Flying Circus, Far West Flight," *Over the Front* 29, no. 4 (Winter 2014): 296; "War Diary," sheet no. 12, April 16, 1919; "The Eastern Flight Victory Loan Flying Circus," War Diary (Victory Loan Eastern Flight), Executive Offices, Training Division, May 19, 1919, 1–3.

11 "Air Battles Over All Big Cities in the Interest of Victory Liberty Loan Drive," *AIR SCOUT* I, no. 21, April 15, 1919, 405.

12 "Twenty-One Aero Squadrons to be Retained," *AIR SCOUT* I, no. 21, April 15, 1919, 418.

13 Special Order No. 1, Flying Circus #2, Mid-West Flight, Ellington Field, Houston, TX, April 2, 1919, by order of Major Stratemeyer.

14 "War Diary," sheet no. 4, April 12, 1919.

15 Alan L. Roesler, "The Victory Loan Flying Circus in Memphis," *Tennessee Historical Quarterly* 73, no. 2 (Summer 2014): 122, 124–26.

16 *Arkansas Gazette*, April 14, 1919, 1; Alan L. Roesler, "Flying Under the Bridges in Little Rock," *Pulaski County Historical Review* 63, no. 1 (Spring 2015): 7–9; https:// encyclopediaofarkansas. net/entries/fort-logan-h-roots-military-post-historic-district-5807/.

17 This section previously published in Alan L. Roesler, "The Victory Loan Flying Circus in St. Louis and Kansas City, April 14 and April 30, 1919," *Missouri Historical Review* 108, no. 1 (October 2013): 52–54, 58–60; ancillary sources include "Proceedings of a Board of Officers Convened Pursuant to … Special Orders No. 169," June 21, 1919, Accident Reports, reel 46003, Belser, George M., Air Force Historical Research Agency, Maxwell Field, Alabama.

18 Lieutenant Frank Carroll's logbook, which is now in the possession of his grandson, Franklin O. Carroll, shows 50 minutes of flight time in his Spad in St. Louis. "Boy Injured at Aero Circus in Forest Park Dies," *St. Louis (MO) Post-Dispatch*, April 15, 1919, 2, shows Carroll taking off at 1:55 p.m., thus placing his return at 2:45 p.m.; J. M. Bruce, "The First Fighting Spads," *AIR Enthusiast 15* (April–July 1981): 76.

19 "10 Injured When German Airplane Crashes Into Crowd," *St. Louis Globe-Democrat*, April 15, 1919, 2, col. 5; "Boy Injured at Aero Circus in Forest Park Dies," *St. Louis Post-Dispatch*, April 15, 1919, 2; Leavitt Grimes was born on December 22, 1904; Certificate of Death, Missouri State Board of Health, Bureau of Vital Statistics, file no. 15569, buried April 18, 1919, New St. Marcus Cemetery, St. Louis.

20 "War Diary," sheet no. 10, April 15, 1919; sheet "ENROUTE," April 19, 1919.

21 Alan L. Roesler, "A Spring Day Like No Other: The Victory Loan Flying Circus Comes to Springfield, April 15, 1919," *Journal of Illinois History* 18, no. 1 (Spring 2015): 48.

22 "Yank Fliers Thrill Big Crowds With Daring 'Stunts,'" *Sunday State Journal* (Madison, WI), April 20, 1919, 13; "War Diary," sheet no. 18, April 20, 1919.

23 "War Diary," sheet no. 23, April 23, 1919; "Thrilling Dare Devil Stunts of Aerial Circus Performers Draw Interest of City Today," *Grand Forks (ND) Herald*, April 22, 1919, 1, 3.

24 Alan L. Roesler, "Flying Machine and War Bonds: The Victory Loan Flying Circus in South Dakota," *South Dakota History* 46, no. 1 (Spring 2016): 47, 51–52.

25 "Aviators in Omaha Give Thrill to Throng," *Omaha (NE) Daily Bee*, April 29, 1919, 4.

26 Alan Roesler, "Victory Loan Flying Circus at Ak-Sar-Ben Field: No Horseplay on April 28, 1919," *Nebraska History Magazine* 100, no. 1 (Spring 2019): 48–49.

27 Franks & Bailey, *Over The Front*, 20, 29, 32–33, 42, 72, 74, 82; "American 'Aces'," *Air Service News Letter* 2, O.S. 1216, January 18, 1919, 2.

28 "War Diary," sheet no. 37, April 30, 1919.

29 "Sky Extra Rains Upon Crowds," *Wichita (KS) Eagle*, May 2, 1919, 2.

30 Alan L. Roesler, "The Victory Loan Flying Circus in Wichita, May 1, 1919, and the Victory Loan Campaign That Brought It There," *Kansas History: A Journal of the Central Plains* 43, no. 2 (Summer 2020): 94–95.

31 Alan L. Roesler, "The Victory Loan Flying Circus: 'The Spectacle Was The Greatest Ever Witnessed Here,'" *Journal of the Fort Smith Historical Society* 37, no. 1 (April 2013): 31–32.

32 "War Diary," sheets no. 14–15, April 18, 1919; no. 37–38, April 30, 1919; no. 52–55, May 8–11, 1919.

33 "Aerial Acrobat, Mile Up, Fools Undertakers," *Chicago Daily Tribune*, May 10, 1919, 1.

34 "War Diary," sheet no. 54, May 10, 1919.

35 "Germans Feared Night Bombing," *Air Service News Letter* I, no. 4, October 31, 1919, 10; "Kelly Field, San Antonio, Texas, April 8," *Air Service News Letter* VI, no. 14, May 10, 1922,

10; "War Diary," sheet no. 51, May 7, 1919; sheet, no. 55, May 12, 1919; Dewey, "Erwin: From the War Letters and Diaries of an American Ace," part XXIII, *Dallas Morning News*, October 22, 1928, 6.

36 "War Diary," sheet no. 55, May 12, 1919; "18,711 Mile Tour for Flying Circus," *Air Service News Letter* II, V–372, May 24, 1919, 2; War Diary (Victory Loan Eastern Flight), May 19, 1919, 2.

Chapter 7: "Lone Star Bill" and the Dole Air Race

1 Joseph A. Weisberg Papers, manuscript notes, UTD; Gorrell's History, E–3, 4, Koons reported to the 11th Aero Squadron on November 5, 1918.

2 Joseph A. Weisberg Papers, manuscript notes, UTD; Gorrell's History, E–9, 75, Cook reported to the 88th Aero Squadron on November 2, 1918.

3 Joseph A. Weisberg Papers, manuscript notes, UTD; "New Texas Charters," *San Antonio Express*, April 7, 1920, 8; "Corporations Chartered," *Houston Post*, April 8, 1920, 7.

4 Joseph A. Weisberg Papers, manuscript notes, UTD; Gorrell's History, N–19, 125, Long reported to the 93rd Aero Squadron on August 29, 1918.

5 "Aviator and Musician Wed," *Dallas Morning News*, July 28, 1926, 7; *Dallas City Directory*, 1927 (Dallas, TX: John F. Worley Directory Co., 1927), 2006–07.

6 "Distinguished Service Cross," *Air Service News Letter* II, V–418, May 29, 1919, 4; "Erwin Famous in World War as 'Terror of Western Front,'" *Evening Star* (Washington, D.C.), August 21, 1927, 3; "Decade of Flying," *Dallas Morning News*, August 21, 1927, 4.

7 "Texas Suited As Greatest Air Center," *Texas Mesquiter* (Mesquite, TX), June 10, 1927, 1.

8 "Given Honorable Mention in Contest," *Texas Mesquiter*, August 19, 1927, 2; "Dallas Spirit Soars Away On Initial Flight," *Dallas Morning News*, August 4, 1927, 1; "Dallas Spirit Makes Record for Take-Off," *Dallas Morning News*, August 5, 1927, 1; "Captain Lands His Ship At Love Field," "How Dallas Spirit Is Built," *Dallas Morning News*, August 6, 1927, 1, 10; "Speedy Construction Marks Completion of Capt. Erwin's Plane," *Dallas Morning News*, August 7, 1927, 4; "Erwin Ready For Dole Hop," *Dallas Morning News*, August 12, 1927, 1–2.

9 "10,000 Cheer Bill Erwin at Dedication of Dallas Spirit," *Dallas Morning News*, August 7, 1927, 1, 7.

10 "Dallas Spirit Makes First Flight Here," *Dallas Morning News*, August 9, 1927, 1, 11; "Erwin Forced to Return as Engine Pump Fails to Work," *Dallas Morning News*, August 10, 1927, 1, 8; "Capt. Erwin Entered In Two Air 'Derbies,'" *Dallas Morning News*, August 10, 1927, 1.

11 "Erwin Ready For Dole Hop," *Dallas Morning News*, August 12, 1927, 2.

12 "Erwin Ready For Dole Hop," *Dallas Morning News*, August 12, 1927, 2.

13 *Ibid.*; Dewey, "Erwin: From the War Letters and Diaries of an American Ace," *Dallas Morning News*, part XXIV, October 23, 1928, 20.

14 "Sponsors With Erwin Given Full Authority," Ted Dealey, "Working Over Dallas Spirit," *Dallas Morning News*, August 13, 1927, 1, 8.

15 Ted Dealey, "Erwin Lose Derby Place," *Dallas Morning News*, August 14, 1927, 1, 16.

16 Ted Dealey "Final Test of Dallas Spirit Monday," *Dallas Morning News*, August 15, 1927, 1–2; Ted Dealey, "Dallas Spirit Ready for Gun In Air Derby," *Dallas Morning News*, August 16, 1927, 1, 8.

17 Ted Dealey, "Forced Return After Making Perfect Start," *Dallas Morning News*, August 17, 1927, 1, 12.

18 "Dole Race Facts," Ted Dealey, "Dallas Spirit Will Continue World Flight," *Dallas Morning News*, August 18, 1927, 1; "Protest Made in Dole Air Derby," *Dallas Morning News*, August 19, 1927, 8.

19 "New $25,000 Offer to Erwin," *Dallas Morning News*, August 18, 1927, 1.

20 "New Offer to Erwin Expires 6 P.M. Friday," "Erwin to Seek Missing Flyers," "Rewards Offered," *Dallas Morning News*, August 19, 1927, 1, 12.

21 "Dallas Spirit Starts Flight For Honolulu," "Erwin's First Purpose To Discover Flyers, He Wires Col. Easterwood," *Dallas Morning News*, August 20, 1927, 1, 12.

22 "Dallas Spirit Silent After SOS Call," "Radio Flashes Tell Progress of Capt. Erwin," *Dallas Morning News*, August 20, 1927, 1, 12.

23 Steven A. Ruffin, *Flights of No Return, The Night Camelot Ended* (Minneapolis, MN: Zenith Press, 2015), 84.

24 "Flying Low to Sight Those Adrift, Thinks Southworth," *Dallas Morning News*, August 21, 1927, 4.

25 "Erwin Speeds Away on His Rescue Trip," *Dallas Morning News*, August 20, 1927, 12; Dewey, "Erwin: From the War Letters and Diaries of an American Ace," *Dallas Morning News*, part XXIV, October 23, 1928, 20, and XXV, October 24, 1928, 18.

26 "Erwin Dropped 2,000 Feet At Terrific Speed to Ocean, Radio Engineer Believes," *Dallas Morning News*, August 21, 1927, 12; https://en.wikipedia.org/wiki/Dole_Air_Race.

27 "Forced Return After Perfect Start," *Dallas Morning News*, August 17, 1927, 1, 12. "To Go on to Tokyo," *Dallas Morning News*, August 18, 1927, 10.

Chapter 8: Byrne V. Baucom, the Epitome of a Career Officer Serving His Country

1 Gorrell's History, M–38 (Individual Victory List, Confirmed Credits), 51; Stacy C. Hinkle, "Wings Over the Border, The Army Air Service Patrol, 1919–1921," *American Aviation Historical Society* 17, no. 4 (Winter 1972): 262; "American 'Aces'," *Air Service News Letter* 2, O.S. 1216, January 18, 1919, 2; "Rickenbacker the Premier U.S. Ace," *Temple (TX) Daily Telegram*, January 11, 1919, 1; "Three Texans Win Title of 'Ace'," *Houston Post*, January 11, 1919, 1; "Milford, Texas, Soldier Awarded D.S. Cross," *Houston Post*, May 11, 1919, 3; "American Ace Will See Regular Army Service," *Daily Herald* (Weatherford, TX) August 26, 1919, 1; "Capt. Baucom Honored By His Brother Officers," *San Antonio Express*, November 7, 1919, 11.

2 "Corporations Chartered," *Houston Post*, April 8, 1920, 7; "New Texas Charters," *San Antonio Express*, April 7, 1920, 8; "Eight Run-Offs Needed to Settle Lawmakers' Race," *San Antonio Express*, August 8, 1920, 66; "Special Election Authorized," *San Antonio Express*, December 7, 1920, 5.

3 Hinkle, "Wings Over the Border, The Army Air Service Patrol, 1919–1921," 264; "Squadron News," *Air Service News Letter* V, no. 14, April 12, 1921, 13; "Squadron News," *Air Service News Letter* V, no. 15, April 15, 1921, 8; "Squadron News," *Air Service News Letter* V, no. 17, April 29, 1921, 18; "Squadron News," *Air Service News Letter* V, no. 22, June 10, 1921, 17; "Squadron News," *Air Service News Letter* V, no. 44, December 9, 1921, 16; http://www:waruntold.com/stories/frank_white.php; see photographs of these ships during bombing maneuvers at San Diego Aerospace Museum, Photostream, 1509, https://www.flickr.com/photos/sdasmarchives/with/.

4 "Squadron News," *Air Service News Letter* VI, no. 5, February 20, 1922, 19; "Squadron News," *Air Service News Letter* VI, no. 7, March 9, 1922, 12; "Squadron News," *Air Service News Letter* VI, no. 24, August 29, 1922, 13; "Squadron News," *Air Service News Letter* VI, no. 32, November 16, 1922, 13; "High Wind Delays Arrival of Chief of U.S. Air Service," *Houston Post*, March 14, 1922, 1.

5 "Squadron News," *Air Service News Letter* VII, no. 11, June 4, 1923, 17.

6 "Planes to Drop Poppies," *Sunday Star* (Washington, D.C.), May 24, 1925, Part 1, 32; photograph, *Evening Star* (Washington, D.C.), October 31, 1925, 16; "52 Aviators Are Rated As Aces," *Sunday Star* (Washington, D.C.), November 1, 1925, Part 1, 28; "Crisis in Mitchell Case May Be Near," *Sunday Star* (Washington, D.C.), November 8, 1925, 5; John J. Pershing, *My Experiences in the World War* (New York: Frederick A. Stokes Company, 1931), 260; William Mitchell, United States Army General, https://www.britannica.com/biography/William-Mitchell.

7 "Notes From Air Corps Fields," *Air Corps News* X, no. 16, December 13, 1926, 23; "Key Bridge Rites For Dead Flyers," *Evening Star* (Washington, D.C.), May 31, 1926, 3. "Air Board Named," *Evening Star* (Washington, D.C.), December 11, 1926, 9.

8 "Army and Navy News," *Sunday Star* (Washington, D.C.), May 8, 1927, Part 3, 11. "Air Corps Officers Under Orders For March Field, Calif.," *Air Corps News* XI, no. 13, October 15, 1927, 298.

9 "Capt. Baucom Dies in Crash; Terrorized Enemy in War," *Evening Star* (Washington, D.C.), May 31, 1928, 2; "Flier Burned to Death When Plane Crashes," *San Bernardino County Sun*, May 31, 1928; "San Antonio Air Depot, Duncan Field, Texas, May 17th," *Air Corps News* XII, no. 8, June 5, 1928, 216; "San Antonio Air Depot, Duncan Field, Texas, June 16," (listing airplanes overhauled and repaired during May by the Engineering Department), *Air Corps News* XII, no. 10, July 10, 1928, 266; per these reference sources, the DH-4 variants then operating at Kelly Field in May 1928 included the DH-4M-1, DH-4M-1T, DH-4M-2, and DH-4M-2T; "Mather Field Boys Average High in Shooting," *Air Corps News* XV, no. 12 (Washington, D.C.: Information Division, October 17, 1931), 354; http://dmairfield.org/people/burt_bt/index.html.

10 "Milford Pays Baucom Honor," *Dallas Morning News*, June 4, 1928, 3; also see http://www.tshaonline.org/handbook/entries/milford-tx.

11 "Erwin Famous in World War as 'Terror of Western Front,'" *Evening Star* (Washington, D.C.), August 21, 1927, 3.

Chapter 9: Easterbrook, Observer Ace, Army Infantry Officer to Air Force General

1 Dewey, "Erwin: From the War Letters and Diaries of an American Ace," part XVII, *Dallas Morning News*, October 16, 1928, 18.

2 "Released for Afternoon Newspapers of Saturday, March 8, 1919," *D.M.A. Weekly News Letter* I, OS 1393, March 1, 1919, 7.

3 "Lieut. Easterbrook Honor Guest," *Seattle Star*, July 2, 1919, 8; "Personal," *Seattle Star*, July 9, 1919, 8; "Border Situation," *Air Service News Letter* I, no. 7, November 22, 1919, 1; "Retirement of Major Easterbrook," *Air Corps News Letter* XXII, No. 20, October 15, 1939, 17.

4   "Awards of Distinguished Service Cross," *Air Service News Letter* III, no. 12, November 7, 1919, 9.

5   "Lt. Easterbrook, Seattle Ace, Here Visiting Mother," *Seattle Star*, December 30, 1919, 3.

6   Olmsted, "Lieut. Arthur Easterbrook and the 1st Aero Squadron," 21; "Kelly Field Organizes Polo Team," *Air Service News Letter* III, no. 22, January 15, 1920, 6. "Officers of the 166th Aero Squadron Complimented for Excellent Work in Conducting Artillery Shoot at Ft. Crockett, Texas," *Air Service News Letter* IV, No. 5, January 27, 1920, 3–4; "Lieut. Arthur E. Easterbrook Transferred to the Infantry," *Air Service News Letter* IV, No. 11, March 9, 1920, 16; "Retirement of Major Easterbrook," *Air Corps News Letter* XXII, No. 20, October 15, 1939, 17.

7   "Squadron News," 11, "Ellington Field, Houston, Texas," 15, *Air Service News Letter* IV, No. 41, November 9, 1920; "First Day Bombardment Group Cooperation With Coast Artillery," *Air Service News Letter* II, No. 38, November 20, 1920, 10; Wedding announcement, 1920, https://digitalcollections.museumofflight.org/collections/show/29157; "Retirement of Major Easterbrook," *Air Corps News Letter* XXII, No. 20, October 15, 1939, 17.

8   "Squadron News," *Air Service News Letter* V, no. 32, August 24, 1921, 9; "Squadron News," *Air Service News Letter* V, no. 37, October 19, 1921, 15.

9   "Squadron News," *Air Service News Letter* VI, no. 6, February 28, 1922, 19; a comprehensive history of this airplane is at: https://oldmachinepress.com/2019/03/20/lwf-model-h-owl-mail-plane-bomber/.

10 "Notes From Air Service Fields," *Air Service News Letter* VIII, no. 22, December 18, 1924, 20; "41st Division Aviation, Washington National Guard," *Air Corps News Letter* XIX, no. 10, May 15, 1936, 22; "Retirement of Major Easterbrook," *Air Corps News Letter* XXII, No. 20, October 15, 1939, 17.

11 "Retirement of Major Easterbrook," *Air Corps News Letter* XXII, No. 20, October 15, 1939, 17.

12 "Notes From Air Corps Fields—Kelly Field, San Antonio, Texas, October 31st," *Air Corps News* XIII, no. 15, November 9, 1929, 395.

13 "War Department Orders Effecting Air Corps Officers—Changes of Station," *Air Corps News* XV, no. 11, September 18, 1931, 334.

14 "Retirement of Major Easterbrook," *Air Corps News Letter* XXII, no. 20, October 15, 1939, 17.

15 "Service Orders," *Evening Star* (Washington, D.C.), March 21, 1935, C–4; "Temporary Promotions In the Air Corps," *Air Corps News Letter* XVIII, no. 6, April 1, 1935, 135.

16 "Distressing Accident At Luke Field," *Air Corps News Letter* XIX, no. 3, February 1, 1936, 24; "Wife of Vice President Entertained by Cabinet Hostess at Luncheon," *Evening Star* (Washington, D.C.), February 22, 1936, A–9; "Personnel Notes, O.C.A.C.," *Air Corps News Letter* XIX, no. 5, March 1, 1936, 11; "Washington Office Notes," *Air Corps News Letter* XIX, no. 12, June 15, 1936, 15; "Washington Office Notes," *Air Corps News Letter* XIX, no. 13, July 1, 1936, 20; "Washington Office Notes," *Air Corps News Letter* XIX, no. 18, September 15, 1936, 17; "Washington Office Notes," *Air Corps News Letter* XIX, no. 20, October 15, 1936, 14.

17 "Advanced Flying School, Kelly Field, May 6th," *Air Corps News Letter* XX, no. 10, May 15, 1937, 22; "46 Army Officers Get Temporary Advances," *Evening Star* (Washington, D.C.), October 21, 1937, A–18; "Promotion of Air Corps Officers," *Air Corps News Letter* XX, no. 22, November 15, 1937, 2; "Monument Dedicated to War-Time Flyer," *Air Corps News Letter* XX, no. 24, December 15, 1937, 7.

18   "Duty Assignments of Graduates of the Army War College," *Air Corps News Letter* XXII, no. 9, May 1, 1939, 5; "Retirement of Major Easterbrook," *Air Corps News Letter* XXII, no. 20, October 15, 1939, 17.

19   http://www.af.mil/About-Us/Biographies/Display/Article/108060/brigadier-general-arthur-e-easterbrook/.

20   Olmsted, "Lieut. Arthur Easterbrook and the 1st Aero Squadron," 21; "Gen. Easterbrook, Retired, Dies," unknown publication, https://digitalcollections.museumofflight.org/collections/show/29155; "Gen. Easterbrook Buried in Arlington," unknown publication, https://digitalcollections.museumofflight.org/collections/show/29154.

Chapter 10: Byrne Baucom Gets the Last Word

1   Dewey, "Erwin: From the War Letters and Diaries of an American Ace," part III, *Dallas Morning News*, October 2, 1928, 15.

2   Dewey, "Erwin: From the War Letters and Diaries of an American Ace," part I, *Dallas Morning News*, September 30, 1928, 27.

3   "3000 Shout Farewell to Local Flyer," *Dallas Morning News*, August 11, 1927, 5.

Abbreviations

AEF	American Expeditionary Forces
AIC	Aviation Instruction Center
Archie or AA	German antiaircraft fire
AS	Air Service
Brig. Gen.	Brigadier General
Capt.	Captain
CO	Commanding Officer
DOW	died of wounds
DSC	Distinguished Service Cross
EA	Enemy Aircraft
EP	Enemy Plane or Pilot
Fl. Abt.	*Flieger Abteilung* (German aviator's or flyer's detachment or section)
GHQ or GH	General Headquarters
hp	horsepower
hrs	hours
Inf.	Infantry
JMA	junior military aviator
KIA	killed in action
km	kilometer
Lieut. or Lt.	Lieutenant
Lt. Col.	Lieutenant Colonel
Ltn.	*Leutnant* (German 2nd Lieutenant)
Ltn. d. R.	*Leutnant der Reserve* (German Lieutenant of the Reserve)
Luftstreitkräfte	German Air Service
Maj.	Major
mg or MG	machine gun
mm	millimeter
mph	miles per hour
NWLLC	National Woman's Liberty Loan Committee

P.C.	command post
POW	prisoner of war
RAF	Royal Air Force
Rev.	Reverend
ROTC	Reserve Officers' Training Corps
Sal.	Salmson
SC	Signal Corps
Sergt. or Sgt.	Sergeant
SO	Special Order
Sop.	Sopwith
SOS	help – the International Morse code distress signal
U.S.	United States
VLFC	Victory Loan Flying Circus
Vzfw.	*Vizefeldwebel* (German Sergeant 1st Class)
WD	War Department
WIA	wounded in action

Bibliography

Articles

Brown, Bowman A. Jr. "*Jasta* 11 Revisited." *Over the Front* 2, no. 3 (Autumn 1987): 270–273.

Bruce, J. M. "The First Fighting Spads." *AIR Enthusiast* 15 (April–July 1981): 76.

Dealey, Ted. "The *Dallas Spirit*, the Last Fool Flight." *Southwestern Historical Quarterly* 63 (April 1960): 16–28.

Duiven, Richard, and Jeffrey Sands. "The Original Flying Circus: The Combat Log of Royal Prussian *Jagdstaffel* 11." *Over the Front* 2, no. 1 (Spring 1987): 38.

Frank, Dr. Sam H. "Air Service Combat Operations, Part 7, Operations on the Marne Salient—Château-Thierry." *Cross & Cockade* Journal 7, no. 4 (Winter 1966): 368–374.

Frandzen, Eugene M. "Lives of the Aces in Pictures: William P. Erwin, Yank Observation Ace." *Flying Aces* (May 1934): 27.

Hinkle, Stacy C. "Wings Over the Border, The Army Air Service Patrol, 1919–1921." *American Aviation Historical Society* 17, no. 4 (Winter 1972): 262.

Kingston, Donald M. "The Plattsburg Movement and its Legacy." *Relevance* 6, no. 4 (Autumn 1997).

Lucas, Stephen, and Alan D. Toelle. "Ten Days – Lt. Charles B. Sands, 27th Aero Squadron." *Over the Front* 19, no. 2 (Summer 2004): 106.

Miller, Thomas G., Jr. "Air Service Combat Organization." *Cross & Cockade* Journal 3, no. 1 (Spring 1962): 2.

Olmsted, Merle C. "Lieut. Arthur Easterbrook and the 1st Aero Squadron." *Cross & Cockade* Journal 20, no. 1 (Spring 1979): 2–21.

Puglisi, William R. "The 27th Squadron's Black Day." *Cross & Cockade* Journal 3, no. 3 (Autumn 1962): 230–233.

Roesler, Alan L. "A Spring Day Like No Other: The Victory Loan Flying Circus Comes to Springfield, April 15, 1919." *Journal of Illinois History* 18, no. 1 (Spring 2015): 48.

Roesler, Alan L. "Flying Machine and War Bonds: The Victory Loan Flying Circus in South Dakota." *South Dakota History* 46, no. 1 (Spring 2016): 47–52.

Roesler, Alan L. "Flying Under the Bridges in Little Rock." *Pulaski County Historical Review* 63, no. 1 (Spring 2015): 7–9.

Roesler, Alan L. "The Victory Loan Flying Circus in Memphis." *Tennessee Historical Quarterly* 73, no. 2 (Summer 2014): 122–126.

Roesler, Alan L. "The Victory Loan Flying Circus in St. Louis and Kansas City, April 14 and April 30, 1919." *Missouri Historical Review* 108, no. 1 (October 2013): 52–60.

Roesler, Alan L. "The Victory Loan Flying Circus in Wichita, May 1, 1919, and the Victory Loan Campaign That Brought It There." *Kansas History: A Journal of the Central Plains* 43, no. 2 (Summer 2020): 94–95.

Roesler, Alan L. "The Victory Loan Flying Circus: 'The Spectacle Was The Greatest Ever Witnessed Here.'" *Journal of the Fort Smith Historical Society* 37, no. 1 (April 2013): 31–32.

Roesler, Alan L. "Victory Loan Flying Circus at Ak-Sar-Ben Field: No Horseplay on April 28, 1919." *Nebraska History Magazine* 100, no. 1 (Spring 2019): 48–49.

Ruffin, Steve. "'Dutch Girl' Over the Argonne, The 50th Aero Squadron in WWI." *Over the Front* 25, no. 2 (Summer 2010): 122.

Ruffin, Steve. "Flying in France with the Fiftieth, 1/Lt. Floyd M. Pickrell, USAS." *Over the Front* 25, no. 2 (Summer 2010): 164.

Ruffin, Steve. "'The Luckiest Man in the Army,' Milton K. Lockwood, Aerial Observer, 50th Aero Squadron." *Over the Front* 25, no. 2 (Summer 2010): 172–173.

Skelton, Marvin L. "*Jagdgeschwader* Nr. 1 Pilots." *Cross & Cockade* Journal 18, no. 4 (Winter 1977): 326–329.

Toelle, Alan D. "Wings Over America, Victory Loan Flying Circus, Far West Flight." *Over the Front* 29, no. 4 (Winter 2014): 292–359.

Books

American Battle Monuments Commission. *American Armies and Battlefields in Europe*. Washington, D.C.: United States Government Printing Office, 1938.

American Battle Monuments Commission. *80th Division Summary of Operations in the World War*. Washington, D.C.: United States Government Printing Office, 1944.

Andrews, C. F. *The Spad XIII C.1, Aircraft in Profile* 1, part 2. Garden City, NY: Doubleday and Company, Inc., 1965.

Archibald, Norman. *Heaven High—Hell Deep*. New York: Albert and Charles Boni, Inc., 1935.

Bowers, Peter M. *The Nieuport N.28C-I, Profile Publications*. London: Hills and Lacey Ltd., 1966.

Franks, Norman L. R., and Frank W. Bailey. *Over The Front*. London: Grub Street, 1992.

Gray, Peter, and Owen Thetford. *German Aircraft of the First World War*. Garden City, NY: Doubleday and Company, Inc., 1970.

Guttman, Jon. *Salmson 2A2, Windsock Datafile* 109. Hertfordshire, Great Britain: Albatros Productions, 2005.

Guttman, Jon. *USAS 1st Pursuit Group*. Oxford, Great Britain: Osprey Publishing, 2008.

Owers, Colin A., Jon S. Guttman, and James J. Davilla. *Salmson Aircraft of World War I*. Boulder, Colorado: Flying Machines Press, 2001.

Ruffin, Steven A. *Flights of No Return, The Night Camelot Ended*. Minneapolis, MN: Zenith Press, 2015.

Sloan, James J., Jr. *Wings of Honor, American Airmen in World War I*. Atglen, PA: Schiffer Publishing, 1994.

Society of the First Division. *History of the First Division During the World War, 1917–1919*. Philadelphia, Pennsylvania: John C. Winston Company, 1922.

VanWyngarden, Greg. *'Richthofen's Circus' Jagdgeschwader Nr 1*. New York, NY: Osprey Publishing, 2004.

VanWyngarden, Greg. *Geschwader 'Berthold' Jagdgeschwader Nr II*. Oxford: Osprey Publishing, 2005.

Newspapers

Amarillo (TX) Daily News. "Society, Presbyterian Church Men to Entertain." January 3, 1912.

Amarillo Daily News. "Society, Chapel Program." February 18, 1912.

Cent Soixante Six. "Costly Honors." March 1, 1919.

Chicago Daily Tribune. "Aerial Acrobat, Mile Up, Fools Undertakers." May 10, 1919.

Daily Herald (Weatherford, TX). "American Ace Will See Regular Army Service." August 26, 1919.

Dallas (TX) Morning News. "Aviator and Musician Wed." July 28, 1926.

Dallas Morning News. "Dallas Spirit Soars Away On Initial Flight." August 4, 1927.

Dallas Morning News. "Dallas Spirit Makes Record for Take-Off." August 5, 1927.

Dallas Morning News. "Captain Lands His Ship At Love Field," 1, 10; "How Dallas Spirit Is Built," 10. August 6, 1927.

Dallas Morning News. "10,000 Cheer Bill Erwin at Dedication of Dallas Spirit," 1, 7; "Speedy Construction Marks Completion of Capt. Erwin's Plane," 4. August 7, 1927.

Dallas Morning News. "Dallas Spirit Makes First Flight Here." August 9, 1927.

Dallas Morning News. "Capt. Erwin Entered In Two Air 'Derbies,'" 1; "Erwin Forced to Return as Engine Pump Fails to Work," 1, 8. August 10, 1927.

Dallas Morning News. "Erwin Ready For Dole Hop." August 12, 1927.

Dallas Morning News. Ted Dealey. "Working Over Dallas Spirit;" "Sponsors With Erwin Given Full Authority," both 1, 8. August 13, 1927.

Dallas Morning News. Ted Dealey. "Erwin Lose Derby Place." August 14, 1927.

Dallas Morning News. Ted Dealey. "Final Test of Dallas Spirit Monday." August 15, 1927.

Dallas Morning News. Ted Dealey. "Dallas Spirit Ready for Gun In Air Derby." August 16, 1927.

Dallas Morning News. Ted Dealey. "Forced Return After Making Perfect Start." August 17, 1927.

Dallas Morning News. Ted Dealey. "Dallas Spirit Will Continue World Flight;" "New $25,000 Offer to Erwin;" "Dole Race Facts," all on 1. August 18, 1927.

Dallas Morning News. "New Offer to Erwin Expires 6 P.M. Friday," 1; "Erwin to Seek Missing Flyers," 1; "Protest Made in Dole Air Derby," 8; "Rewards Offered," 12. August 19, 1927.

Dallas Morning News. "Dallas Spirit Silent After SOS Call," 1; "Radio Flashes Tell Progress of Capt. Erwin," 1, 12; "Dallas Spirit Starts Flight For Honolulu," 1, 12; "Erwin Speeds Away on His Rescue Trip," 12; "Erwin's First Purpose To Discover Flyers, He Wires Col. Easterwood," 12. August 20, 1927.

Dallas Morning News. "Decade of Flying," 4; "Flying Low to Sight Those Adrift, Thinks Southworth," 4; "Erwin Dropped 2,000 Feet At Terrific Speed to Ocean, Radio Engineer Believes," 12. August 21, 1927.

Dallas Morning News. "Milford Pays Baucom Honor." June 4, 1928.

Dallas Morning News. John Peyton Dewey. "Erwin: From the War Letters and Diaries of an American Ace," part I. September 30, 1928.

Dallas Morning News. John Peyton Dewey. "Erwin: From the War Letters and Diaries of an American Ace," part III. October 2, 1928.

Dallas Morning News. John Peyton Dewey. "Erwin: From the War Letters and Diaries of an American Ace," part IV. October 3, 1928.

Dallas Morning News. John Peyton Dewey. "Erwin: From the War Letters and Diaries of an American Ace," part VI. October 5, 1928.

Dallas Morning News. John Peyton Dewey. "Erwin: From the War Letters and Diaries of an American Ace," part VIII. October 7, 1928.

Dallas Morning News. John Peyton Dewey. "Erwin: From the War Letters and Diaries of an American Ace," part X. October 9, 1928.

Dallas Morning News. John Peyton Dewey. "Erwin: From the War Letters and Diaries of an American Ace," part XI. October 10, 1928.

Dallas Morning News. John Peyton Dewey. "Erwin: From the War Letters and Diaries of an American Ace," part XII. October 11, 1928.

Dallas Morning News. John Peyton Dewey. "Erwin: From the War Letters and Diaries of an American

Ace," part XIII, October 12, 1928.

Dallas Morning News. John Peyton Dewey. "Erwin: From the War Letters and Diaries of an American Ace," part XV. October 14, 1928.

Dallas Morning News. John Peyton Dewey. "Erwin: From the War Letters and Diaries of an American Ace," part XVII. October 16, 1928.

Dallas Morning News. John Peyton Dewey. "Erwin: From the War Letters and Diaries of an American Ace," part XVIII. October 17, 1928.

Dallas Morning News. John Peyton Dewey. "Erwin: From the War Letters and Diaries of an American Ace," part XIX. October 18, 1928.

Dallas Morning News. John Peyton Dewey. "Erwin: From the War Letters and Diaries of an American Ace," part XX. October 19, 1928.

Dallas Morning News. John Peyton Dewey. "Erwin: From the War Letters and Diaries of an American Ace," part XXI. October 20, 1928.

Dallas Morning News. John Peyton Dewey. "Erwin: From the War Letters and Diaries of an American Ace," part XXII. October 21, 1928.

Dallas Morning News. John Peyton Dewey. "Erwin: From the War Letters and Diaries of an American Ace," part XXIII. October 22, 1928.

Dallas Morning News. John Peyton Dewey. "Erwin: From the War Letters and Diaries of an American Ace," part XXIV. October 23, 1928.

Dallas Morning News. John Peyton Dewey. "Erwin: From the War Letters and Diaries of an American Ace," part XXV. October 24, 1928.

Evening Star (Washington, D.C.). Photograph. October 31, 1925.

Evening Star (Washington, D.C.). "Key Bridge Rites For Dead Flyers." May 31, 1926.

Evening Star (Washington, D.C.). "Air Board Named." December 11, 1926.

Evening Star (Washington, D.C.). "Erwin Won Fame For Valor in War." August 20, 1927.

Evening Star (Washington, D.C.). "Erwin Famous in World War as 'Terror of Western Front.'" August 21, 1927.

Evening Star (Washington, D.C.). "Capt. Baucom Dies in Crash; Terrorized Enemy in War." May 31, 1928.

Evening Star (Washington, D.C.). "Service Orders." March 21, 1935.

Evening Star (Washington, D.C.). "Wife of Vice President Entertained by Cabinet Hostess at Luncheon." February 22, 1936.

Evening Star (Washington, D.C.). "46 Army Officers Get Temporary Advances." October 21, 1937.

Grand Forks (ND) Herald. "Thrilling Dare Devil Stunts of Aerial Circus Performers Draw Interest of City Today." April 22, 1919.

Houston (TX) Post. "Three Texans Win Title of 'Ace.'" January 11, 1919.

Houston Post. "Milford, Texas, Soldier Awarded D.S. Cross." May 11, 1919.

Houston Post. "High Wind Delays Arrival of Chief of US Air Service." March 14, 1922.

Omaha (NE) Daily Bee. "Aviators in Omaha Give Thrill to Throng." April 29, 1919.

Osage Journal (Pawhuska, OK). "Presbyterian Church." May 2, 1912.

Osage Journal. "Union Meeting." May 9, 1912.

Osage Journal. "Union Meeting." May 16, 1912.

Osage Journal. "The Methodist Church." May 23, 1912.

Out of Control. "McElvain Was 'Out of Luck' For His 'Twenty-Three Carrot' Soup." December 13, 1918.

Plane News II, no. 12. "Intensive Combat Work at Field 8 Cram Full of Exciting Incidents." February 8, 1919.

Plane News II, no. 13. "Issoudun Products Constitute Major Portion of Flyer Aces." February 15,

1919.

Plane News II, no. 18. "Aviators Receive Goodly Number *Croix de Guerre* and French Citations." March 22, 1919.

San Antonio (TX) Express. "Reserve Officers on Furlough Will Return August 29." August 16, 1917.

San Antonio Express. "Standing of Class in Equitation is Given." November 22, 1917.

San Antonio Express. "New Texas Charters." April 7, 1920.

San Antonio Express. "Eight Run-Offs Needed to Settle Lawmakers' Race." August 8, 1920.

San Antonio Express. "Special Election Authorized." December 7, 1920.

Seattle Daily Times. "A. E. Easterbrook Tells of His Work." October 25, 1918.

Seattle Star. "Plan Eight Aerial Lines in United States." October 19, 1918.

Seattle Star. "Lieut. Easterbrook Honor Guest." July 2, 1919.

Seattle Star. "Personal." July 9, 1919.

Seattle Star. "Lt. Easterbrook, Seattle Ace, Here Visiting Mother." December 30, 1919.

St. Louis (MO) Globe-Democrat. "10 Injured When German Airplane Crashes Into Crowd." April 15, 1919.

St. Louis (MO) Post-Dispatch. "Boy Injured at Aero Circus in Forest Park Dies." April 15, 1919.

Sunday Star (Washington, D.C.). "Planes to Drop Poppies." May 24, 1925.

Sunday Star (Washington, D.C.). "52 Aviators Are Rated As Aces." November 1, 1925.

Sunday Star (Washington, D.C.). "Crisis in Mitchell Case May Be Near." November 8, 1925.

Sunday Star (Washington, D.C.). "Army and Navy News." May 8, 1927.

Sunday Star (Washington, D.C.). "Erwin's Father Calm" (Pawhuska, OK), "Mother of Erwin Calm" (Dallas, TX). August 21, 1927.

Sunday State Journal (Madison, WI). "Yank Fliers Thrill Big Crowds With Daring 'Stunts.'" April 20, 1919.

Texas Mesquiter (Mesquite, TX). "Texas Suited As Greatest Air Center." June 10, 1927.

Texas Mesquiter. "Given Honorable Mention in Contest." July 22, 1927.

Twice-a-Week Herald (Amarillo, Texas). "Local News Items." December 26, 1905.

Twice-a-Week Herald (Amarillo, Texas). "Local News." July 24, 1906.

Twice-a-Week Herald (Amarillo, Texas). Advertisement. August 17, 1906.

Twice-a-Week Herald (Amarillo, Texas). "Local News." August 24, 1906.

Twice-a-Week Herald (Amarillo, Texas). Advertisement. September 28, 1906.

Weekly Herald (Amarillo, TX). "To Take Postgraduate Course." April 11, 1907.

Weekly Herald (Amarillo, TX). "Personal Mention." April 11, 1907.

Wichita (KS) Eagle. "Sky Extra Rains Upon Crowds." May 2, 1919.

Wichita (KS) Eagle. "Wichita Kept Record Clear in Bond Drive." May 11, 1919.

World Herald (Omaha, NE). "Captain Erwin, 'Ace', Saw Fierce Fighting." April 29, 1919.

Official Publications

AIR SCOUT I, no. 21. Garden City, NY: U.S. Aviation Fields. 1919.

Dallas City Directory, 1927. Dallas, TX: John F. Worley Directory Co. Published annually.

Gorrell's History of the American Expeditionary Forces, Air Service 1917–1919. National Archives and Records Administration (NARA), Washington, D.C.: 1975.

War Diary (Victory Loan Eastern Flight). NARA, Washington, D.C.: 1919.

War Diary (Victory Loan Mid-West Flight). NARA, Washington, D.C.: 1919.

U.S. Air Service/Air Corps Newsletters (Washington, D.C.: War Dept.)

Air Corps News X, no. 16. "Notes From Air Corps Fields." December 13, 1926.

Air Corps News XI, no. 13. "Air Corps Officers Under Orders For March Field, Calif." October 15, 1927.

Air Corps News XII, no. 8. "Captain Baucom Dies in Airplane Crash." June 5, 1928.

Air Corps News XII, no. 8. "San Antonio Air Depot, Duncan Field, Texas, May 17th." June 5, 1928.

Air Corps News XII, no. 10. "San Antonio Air Depot, Duncan Field, Texas, June 16." July 10, 1928.

Air Corps News XIII, no. 15. "Notes From Air Corps Fields – Kelly Field, San Antonio, Texas, October 31st." November 9, 1929.

Air Corps News XV, no. 11. "War Department Orders Effecting Air Corps Officers—Changes of Station." September 18, 1931.

Air Corps News XV, no. 12. "Mather Field Boys Average High in Shooting." October 17, 1931.

Air Corps News Letter XVIII, no. 6. "Temporary Promotions In the Air Corps." April 1, 1935.

Air Corps News Letter XIX, no. 3. "Distressing Accident At Luke Field." February 1, 1936.

Air Corps News Letter XIX, no. 5. "Personnel Notes, O.C.A.C." March 1, 1936.

Air Corps News Letter XIX, no. 10. "41st Division Aviation, Washington National Guard." May 15, 1936.

Air Corps News Letter XIX, no. 12. "Washington Office Notes." June 15, 1936.

Air Corps News Letter XIX, no. 13. "Washington Office Notes." July 1, 1936.

Air Corps News Letter XIX, no. 18. "Washington Office Notes." September 15, 1936.

Air Corps News Letter XIX, no. 20. "Washington Office Notes." October 15, 1936.

Air Corps News Letter XX, no. 10. "Advanced Flying School, Kelly Field, May 6th." May 15, 1937.

Air Corps News Letter XX, no. 22. "Promotion of Air Corps Officers." November 15, 1937.

Air Corps News Letter XX, no. 24. "Monument Dedicated to War-Time Flyer." December 15, 1937.

Air Corps News Letter XXII, no. 9. "Duty Assignments of Graduates of the Army War College." May 1, 1939.

Air Corps News Letter XXII, No. 20. "Retirement of Major Easterbrook." October 15, 1939.

Air Service News Letter 2, O.S. 1216. "American 'Aces'." January 18, 1919.

Air Service News Letter II, V–100. "Army Aviators to Fly for Loan (Central or No. 2 Flight Personnel)." April 5, 1919.

Air Service News Letter II, V–277. "Awards of French *Croix de Guerre*, With Palm." May 10, 1919.

Air Service News Letter II, V–372. "18,711 Mile Tour for Flying Circus." May 24, 1919.

Air Service News Letter II, V–418. "Distinguished Service Cross." May 29, 1919.

Air Service News Letter I, no. 4. "Germans Feared Night Bombing." October 31, 1919.

Air Service News Letter III, no. 12. "Awards of Distinguished Service Cross." November 7, 1919.

Air Service News Letter I, no. 7. "Border Situation." November 22, 1919.

Air Service News Letter I, no. 11. "Promotions." December 22, 1919.

Air Service News Letter III, no. 22. "Kelly Field Organizes Polo Team." January 15, 1920.

Air Service News Letter IV, No. 5. "Change of Border Organization;" "Officers of the 166th Aero Squadron Complimented for Excellent Work in Conducting Artillery Shoot at Ft. Crockett, Texas." January 27, 1920.

Air Service News Letter IV, No. 11. "Lieut. Arthur E. Easterbrook Transferred to the Infantry." March 9, 1920.

Air Service News Letter IV, No. 41. "Squadron News;" "Ellington Field, Houston, Texas." November 9, 1920.

Air Service News Letter II, No. 38. "First Day Bombardment Group Cooperation With Coast Artillery." November 20, 1920.

Air Service News Letter V, no. 14. "Squadron News." April 12, 1921.

Air Service News Letter V, no. 15. "Squadron News." April 15, 1921.

Air Service News Letter V, no. 17. "Squadron News." April 29, 1921.

Air Service News Letter V, no. 22. "Squadron News." June 10, 1921.

Air Service News Letter V, no. 32. "Squadron News." August 24, 1921.

Air Service News Letter V, no. 37. "Squadron News." October 19, 1921.

Air Service News Letter V, no. 44. "Squadron News." December 9, 1921.

Air Service News Letter VI, no. 5. "Squadron News." February 20, 1922.

Air Service News Letter VI, no. 6. "Squadron News." February 28, 1922.

Air Service News Letter VI, no. 7. "Squadron News." March 9, 1922.

Air Service News Letter VI, no. 14. "Kelly Field, San Antonio, Texas, April 8." May 10, 1922.

Air Service News Letter VI, no. 24. "Squadron News." August 29, 1922.

Air Service News Letter VI, no. 32. "Squadron News." November 16, 1922.

Air Service News Letter VII, no. 11. "Squadron News." June 4, 1923.

Air Service News Letter VIII, no. 22. "Notes From Air Service Fields." December 18, 1924.

Air Service Weekly News Letter. "For Immediate Release." October 26, 1918.

D.M.A. Weekly News Letter I, OS 1311. "Cited for Distinguished Service." February 8, 1919.

D.M.A. Weekly News Letter I, OS 1345. "Advanced Ratings for Overseas Flying Officers for Distinguished Service;" "Honor Roll of the Air Service." February 15, 1919.

D.M.A. Weekly News Letter I, OS 1393. "Released for Afternoon Newspapers of Saturday, March 8, 1919." March 1, 1919.

D.M.A. Weekly News Letter I, V–16. "'Aces' to Fly for Loan." March 22, 1919.

D.M.A. Weekly News Letter I, V–37. "French Citations." March 29, 1919.

Index